CLEAR AS GLASS

By Wendy Daudelin

Wendy Daudelin

CLEAR AS GLASS

This book is a work of fiction. References to real people, events and establishments are intended to provide a sense of authenticity and are used fictitiously. All other characters and dialogue are drawn from the author's imagination.

Library of Congress Cataloging in Publication Number: 2018907380

ISBN: 978-1-7324817-0-1 (ebook Edition)

ISBN: 978-1-7324817-1-8 (Paperback Edition)

First Edition

Cover drawing by Kyla Daudelin

Cover design by Wendy Daudelin

Photo and other artwork by Wendy Daudelin

Preface

I grew up near Toledo and lived in the area my whole life. Over those many years I learned bits and pieces from family, friends, neighbors and co-workers about how and why Toledo became known as The Glass City. For a quarter of a century I have had the privilege to work at the legendary Libbey Glass in Toledo with many great people. My company is the reason Toledo got its nickname. Glass became synonymous with Toledo because of Edward Drummond Libbey.

Edward moved his one glass company to Toledo in 1888 and from there he started a revolution. He took that one tabletop glass company and created several others with his business partners which produced other items made of glass. Owens Bottle Company (today known as Owens-Illinois), Owens-Corning, and Libbey-Owens-Ford (today a part of Pilkington) were just a few of those businesses.

Edward's ingenuity and industrious spirit is something I admire dearly. I only wish I had the opportunity to meet this amazing man.

IN MEMORY OF MY MOTHER

Mom's burning passion for books sparked
my interest in reading at an early age.
Mom was my loudest cheerleader in life and
first fan of my early creative writing endeavors.

Although our paths didn't cross I feel like I have come to know Edward as an "Uncle" over these many years working at the factory that he created. I feel his presence in the halls and feel he is still there in spirit cheering us on. Whenever something goes especially well at work, you can often hear someone sincerely say, "Thank you Uncle Libbey!"

Edward's picture is hanging on our walls, his name is on the door, his signature ℒ is on the glass, and his spirit is in our heart. His story is one that inspires me and I wanted to share it with you.

Edward has been gone so long that he has become like a mythical, legendary person. I have added some fiction into the story but I think my "Uncle Libbey" would appreciate and enjoy it. I hope you do too.

Happy 200th Anniversary Edward!

Chapter 1

Holy Toledo, do I have a story for you! I hope you are sitting down because this may just blow you off your feet. No, I'm not kidding, it is truly that explosive! My family has been guarding a closely held secret for several generations. This incident, which started with my great, great, great grandfather, has been passed down among my family. Each generation eventually learns our family secrets that are too wild, dangerous and risky to share with more than a few.

Why would I reveal it now, you may ask? Well, this secret has been both a blessing and a curse for us. You know what it is like when you have a secret, right? You always worry about someone finding it out. You lose sleep over it. You feel like you have to always be so careful about what you say, where you go, who you talk to, for fear of letting your guard down and spilling out too much information.

The news I'm going to tell you was held hush-hush because at the time it started, it just would have been too perilous to let it be known by others. Time and circumstances have changed now. I think the hour has come to let the world in on our well-kept and fascinating secret. I trust that I will not regret my decision.

Instead of just blurting out the secret, I need to be fair to those who put it in motion. In order to help you understand the history of how it began it is essential to start at the very beginning. I implore you to keep an open mind and try and understand the conditions of how this happened and why the few secret keepers thought it was so important to keep it confidential for so long.

My story begins way back in the 1800's in America. My great, great, great grandfather agreed to take on this secret because his boss asked him to do it. He couldn't resist and felt honored that he was entrusted with such a confidential assignment. Little could he have envisioned that it would have been passed down for so many generations.

I have agonized over my decision to tell you this tale but I feel it is the best way to honor my ancestors. Plus, I'm ready to emerge from all this cloak and dagger business that has placed such a huge responsibility upon my family. And after all, I have always thought the best secrets are those that are shared! Don't you agree?

If you have ever taken it upon yourself to pick up your drinking glass and found an "***L***" on the bottom you may be familiar with Libbey. William Libbey and his son Edward Drummond Libbey were my great, great, great grandfather's bosses. Essentially my ancestor was lucky enough to secure a job at the glass factory and eventually became a good friend to William's son, Edward, which brought about our family business.

My father, who told me this story, was born with the gift of gab and could yarn a tale with the best of them. He'd become especially gabby with a little Irish beer in him for encouragement. So I warn you, you may want to sit down and enjoy a tall drink, served in your favorite glass, hopefully one of ours made in Toledo, as you settle in to read this story.

This account, as told to me by my father, and told to him by his father and so on back to the one who started it all my great, great, great grandfather, Redmond, or Red as he was called by his friends.

The name Red fit him well as he had a full head of bright red curly hair from the day he was born, or so I was told. The name Redmond, I realized later, was quite an appropriate for him for another reason. The name means protector. Red took on the protector role early in his life as you will soon learn.

I think our Irish heritage makes us naturally talented at grand storytelling, but you know as well as I do, that sometimes stories do get some embellishments added along the way. So I advise you to enjoy the story in the spirit in which it is told and if some facts of dates, times, or other minor details aren't quite exact, please forgive me. I will attempt to relay the story in Red's words.

Chapter 2

I never expected to have the kind of life to write about but then one time, being in the right place at the right time, changed everything. My actions and the unexpected change in my life would impact generations of my family, and for the better, I hoped.

I grew up in a small farming part of town near the Charles River. I lived on the farm with my mother and her brother's family ever since I was a knee high to a mosquito. My father died when I was young and sadly I really have no memory of him.

Unfortunately, my father's death put my mother in a grief-stricken tailspin in which she never fully got over. There was always a cloud of sadness around her that festered just beneath the surface. I too felt a sadness for the father I didn't know, and the mother I longed to know better. I was grateful and fortunate that my Uncle Gavin found room in his heart and home to take us in.

Although Uncle Gavin was a wonderful caring person, I grew up never quite feeling right about living with his family. My two cousins were several years older than me when we arrived on their doorstep with just a small trunk containing all our belongings. It was soon clear to me that they weren't excited to be getting new long-term residents in their home. My aunt never looked happy and barely talked to me or my mother. The home was big enough for all of us, but times were rough, and they were all likely concerned that we would become a burden to their family.

I knew the ways of the world, or so I thought, and as I grew older I didn't expect much excitement could happen in my life. I expected little and figured the best thing to do was stay quiet and out of the way.

Uncle Gavin's farm consisted of several acres of land. He also had some cows, sheep, chickens and a goat. His sons were expected to take over the family farm someday. However, they had grown weary of farm life early in their youth and secretly longed to move to the city when they grew up.

Shortly after my arrival, my cousins let me know that I needed to earn my keep (and my mother's too). They quickly created a list of chores for me. I soon realized this was all the work they were expected to do, but I didn't mind so much. I wanted to show them I was big and strong and smart.

My uncle often worked in the fields from sun up to sun down. He was pleasant enough but not much of a talker. He was more the strong, silent type. He preferred his work to talking and socializing. He claimed he was this way because while growing up my mother never gave him a chance to talk. She would talk continuously, barely taking a break to catch her breath, he muttered to me once when I pestered him with questions. Sadly, my mother's mood changed drastically when my father died. Upon his death, she became quiet and withdrawn. I longed to know the talkative girl Uncle Gavin described.

When we settled in at the farm, I saw less and less of my mother. It seemed like she didn't want to be around me. I wondered if I was too much of a reminder to her of my father, or if she was just so depressed she couldn't see the pain I was in too.

I decided early on to try and make the best of the situation. What other choice did I have? I did my chores, without complaint, did my homework and got decent marks, and eventually broke through to my uncle. I would sneak into the barn when he was working on a machine and watch in amazement as he took a broken object and gave it new life.

At first, I think he would pretend not to notice me, and probably expected me to grow bored and slither away. The day he turned to me and said, "come a little closer and you can see how this works" was a turning point in our relationship. From that day forward he taught me everything he knew about machinery.

I don't mean to brag, but I was a quick learner. I took what he taught me and would seek out broken objects, or objects in good working order, to tear apart and put back together. As I got older neighbors would bring over items by for me to fix. I loved the challenge. I also enjoyed the look of amazement on their faces when I returned the castoffs into their former working condition. A few times I even added parts and features to make the item work in better ways.

In my limited free time I enjoyed hiking through the woods at the edge of the farm. The woods were a place I could be alone with my thoughts and just explore. My mother often complained that I was a bit of a dreamer. "Get your head out of the clouds," she'd often say when she caught me daydreaming. I wasn't doing nothing nor being lazy. No, I just was always trying to imagine better ways of doing whatever task was at hand.

In my mind, I mulled over various ideas of how to make some kind of contraption that would make tough tasks simpler. Take plowing for example, pulling blades behind a donkey was back-breaking work. Why couldn't someone invent some kind of machine that would do more of the work for you? Why couldn't it be me to invent it? I knew one day I would be an inventor of something majestic!

I would frequently talk to the rabbits and other creatures I came across divulging my plans to their attentive stares. I read anything I could find and marveled at all the inventions that were being introduced. It gave me plenty to think about as I meandered through the woods. Sometimes, if I was lucky, I would find some discarded parts of old treasures that I would haul back to my room and hide away. These old parts would wait patiently to be used again when I was ready to fix something.

On one occasion I found someone in trouble and rushed to help him. I didn't know it then, but by coming to his aid, my life would someday change in many splendid ways that I could never have dreamed.

On that particular day I was on an errand for my mother when I came upon a man on the side of the road. With just one look I could see the man looked very distraught. What struck me the most was that the man was impeccably dressed. I could tell straight away this man was not from around here. I was so struck by his regal appearance. As I got closer I saw that the man was holding the reins that should have been around a horse. I also noticed an overturned carriage down the embankment. The man looked at me, and I saw right away the embarrassment and shame on his face.

"Where's your horse?" I asked.

The man stared at me a minute without saying a word. As I approached him, I realized how awful I must have looked. I was all haggard and sweaty from my jaunt through the woods. The man continued looking at me and then just pointed towards the woods.

I turned and started down the hill towards the carriage. As I descended, I spotted the horse in the field just east of the woods. I looked back at the man and motioned him to come towards me. When the man drew closer I signaled for him to walk to the left side of the horse as I walked around the other side. I showed no fear, although it wasn't easy. I had never needed to capture a horse before and wasn't sure I'd be able to grab him but I knew I had to help this man.

Soon we got close enough to the horse to get the reins on him and tied him up to a tree. With the horse secure, I turned my attention back to the carriage. After several moments of frustration we were finally able to get it upright and reloaded. The man stood near the carriage, dusting himself off, as I went back for the horse and got him hooked up to the carriage. I walked behind the carriage as the horse pulled it back up to the road.

When the man, the horse, and the carriage were back on the road where they belonged, the man smiled a huge sigh of relief and waved me to come closer to him. "My name is William. What's your name?"

"I'm Redmond. Pleased to meet you sir. Are you lost? You don't look like you're from around here."

"Not exactly. I wanted to get this rocking chair as a surprise for my wife," William said. "You really helped me out of a jam, let me pay you for your trouble…"

"Oh no sir, I couldn't take any money from you. I was glad to help, no thanks necessary," I said shaking my hand and stepping back from the carriage.

The man seemed surprised that I didn't want any money, but must have felt he needed to pay for my services in some way. He reached his hand into a box behind his seat and pulled out a fancy glass vase. I didn't feel I should accept it, but he was so insistent that I graciously took it and thanked him. I didn't realize until much later that this was something that was made at the man's factory.

I picked flowers for my mom that day and presented them to her in the glistening vase. My mom cherished the beautiful container and never quizzed me about how I came into enough money to give her such a gift. I figured she must have thought I found it in Uncle Gavin's closet.

Every now and then, over the years, I would spot the vase in the cupboard and remember that finely dressed stranger.

So that was the way I met William. I didn't dare tell anyone about my encounter with William that day. Some things are better kept to yourself.

Chapter 3

My chance meeting with the mysterious traveler, known as William, did have me wondering about him all the way home. I couldn't imagine where he came from and why someone with his obvious wealth wouldn't just hire someone to pick up the chair and deliver it. I figured if went to all that trouble for his wife, he must really love her. I wondered if my dad ever did anything like that for my mother. I probably wouldn't ever know since the topic of my father had become an unspoken subject.

When I was sixteen my beloved Uncle Gavin passed away. He died peacefully in his sleep, which was a blessing for him, but not so much for me. His passing left me devastated. I had come to adore my uncle and I took the news very hard. His death also took an additional toll on my mother and I worried she would fade away too. She was already so much weaker and frailer than when we had arrived at her brother's home years ago.

When my uncle was put to rest I knew I would have to discuss my fate with my cousins. They both lived in another town now and had small families. I didn't see them much anymore and that was alright with me.

"Mom wants me to come back home and take over the family farm…" I heard one of them say to his brother as I neared the room they were in.

I stopped in the hallway abruptly, my heart raced as I quickly realized the gravity of their words. Did they now own the house I was living in with my mother? Would they kick us out? Surely they wouldn't do that. No, my aunt must have ownership of the house, she wouldn't do that, I thought hopefully as I tried to get over my anxiety.

"No way am I coming back from the city to live on a farm again…" I heard the other one say.

I looked up optimistically as they complained that their *city* wives would never want to move to this town. However, my optimism faded as they decided they could now charge my mother and I rent if we wanted to stay in the house. They saw me lingering near the door and pulled me in to reiterate the dreaded conversation I just overheard. My cousins also quickly agreed that they would sell some, or most of the land, so my offer to continue working in the fields was not an option. My mother was in no condition to work so I had no choice, I would just have to find a way to pay the rent.

My dream of someday going to college, which was really just a fantasy anyway, I reasoned, was now a fast fading memory.

I decided not to worry my mother about my cousin's demands until I had a solution.

After a restless night I got up the next morning and set out to find a job. Those first days looking for work were dreadful. It's not easy to take rejection, but I soldiered on, I had no choice.

One morning I spotted a number of boats filled with cargo gliding down Miller River. I decided to follow them a while.

Eventually I stopped to watch them when they looked to be stopping near Lechmore Point. Then I could sec why.

A stream of smoke billowing out of a chimney caught my eye. The structure looked at least 200 feet tall. Its size rivaled that of the monument at Bunker Hill, just to east. I had to get a closer look.

Finally, I came up to the looming factory by the river's edge. "Land sakes, would you look at that? Surely they must be in need of a young, strong man," I said aloud as I straightened my hair, put out my cigarette, and headed towards the building.

It was a splendid sight to behold. Having grown up in the country, I wasn't used to seeing such massive buildings. Workers briskly walked by me as I drew nearer. I tried to say hello, but I was greeted with a cool reaction or a nudge to get out of the way. I guess I was in their way. I was the stranger here.

I had my eyes glued on the huge tower near the building. Steam was coming from the chimney, and I wondered what it would be like to climb that tower. What a view that would be I thought as I nearly smashed into another guy. I couldn't help it, I was just a country boy, in awe of this view. I heard and read about places like this but I'd never seen anything like it in person.

My imagination ran wild as I tried to envision what was inside. As I made my way to the front door I tried not to lose my nerve. Getting inside was easy, but now what I wondered?

I quietly began following a couple men down the main corridor. Along the way I stopped to admire the numerous medals that adorned the walls. I noticed an office door to the left and before I lost my courage, I took a deep breath, knocked on the door and went inside. An old lady looked up at me and frowned as she studied my attire and my rugged good looks, I assumed.

I put on a brave smile but before I could get a word out she lowered her glasses and said, "Are you lost, sonny?"

I was outraged, of course I was lost, sort of, and young enough to be her grandson, but I bit my tongue and said as cheerfully as possible, "No, ma'am, I'm here to apply for a job. I can fix just about anything and by the looks of this place--"

She cut me off, waving her hand and snickering, "We're not hiring, and what makes you think we need anything fixed?"

She must have seen from my reaction that she hadn't been very nice. She started to apologize but before she could finish we were interrupted by a very cheerful voice.

"Millie, what have you been telling this young man? We should not turn someone away so quickly that wants to join us. Sir, let's go see the gaffers, I'm sure one of them could use another knocker-upper." He said with a bellowing laugh.

I was stunned and turned around to see who would come to my defense. Standing behind me was a tall distinguished gentleman. I couldn't believe it. It was none other than the man I had met on the road many years ago. I would have recognized him anywhere. But why in the world did he want to help me, and secondly what is a gaffer? I know a knocker-upper is used to wake people up, but I couldn't picture he'd need someone to wake employees up at this wonderous factory.

William must have recognized me right away too. Maybe it was my bright red hair that gave me away. William clapped and bellowed, "Well, I never thought I'd see you again. How have you been Red?"

I just stared at him and back at the lady who now looked very puzzled.

"Mr. Libbey you know this boy?"

And then it struck me. The vase he gave me that day was made here in this factory. This must be his factory. I often wondered if William got into any further trouble that day or if his wife ever found out about the events of that wild day. "How does your wife like that rocking chair, sir?" I asked sincerely, while looking smugly at the lady who was still stunned that I could know Mr. Libbey.

A couple other men stopped in the hallway and looked at us. They too seemed surprised that someone that looked like I did could know such an important man. I could barely hear their whispers, but I caught their bewildered looks as they gazed at me in confusion.

William just laughed recalling the day he took that carriage on his own to fetch that chair for his wife. He hadn't thought of that in years. Although his wife enjoyed that rocking chair every day, William confided to me that he had worked hard to forget that stressful day. "I don't know that I ever thanked you properly that day. You took off so quickly…." William said as he got a faraway look in his eye.

"Red, you come with me," he said and gestured to me to follow him down the hallway.

What could I do but stand tall and make a sheepish grin at Millie! As I strode past her I couldn't help but smirk as she mumbled something about me being too high for my nut.

I'm not sure why, but William seemed anxious to show me the factory that he must have worked so hard to establish. I was quite impressed as we walked around. I had never seen anything like it. Surprisingly, William talked to me about the finances of the company and I struggled to listen as the whirl of machines buzzed around us.

I was awestruck as we walked near the furnace and saw the teams of workers so engrossed in their work. The fella that really took my breath away was the one standing on top of a crate with a large thin pipe in his mouth. He blew into the pipe and worked a gob of glass on the end into shape. The gob was extremely hot, I could tell, because it was a fiery shade of orange, like fire. I asked William how long it took to learn that skill and he laughed saying it was a senior level position which took many years. There was much to learn about working with molten glass before reaching that role.

Eventually we made our way the cutting room on the second floor. It consisted of a long row of carvers each sitting next to a carving wheel. I walked closer to inspect what they were doing. "What are they dropping from their hand?"

"Oh, that is sand, it is mixed on with the spray of water that drips from that container above, see, and they apply the sand, as needed, which helps in the cutting process."

The third floor operations surprised to me. A long table was on each side of the room. Ladies sat in a line on a long bench across from each table. They each had what looked like a fancy carving machine in front of them which I desperately wanted to pull apart and inspect. Their right elbows rested on a pillow as they sat engraving beautiful scenes or fancy flowers and designs on their glass piece. I was so enthralled with the etcher, that I got right up in one woman's face to inspect close up how she was using it. William just chuckled, and gently pulled me back out of her way.

"I'm just blown away Mr. Libbey. I never thought about how those designs were put on the glass."

William led me back down to another area of the ground floor where there were several dozen men selecting glass, inspecting them a final time, and packing them gently into barrels.

"The barrels are the sturdiest way we have found to send our products on the railroads and across the country."

"Wait, are you kidding me? How did you learn and make all this, Mr. Libbey?"

"One man cannot do it alone as you can plainly see. It takes many skilled people. I also had a great mentor and partner in Deming Jarvis. He taught me so much about the fundamentals of the glass business."

I walked over and peeked into one of the barrels. I couldn't believe it. Inside were several colored lenses. "You even make the signals for the railroad signs? That is so neat, but how do you get them different colors?"

William proudly smiled and went into a long explanation about how he played around with different formulas of frit to get different colors of glass. "Unfortunately there can be a slight variation in the color of each piece if the raw materials in the batch aren't mixed just right. We use a colored powder mixture, and fire it into the mold at the precise temperature to get the right hue of glass color. Consistency is what I strive for."

The great bottom fact was that I knew William must have had a good education. He certainly lived in a much different world than I grew up in. I wasn't jealous, mind you, I was grateful for my life. Although I didn't have a father growing up, I was especially thankful for the kindness my uncle had shown me. However, as William continued talking to me it made me wonder how different my life could have been if my father had been around. Would he have been as successful as William?

When walking through the woods as a child, I often found myself pretending to talk to my father. In my mind, over the years since I first ran into William, the father I talked to took on his image. I would replay that fateful day I found him stranded on the side of the road and pretend that he revealed that he was looking for his long lost son. To be standing here now as William showed me about his business was really something.

In my current situation I knew I wouldn't have the opportunity to get a secondary education. My uncle saw that I was a very intelligent person, but with him gone and my mother unable to work, I was going to have to find a way to pay our expenses and get through my last year of high school.

From an early age I could look at any machine and figure how it ran and make improvements if needed. Mechanics just came natural to me. I was always looking for things to fix. The fun for me was in solving the problem. Little did I know then that over time this gift would be my ticket to a new life.

William seemed to take a shining to me to the dismay of the workers standing nearby. I couldn't really figure out why someone as important as William would take the time to talk with me. Sure, I was charming of course, but I would have never suspected we could become friends. Our paths re-uniting on this day, would bind our families together in ways we would have never guessed.

Chapter 4

I left the factory feeling like the luckiest guy in the world. I yelled out, "Yahoo!" and jumped pumping my fist in the air. I got a few strange looks but I didn't care. The goofy smile on my face was plastered there the rest of the day.

I felt down on my luck for most of my life and now I felt like I was in a dream. While I grew up in a family without much money I did have their love and support. It was just tragic when my father died when I was so young. I was lucky to have my uncle there to help my mother and me through those toughest years.

I learned early that I had to help my mother as best I could. I was a pretty smart boy but could only dream of going onto college. There was no money for such extravagances. I knew that kind of opportunity was out of reach, so I turned my energy to finding any little jobs to help my mother.

I was always a very inquisitive lad and learned much from my uncle. I now had a way that I could put it to good use. Since we never had much money we had to use our wits to fix anything that broke or do without. There wasn't much dough to buy new things so pulling something apart and finding a way to make it work again was just the way I grew up. I had a knack for it too. Ever since I was a young lad neighbors would come looking for me to fix this or that around their home. I was always happy to oblige. I knew my uncle felt a sense of pride in this too, especially since his boys didn't share his interests.

I always enjoyed a challenge. Now I would get a chance to put my skills to work on a large scale. As I walked away from the factory that day I couldn't help but get chills as I looked back over my shoulder at the great structure.

I hurried along, anxious to share the news with my mother, and thought of all the wonderful pieces of machinery I saw that day. I couldn't wait to get my hands on them. Although that was not the job I was hired for, I knew I would soon show Mr. Libbey how lucky he was to have hired me.

I worked hard every day. There was so much to learn. The gang I was assigned to was pleasant enough to me. The gaffer, who was the glass master and the head of the gang, had the final say in hiring me for his team and I wasn't going to let him down. I started out as a taker-in. It was my job to take the glassblowers final product and carefully get it in the annealing furnace, or lehr as they called it. This annealing process, I soon learned the hard way, was a critical part of the glassmaking procedure. If a glass wasn't annealed it could essentially burst as it cooled. Witnessing a glass break and seeing all the glassmaker's hard work shatter into pieces was not something I wanted happening on my watch.

I also made myself useful by anticipating the gang's needs and always being ready to grab this or that and bring them what they needed. Other tasks I soon carried out involved cleaning blowpipes and other tools, preparing the molds and keeping the furnace fueled.

Observing the master artisans blow the pipes and craft their gob into a work of art was a fascinating bonus. I was both amazed and intimidated by their talent. I was sure I'd never be able to make something so beautiful, even if I worked here a hundred years.

I rarely saw Mr. Libbey again in those first few months. I had hoped to thank him for giving me a job but I soon realized that he was likely much too busy to deal with a taker-in like me. I would find a way to get his attention someday and make him glad he hired me, I vowed to myself.

When a machine broke down one day, I saw this as an opportunity and seized it. You see, with a machine down everyone stopped working. One machine could halt all the production. When nobody was working, the company was losing money. Obviously that is not good for business. I was ready to make my move and save the day.

While a few of the older workers began looking over the machine and arguing about what to do first, I quietly stepped around them and quickly assessed the situation. I grabbed a couple tools that were laying nearby and started pulling things off the machine. This got the attention of the arguing workers who stopped bickering and stood looking stunned at what I was doing.

The men looked around at each other and before they could turn to yell at me, one of them burst out laughing and hollered loudly, "What do you think you're doing lad? This is a very complicated piece of machinery. Do you have enough money to buy a new one after you wreck it?"

I ignored the men as they all started laughing and mocking me for what I was doing. I could tell they all thought I was doing something terribly wrong and they wanted to see me fail. That would teach him a lesson I heard them all whispering and snickering to each other.

A short while later it was me who was laughing, but just on the inside, as I fixed the machine up and it worked.

It wasn't long before Mr. Libbey heard about the incident and summoned me down to his office. Mr. Libbey started by asking me about what my job was there and that he didn't think fixing machines was in my job description. I felt my cheeks swell with heat. Perspiration flowed from my forehead and I was trying to gain my composure to apologize, but Mr. Libbey abruptly stopped me and said, "Where did you learn to do that? I know you didn't hire you for such a position, but maybe I need to rethink that! Why don't you tell me more about what you can do and I may find a better suited position for you."

I went on to explain how much I learned from my uncle on the farm and how I loved figuring out how to make things work. I tried to gloss over the fact that I had no formal training and little education, but Mr. Libbey already knew that and didn't seem to mind.

Don't ask me why, but from that day forward, Mr. Libbey took me under his wings and began mentoring me about his business. It was like William saw a rare, special quality in me and knowing that I was without a father so young in life, he tried to fill that role and guide me along.

I was so grateful to have the job and never expected to spend any time with the boss. I certainly could never have imagined that we would form such a special friendship that would last a lifetime. I learned so much from William and worked hard to repay him for his kindness.

While I enjoyed my time with William, I also forged a special connection to William's son. I would soon relish the days when his little boy, Edward, would come in to work with him. Edward often said he found his dad's job *boring* so he would sneak away to hunt me down. Edward would come up to me and pull on my shirt to get my attention. I was usually climbing around under one machine or another tweaking with something.

Edward was so easily amused by my wild, imaginative stories. He would hang onto every word and laugh as he handed me tools and begged to hear just a little more. I didn't have a little brother. I was the youngest in the house when I grew up and having this little scamp eager to listen to me was truly quite enjoyable.

I came to feel like a big brother to Edward. I promised myself I would always be there to encourage him and guide him, like his father did for me. When Edward grew older he confided to me how he enjoyed seeing the business his father owned, but that he didn't want to do that with his life. I would listen and encourage him to follow his heart. I just knew in time that he would realize the glass business was just a part of him and that he couldn't deny his destiny.

The Libbey's became like dear family to me. They were there through all the good and bad times in my life. Luckily there was way more good than bad. They all were there in my two happiest times, my marriage and a few years later when I welcomed my only child Robert into the world.

Mr. Libbey was fortunate and knew that his station in life was partly due to his parentage. Although William humbly bowed to his wife Julia's family, because she could trace their roots all the way back to the Mayflower. I was so fascinated with that fact because I enjoyed history. Naturally, since I grew up near Plymouth Rock I often imagined what it must have been like for those brave pilgrims to leave their homes and travel to a new land. I could never imagine myself leaving Cambridge, let alone journeying across the world to a new country. I figured my family would remain here in Massachusetts for generations.

I wasn't exactly sure what Mr. Libbey saw in me, but I hoped it was a young, energetic, smart boy with a lot of potential. *Who knows where I would have been if I had been born to different circumstances.* That fact apparently weighed on William over the years and even more as his own three children grew and had different opportunities than my son.

I didn't know it at the time but William did something that would help my son get the education that I missed out on and that truthfully I would have found difficult to provide for my son.

Chapter 5

William secretly made arrangements to pay for college for my son when the time came. He did it anonymously because he knew I wouldn't have accepted the help. My pride would have gotten in the way. Instead, the college approached my son Robert about a special trial program they had launched and advised that he was selected to be the first recipient. I was so ecstatic about the news that the thought never occurred to me that Mr. Libbey was behind it all.

(Edward would learn about this arrangement when he took over the business from his father. He was so pleased that his father did this for me. Edward would ensure it was fully executed as intended.)

Edward had the opportunity to grow up in a rich, cultural environment. His love of art, music, and literature influenced his life tremendously and he longed to implant that love and appreciation in others. He grew up and went to Boston College with the intent of becoming a minister. However, the world had other plans for his talents and at the age of twenty he found himself working at his father's company, The New England Glass Company.

"Red, I know what I said all these years, but I just couldn't fight it anymore. I feel that my dad needs me here and I will make the most of it."

I just smiled as I watched William, grinning from ear to ear, as his son Edward showed up for work that first day. Edward followed behind his father, as they walked down the familiar halls where he spent much of his childhood.

Everyone smiled and welcomed the newest employee. William surprised Edward with a small plaque engraved with his name on it. His first office wasn't much bigger than a broom closet but Edward looked back at me and winked before he stepped inside.

William wanted Edward to gain experience in all areas of the business. There was no better way to learn it except from the bottom to the top. Edward started out as a clerk and over the years he learned to appreciate the business more and more. He worked hard to move up the ranks. I watched in awe as Edward seemed to go from that inquisitive fun loving child that followed me around to a serious apprentice eager to please and impress his father.

Not long after Edward joined the company, William's business partner abruptly left the struggling business. William wasted no time in changing the name of the company to William Libbey & Son. That seemed to be a real turning point for Edward. From that day forward he seemed more determined than ever to make the business thrive.

Edward wasn't a skilled artisan and regretted that he could never make the beautifully sculpted glassware pieces that their best employees could, but he was talented in other ways. He used his charm and charisma and knowledge of the business to his advantage. He was determined to establish a foothold in the industry by selling high quality glassware that would be sought out by investors and collectors for generations.

There were many, many competitors to contend with which made his mission difficult. Glassmaking was one of the oldest professions in the country. In fact, it was the first industry started at Jamestown, Virginia by the pioneers. Glassmaking had been around for centuries and Europeans also had many glass companies. This fact would prove challenging as the Europeans would often infiltrate America with shiploads of glassware products.

In Massachusetts we struggled to compete against businesses from other states. Some of these competitors were able to sell their product at a cheaper price because they were closer to critical supplies. Shipping costs for material plus the union wages Libbey was paying its workers was putting a huge strain on the business. We were at a crossroads. It was getting nearly impossible to stay afloat and drastic measures or a miracle were needed. And then the most distressing thing happened.

Chapter 6

Tragedy unexpectedly struck the Libbey family in 1883. Edward was just 30 when his father suddenly and without warning passed away. This left Edward in mourning and in charge of a struggling business. William's death struck everyone with grief, especially Edward. But then again, I took it almost as hard as Edward. William had been such a wonderful supporter and friend to me since I was young.

Edward told me later how he prayed for a miracle, but little did he know how that miracle would present itself.

This part of the story is really no different than many others you have read or heard about over the years. Maybe this part of the story will have you reflecting on your own life and what grand gestures you made over love.

The year after his father's death Edward found himself making a lot of trips around the country. He was determined to find a way to keep the business going. He felt he owed a great debt to his father. Since his father left him the company he felt a tremendous obligation to make it successful as a tribute to his father's lifetime of work. Edward had a few good people watching out for him and they would share their concerns with me. I felt helpless at times, but did my best to remain positive.

Edward's stepmother was so terribly worried about the burden put on the young man's shoulders. "I wish I knew what to do for Edward. William has worked so hard for years to keep this business afloat, and without him I'm so afraid –"

I interrupted her to put her at ease, "Don't fret, Mrs. Libbey. Edward will do just fine. You know I'm here and I will do whatever I can to help."

I sat with her while she pulled herself together. Having lost my wife not so long ago, I could understand the pain she was in. Edward's stepmother was awfully proud of Edward and grateful that he chose to alter his plans and work side by side with his father all these years.

Edward's sisters, Sarah and Alice, also looked troubled about the extra strain the loss of their father was having on Edward. They stopped into the plant more frequently to check up on their brother now. "Edward you need to take time to enjoy yourself, find a wife and settle down with children" the sisters would say repeatedly. Edward would just smile and tell them he was going to handle everything.

It was a difficult time and Edward did his best to run the company and put the workforce at ease. However, the workers soon rallied together and voted to strike for better wages and working conditions. Edward demonstrated a great deal of respect for his workers and they gave him the respect he deserved. They were willing to compromise and give Edward a chance. Soon enough they learned to appreciate his new role in the company. They found that Edward took their issues and concerns seriously and worked hard to negotiate with them fairly. He was persuasive in convincing them that they all needed to work together in order to prosper.

Alice's husband, William, was a good friend that Edward could count on during these rough times. William was a businessman too. He was in the furniture business and fortunately people were always in need of new furniture and his business was thriving. When times became really tough William loaned Edward money to keep the glass business afloat. Edward told me that he was awfully grateful to his brother-in-law and was determined to repay him as quickly as possible. I knew he would do it too. Edward was a smart as a steel trap and would find a way to make this business flourish.

Edward was always an avid reader. He would read any book he could get his hands on as soon as he learned to read as a child. His early mornings nowadays were spent reading every word of the local newspaper. He always wanted to know the latest happenings on the business front. However, he also took notice of the arts and culture sections. He always made it a point of getting to any of the new art shows in town. When he was in college he fell in love with Biblical art and often vowed he would own some famous works someday.

One morning I walked by his office while he was browsing the newspaper. Edward leaped up from his chair and exclaimed, "This is too good to be true! I've been struggling to compete lately and the energy prices I'm paying are a huge portion of my costs. Here's a place boasting they are giving away gas for free!"

I couldn't help but stop to see if he was pulling my leg. Edward walked towards me and started shaking the paper at me. Then I noticed Sarah sitting there across from his desk. She grabbed the paper from Edward's hand and began reading the large advertisement that took up half a page of the paper. It touted that new natural gas wells were found in Ohio. The ad was encouraging glass companies to set up shop and enjoy cheap or even free gas she confirmed.

Sarah and I let out a laugh as we had not seen Edward so excited in months. Sarah was one of the few people that knew that if Edward couldn't get costs under control he would probably be bankrupt in a year or two. Competitors who were located in the coal mine states, with access to cheap coal, were killing him on pricing. People loved the products our company manufactured but they were more expensive and we all knew we were being priced out of the market.

As Edward thought more about that article that day, he decided it was worth making a trip to Ohio. What did he have to lose?

Edward stopped by my desk later that day and filled me in on his travel plans. When he asked me to accompany him to Ohio, how could I refuse?

I felt honored to travel with Edward. He had other managers that he could have easily taken, but he valued my judgement and knew I would give him a fair, honest opinion. I was packed and ready when Edward's carriage came for me the next morning.

"You're going to Toledo? The Great Black Swamp?" one of the train passengers in the seat in front of us said laughing. "What in the world would make a business man like yourself want to go there? Do you have family there?" the man asked. Edward looked at me, with a little grin, and I shook my head knowingly.

"I've heard some great things about the place," Edward said. He cleared his throat and continued in a friendly manner, "I read that some of the business leaders there are working on a major plan to make it the next New York City. The town has an abundance of water from the lake, and rivers and the railways go all through the town."

The man and Edward shared a lively banter back and forth about the virtues of living in Ohio versus Massachusetts. "Well, I'd never live anywhere but Boston. I'm a Bostonian, through and through," the man boasted proudly.

"Generations of my family have lived in Boston and with the culture and night life it's like no other city in the world to me," the man said loudly, determined to get anyone listening to join in and agree with him. Some others just nodded quietly in agreement and went back to reading their books or papers. "When are you headed back to Boston?" the man asked Edward.

"I'll be back on the train on Thursday," Edward answered hoping not to encounter the man again. However, that hope was quickly dashed when he heard the man's reply.

"Great, that's my return date as well. We will meet up and you can tell me how much I was right!" the man laughed loudly.

Chapter 7

It was 1887, and it was my first time leaving Massachusetts. I wiped a tear from my eye as I looked at the "Welcome to New York" sign in the distance. I wasn't sad, or frightened, but I had the feeling Massachusetts wouldn't be my home much longer. I didn't know exactly where I would end up, but it seemed time to seek my future elsewhere.

When we arrived in Toledo the rain showed up as well. We were welcomed with a downpour of rain accompanied by loud thunder. "I'll take that thunderous applause as approval of our arrival," Edward chuckled.

Edward hurried to the hotel to get settled in his room and prepare for our first meeting. Edward had previously made arrangements for us to meet with a local banker that afternoon and was glad he had some time before the appointment to dry off.

I decided to continue on down the street. It was my first visit to Ohio and I wasn't going to let a little rain delay my plans. "I'll be back well before the meeting, I just want to have a look around first," I said hurriedly as I meandered down the street.

The gentleman we had come to meet was George Pomeroy. Mr. Pomeroy was President of the First National Bank and one of the preeminent business leaders of the town. Edward and I headed over to his office later that afternoon. Luckily the rain had mostly subsided so it was a pleasant walk.

As Edward and I walked through the streets he asked me to visualize this as our next home. “Can you imagine our folks living here? I want them to love it as much as Cambridge.”

“It definitely has possibilities,” I said trying to be enthusiastic although my heart was still with Cambridge.

We arrived at Pomeroy’s office a few minutes ahead of our appointment time. The secretary offered us coffee as she motioned for us to sit down in the lobby. The office was rather large and tastefully decorated in French style. Edward stood to admire the painting of a French castle just as George walked up behind him.

“Mr. Libbey I presume? I hope I didn’t keep you waiting too long. So pleased you came all this way to our fair city,” Mr. Pomeroy said cheerfully.

“The pleasure is mine, Mr. Pomeroy,” Edward said extending his hand to greet him properly. “This is my associate, Redmond Wynston.”

“How do you do sir?” I said nervously. I definitely felt a little out of place being at such an important meeting. I would have preferred staying at the factory, but Edward was so insistent that I come along. I was a trusted friend to Edward and he knew if I liked the town I would be a great advocate to help persuade the rest of the workforce.

“Have you had an opportunity to look around the town Mr. Libbey?” Mr. Pomeroy asked as he escorted Edward down the hall to his office, with me following closely behind. Edward told him we had just arrived earlier in the afternoon so he didn't have much opportunity yet.

Mr. Pomeroy was one of the premier businessmen in town and was interested in finding people that would locate here that could help Toledo grow and prosper. The two talked like old friends, finding that they had much in common. I could tell that Mr. Pomeroy took a quick liking to Edward.

"Gentlemen, you must come to my home tonight for dinner. My wife Hannah is a wonderful cook and is always looking to show off her culinary skills on new people."

Edward found Mr. Pomeroy quite intriguing and couldn't resist a home-cooked meal with a gracious host. He thanked him kindly and asked for the address. "Here's the directions to my house on Huron Street. I look forward to seeing you both at 6:00 p.m." George said as he escorted us out the front door.

Edward and I spent the rest of the afternoon checking out the town. We both found it a charming place with a lot of potential. After walking several blocks Edward let out a sigh and said, "I'm sad to find that there doesn't seem to be any museum's in the town."

I knew that was something he would surely miss about his hometown. "You should just open a museum if you move here, you have enough stuff to fill one," I said half-joking as Edward scoffed off the suggestion as preposterous.

We continued down Madison Avenue and soon found a quaint coffee shop and stopped in for a drink. While we were there we struck up a conversation with a few local men and they were soon laughing at the funny stories we told. "We have a great baseball team. Do you like baseball?" one of the men asked Edward, changing the subjcct.

Before he could respond the other one chimed in, "Of course he does, what American doesn't love baseball? It's one of the greatest sports around."

This led to a raucous conversation about who was the best baseball player and which team was going to beat what team. Edward enjoyed the colorful exchange as he defended the Boston Red Stockings, his team, against any others they mentioned. When it was near dinner time we bid farewell to the locals and left.

Edward spotted the house as soon as we turned onto Huron Street. "That stately Italian Villa brick home must be George's house," Edward said confidently to me. Edward admired the architecture and the columns along the front porch as he opened the gate and walked up to the front door. George greeted us at the door.

"Edward and Red it's so great to see you again, welcome to my home!" George said excitedly as he shook our hands and led us into the foyer. Edward greeted Mrs. Pomeroy as she entered the room.

"How lovely to meet you. You have a beautiful home Mrs. Pomeroy," Edward said with a sincere grin on his face.

"Please you must call me Hannah. I'm so pleased you both could join us tonight. I do hope you like roast, I've been preparing it all day. It's one of George's favorites," Hannah said hopefully.

"It sounds and smells wonderful Hannah," Edward said. With the introductions out of the way Hannah excused herself and returned to the kitchen. George offered us a drink and we headed to the library.

"This is my favorite room," George confessed. "I find it wonderfully inspiring to come in here and be surrounded by all the greats."

I could see how much Edward was impressed with the collection of leather bound classics and other books that lined the shelves. George told a few stories of how his collection of books started and had us both laughing and feeling at ease in no time.

"What music do you enjoy?" Edward asked pointing at the gramophone in the corner.

"Why don't you listen and tell me," George said as he picked up a record and put it on. The music filled the room and sounded wonderful.

"Is it Bach? I admire anyone who can make that kind of sound." Edward said as the doorbell chimed.

"We have a couple other guests joining us tonight. I hope you don't mind, but my dear friend Maurice Scott and his daughter Florence are coming. That is probably them, I'll be right back," George said and walked quickly out of the room before we could say a word.

Edward took the time to walk over and check out the collection of books along the wall. He pulled one off the shelf that caught his eye, but he didn't get a chance to open it before a lovely creature entered his view. He abruptly dropped the book as George introduced him to a most striking lady. I was enchanted to see the subtle glimmer Edward tried to suppress in his eyes. I could tell from that first encounter the two made a handsome couple.

"Florence and Maurice Scott I'd like you to meet Edward Libbey and Redmond Wynston. Edward is from Cambridge and here to consider our town for his business," George said to the newcomers. "Edward, Maurice is one of my oldest and dearest friends. I don't know how with his looks he managed to have such a beautiful daughter, but I suspect his wife gets all the credit," George chided his friend. The compliment to Florence had her blushing. Something in her eyes told me we would become lifelong friends.

(I found out later that George didn't let on to anyone else his special plan for the night. When he found out Edward Libbey wanted to come and check out Toledo he was ecstatic. He knew of Edward's famous company and it was just the kind of business that Toledo wanted here. George figured that meeting some people his age may sway Edward to pick Toledo. George secretly had a lot riding on Florence's charms to do the trick.)

George and a few other prominent business men active in the town had formed a committee. The members met often and over drinks and cigars as they discussed what they wanted to see for the future of Toledo. They were visionary and forward thinking men. They wanted to establish Toledo as more than just a farming town. They wanted industries to set up shop that could help the town prosper. They had already helped build the railways and infrastructure that would rival the other towns. Now they just needed to snare a big company.

In time I found out that when Edward Libbey reached out to George, George was determined he was going to do everything in his power to convince him to move here. When he learned that Edward was single, the first person he thought of for a match was Florence. Anyone could easily see that he adored Florence like she was his own. He had known her for years and watched her grow up into a fine young lady. He knew Maurice had refined her in such a way that there weren't many young men in town that could match her in education and culture.

Florence had been educated abroad and was a very worldly scholar. I imagined this likely intimidated many of the men her age that lived around town. (It certainly intimidated me.) I would quickly learn that the Scott family was known around town as a very generous and wealthy family of privilege. Someone of Edward's caliber and upbringing in Cambridge would most assuredly be a match intellectual wise. Now if they hit it off, that could be a huge advantage for George's plans, he admitted to me later. He also confessed to me that when he saw Edward look glowingly at Florence that first night, he knew his plan was happily in motion.

Florence excused herself and left the library and went to find Hannah in the kitchen. I stepped into the hallway as Florence entered the kitchen. Hannah smiled brightly and I overheard her say, "Florence I'm so glad you could join us for dinner this evening. I know we didn't give you much notice. When George met Edward this afternoon he simply insisted he come for dinner. Edward must have made quite an impression on him. George has been going on and on about him since he got home. He is really hoping we can talk up Toledo and help convince Edward to move here. Just think of what that could mean for our town. The men have been working so hard to try and entice glass manufacturers to come here and now we have the owner of one of the most premiere companies investigating our town." Hannah looked sneakily at Florence trying to gage her reaction to her talk about Edward.

Florence wasn't giving anything away until Hannah boldly said, "That Edward sure is a handsome gentlemen too. I can't believe he isn't married yet." Florence's cheek turned a little crimson as she stopped herself from agreeing out loud and looked down at the floor appearing a little embarrassed.

Hannah was a good friend of Florence's mother and she wanted to see Florence happily married too. I could discern from the conversation that Florence probably had not thought about marriage in a while. She said she had been too busy traveling the world. Florence raved about how she enjoyed the past summer in Germany.

I could see that by society standards, Florence was getting up there in age to be single and perhaps was starting to think that her time had passed to becoming a bride. The men she had met around town were probably nice and all but they likely didn't have the same worldly experience or maybe didn't have the same interests or love of art that Florence did. I took an instant liking to Florence and found myself also wanting to play matchmaker. While Edward had dated, he never took the time to get too serious about anyone. If George wanted my help in this endeavor, I would gladly lend my support!

I made a point of approaching Florence when she left the kitchen alone. It was a little forward of me I know, but for Edward's happiness I was willing to risk it. Florence found me easy to talk too, and having just escaped from the meddling older ladies in the kitchen, she was ready to unleash her frustrations. I just happened to be there and ready to lend an ear.

Florence looked exasperated, let out a sigh and confided that she just didn't find much in common with anyone of late. She relayed that her mother just couldn't believe she could be happy pursuing her interests instead of pursuing a husband. Florence quietly told me that she was so glad her mother had not been able to join them that night. It would have made for an awkward sight, knowing that her mother would have been gushing all over Edward and the thought of playing matchmaker. She cringed and shook off the thought. I just laughed nervously as I secretly planned to do the very thing she didn't want. But she didn't know Edward the way I did. I figured she could thank me later!

Edward, Maurice and George joined me and the ladies in the dining room when they were called. George made sure Edward was seated across from Florence. The more George looked at the two of them the more I could see that he was convinced this would be a good match. I didn't expect to ever play the role of matchmaker, but George and I glanced at each other approvingly as the night wore on. We congratulated each other later thinking that we had struck gold on our common goal.

I could see that Hannah took extra care that afternoon in setting the table. Fine china, with flowers delicately etched around the rims, were elegantly matched with fine silverware. Not surprisingly, several Libbey glassware items, the couple must have purchased over the years, were proudly on display. This consisted of water goblets, wine glasses and as Hannah pointed out the exquisite compote, beautifully engraved flowering around the bowl, she raved that it was her personal favorite. Hannah had the compote brimming with pecans, apparently her husband's favorite snack.

Edward was impressed and pleased with the table setting and remarked, "My Hannah, I'm so pleased to see the wonderful glassware on your table. I hope that you find yourself enjoying them for a long time. The dinner smells delicious. George told me this is his favorite meal and I'm sure it will be one of mine too."

George encouraged Edward to tell them about his travels. Florence seemed impressed that Edward had been to many of the places she enjoyed in Europe. The pair talked back and forth almost forgetting the rest of us in the room. George and I didn't mind and neither did Hannah. I could see the Pomeroy's sharing a few silent glances, confirming they were both pleased the dinner was going so well.

Florence's father also seemed taken with Edward. This was not a surprise to me. It was rare that I would hear of anyone that didn't like Edward. He just had a way of making everyone feel at ease and he so enjoyed an audience. Edward had a gift for storytelling and kept the group entertained and laughing all evening. I was just happy to be there watching it all unfold.

After dinner we made our way to the parlor. "Hannah plays the piano like an angel. Darling, why don't you play us a few verses of that new song you learned, what was it called again?" George asked.

"I don't know that our company wishes to hear me, I'm really not all that good yet. I just play it for fun when nobody is around."

"Nonsense. You have a real talent for that piano. I know you haven't played long, but the sound that comes out is like heaven." George said truthfully.

"Yes, please play us something Hannah, I would love to hear you," Edward said as we all spoke in unison pleading to her.

Hannah couldn't refuse all of us so she sat down at the piano. The rest of us sat down nearby eagerly awaiting the impromptu concert. Hannah took a deep breath, put her fingers upon the keys and tapped away while emitting the most beautiful sound. She was encouraged by the group and ended one song and started another. "Bravo, bravo! You should be playing in a large concert hall Hannah," said Edward sincerely.

"Hannah, I agree, that was outstanding. I can't believe you've picked all that up in such a short time," Florence said.

Then I noticed Florence give Hannah a stern look when I saw Hannah about to reveal loudly that Florence played piano as well. I could tell she was not in the mood to be put on that type of display in front of Edward tonight. She looked rather self-conscious and quietly told Hannah she wasn't good enough to play for an audience. I was sure she was just being modest, but I figured Edward would get a chance to hear her play another day.

Edward turned to me and said he was really enjoying himself and didn't want the evening to end. We agreed that meeting George earlier in the day was very productive and this dinner invitation couldn't have gone better. Edward wouldn't admit it to me then, but he didn't have to, as I could see that he had taken a real shine to Florence.

I could tell he never expected to meet such a beautiful and cultured lady here in Toledo. She knew more than many of the ladies he knew back in Cambridge. I noticed the time and reluctantly reminded Edward that we should go.

"George and Hannah, I do so appreciate your hospitality this evening but we really must be getting back to the hotel. We have to leave early in the morning to get back home." Edward then turned to Maurice and shook his hand, "Mr. Scott, sir, it was such a pleasure to meet you. I thank you for taking the time to tell me all about the virtues of Toledo. I can truly appreciate it all the more now."

Finally Edward turned and smiled at Florence, "It was a great pleasure to meet you as well. I do hope you will be in town if I drop by again. If anyone of you are ever in Cambridge again, please look me up so that I can return the hospitality."

Edward picked up his hat and draped his coat over his arm and headed out the door. The walk back to the hotel gave us time to reflect on the evening. If there was anything else George could have done to convince us of all the reasons to move here I couldn't think of it.

"That George sure tried to pull a fast one didn't he?"

"Whatever do you mean?" I asked sheepishly.

"I know exactly why George invited Florence to dinner, but you know what? I didn't mind one bit." Under his breath I heard him mutter something like, "What a beauty."

Anyone in his right mind would agree that Florence was delightful and utterly charming. I could tell as we walked the rest of the way to the hotel that Edward was figuring out a plan to see her again. But then abruptly he tried to keep a serious tone as he lectured me, "Red, I know what you might be thinking, but trust me, that lady will not be a factor in my relocation decision."

I knew Edward well and could tell he was protesting too much, trying to convince himself, because he was already realizing it was going to be hard to keep that promise. The other towns were going to have to be extraordinary to compete. Could any of them hold a candle to what Toledo could offer?

Chapter 8

Edward was uncharacteristically melancholy on the train ride home. He wouldn't admit it to me, but I could see the longing in his eyes as he stared out the train windows watching the town fade far from view as we headed back to Cambridge the next morning. I tried not to dwell too much on the future, but I could feel big changes coming our way.

The following days for me were fairly routine, working at the factory, and spending time with my family. Edward, however, never stayed at home too long these days. If there was a new business starting up, like a store or hotel, he would be there. He had many salespeople working for him that were more than capable of handling the job, but Edward made it a point to personally meet the owners of these establishments. He would learn all he could about the person and their business as he rode the train from one town to the next.

Edward enjoyed the long train rides where he had the chance to meet his fellow passengers. It seemed before he left the station at the beginning of a trip he was already striking up a friendly conversation with someone.

Edward enjoyed studying other people and places. He was one of those folks that by the time a train ride ended, whether it was an hour or ten, Edward would have made several new friends. I always admired that about him. I was friendly enough, but didn't feel so at ease talking with strangers. Edward's friendly personality was a big advantage for his business too. He was never afraid to talk with people. He had a way of talking with anyone and somehow as soon as they found out what he did, they would be asking him where to buy his wares. He was just a natural born salesperson.

In the mid 1880's there were many new businesses starting up. It was an exciting time to be in America I thought. The economy was going strong and middle to upper class people had money to spend on new-fangled items for the home. Department stores were opening in cities and feeding the people's appetites for products. Our artisans crafted some of the most stunning glass and Edward was personally going to ensure that our glassware would be there and ready for them wherever they shopped.

Edward often traveled alone on his adventures across the country. He left his plant manager Jim in charge while he was away. I'd know Jim for a while now and he was more than capable of running the day to day operations of the factory and handling the men. If he encountered any problems, Edward knew I was there too.

As the year dragged on, some of the other men started to become more rebellious. I overheard several of them grumbling about their paychecks. Their wives were telling them they needed more money to run the household and they heard the rumors of what other glasshouses were paying in West Virginia and Pennsylvania.

Although they probably didn't want to leave their hometown of Cambridge, they likely did want more of the finer things in life. You wouldn't believe all the exciting new things being put on the market at this time that would ease the workload in the home for their wives. Some of the best inventions were the sewing machine, washing machine, dishwasher and vacuum cleaner, and all the housewives longed for them, including mine.

Eventually the topic of conversation turned to a strike. Friends asked me about whether we should strike again. I could understand some of the concerns and felt conflicted. I knew this talk would be a surprise to Edward as felt he treated all the workers fairly and respectfully and didn't think there was a need for a strike. I made an effort to understand the views of all the workers. I wanted to be prepared to discuss these with Edward when he returned from his trip.

Edward left for Chicago by train yesterday. We had a sales office in Chicago and Edward wanted to visit and check on the team. The office consisted of a few salespeople and a secretary. A small display room there glittered with samples of our finest cut glass pieces. It made for an impressive place to bring clients. The salespeople conducted many meetings in that office proudly showing off our products and taking orders from customers. Edward liked to surprise the staff so they never knew when he was coming.

The office was capably run by Tim. Tim, a longtime salesman with the company, was usually happy when Edward came in to town. This gave him the chance to see the boss in person and tell him exactly how business was going and what problems they were encountering in town. Tim had lived in Chicago all his life.

He endured some hardships when the great fire struck the town a few years back. The fire was devastating for the townsfolk but fortunately they were on the way in recovering and rebuilding the grand city.

Edward knew Tim had a big meeting with Mr. Ward and he planned his trip so that he could attend that gathering. Mr. Ward owned a large department store and was a valued client. I suspected Mr. Ward to be impressed that Mr. Libbey would travel all the way from Massachusetts to meet with him. Edward made it a priority to meet with as many of his customers as he could every year.

Edward anticipated Mr. Ward to place a large order for our line of Kenwood glassware to display in his catalog. His catalog business was growing more and more popular with folks in the mid-western states. The railways were growing every year and this made it easier to ship and receive products across the country. Edward was determined to have his products on every track across the land.

Edward also had another motive for going to Chicago. He wanted to congratulate Tim for increasing his sales numbers over the past couple quarters. The city was expanding and Tim was doing his part to grow our company along with it. Edward let Tim know that his Chicago office was bringing in more sales than all the other offices.

When Edward didn't return from Chicago as expected I asked his assistant what happened. She stated, "Oh, he decided to stop in Toledo for a day on the way home."

"No surprise there." I said happily to myself as I turned away. Did Florence have any idea that our future destiny was riding on her? I kind of hoped not, that would be quite a burden for anyone that age to endure.

My thoughts on the matter were kept to myself – I knew how to keep a secret and I sure didn't want to get the workforce riled up prematurely over my suspicions.

Chapter 9

I could see it coming like a train racing off the tracks. The men had fought to organize a union a few years back and now the whispers of another strike was picking up steam. This time it wasn't just a fight for higher wages, they also wanted better working conditions. They heard of concessions workers were getting from other companies and they felt they had a right to the same.

Edward sighed and said to me, "I don't know why they needed a union. Our wages were already above the industry average. And I'm doing everything I can to make this a great place to work."

I felt helplessly in the middle. I was just one of the working guys, not the owner. However, I was also close with Edward and his father and I knew them to be honest, good folk and fair bosses.

"Ed, you know competition is fierce and the most qualified employees have many choices of where to work. Many wouldn't hesitate to leave, even to another state if they get a better offer. I can try and reason with them before this gets out of hand, but what do they want me to tell them?"

Edward knew what he was up against. He himself had traveled to other states to encourage people to join his company. Next to fuel, the second highest of costs to the business was labor. Edward was very concerned and said, "Don't the men know how severe my costs are? I guess I will have to pull the workers together and tell them honestly about our production costs, profits (or lack thereof lately) and projected sales. If the business was doing better, I would gladly pay them more."

I guess he thought that by giving the men all this information they would understand. Unfortunately they didn't want to listen to any of it at first.

Some of them accused Edward of distorting the figures. They knew how much their products sold for and they thought there should be more money coming in. They didn't want to believe the amount of expenses that were incurred each day.

They also dismissed the fact that there were so many glass houses right now and competition was fierce. Unfortunately, several kept dropping their prices below their costs just trying to hold out long enough to put another competitor out of business. This was not a sustainable business practice and the whole industry was suffering as a result.

A few rabble-rousers seemed to be working hard to undermine everything Edward said. I feared they wouldn't give up until they got a strike. I couldn't really blame them. They had their family's best interests in mind and you couldn't fault a guy for that.

Edward didn't threaten, but he bluntly said that another union strike could force him to shut his doors. The ringleaders spoke out, protested, and told everyone he was bluffing, he'd never shut down, he'd never leave his hometown they presumed.

They kept up the heat and worked their agenda through each department until they felt they had enough on their side. They all voted, and to Edward's dismay, the majority overwhelmingly chose to strike.

Edward was worried that an increase of wages would put him out of business. I was at a loss for words. I held my breath as Edward warned me that he wouldn't be staying in town for much longer.

Edward's sisters wanted to know firsthand what was going on with the vote, so they made it a point to stop into the office that morning. Edward didn't look too happy to see them, but he tried to cover that with a forced smile.

"How did the vote go?" Edward's sister Sarah asked, although from Edward's face she didn't need to hear a response, it was written all over his face. His sister looked at me for some reassurance but what could I say?

"Edward worked hard to show the workers the economics of running the factory. The men are just so used to having the company around, you know? It's been here for seventy years, that's more than their whole lives. Many had fathers who worked here before them, and they are sure their sons will carry on the tradition."

"I know how hard our father worked to make the business stay afloat and I know what a challenge you have on your hands," Sarah said, turning towards Edward.

"I've already contacted some businessmen in Ohio and West Virginia and I will go out again next week to meet with some of them. Nobody really thinks I'll leave, but I'm already packing my bags. We will not survive if we stay here another year," Edward said sadly.

"You know I support your decision. Anything I can do to help I will do," I said reassuringly as his sister Sarah nodded her head in agreement.

Sarah always looked up to her big brother, especially ever since their father had passed away. Edward changed his whole life's plan to help his dad in the business. She looked uncomfortable seeing him so dejected.

When Alice's husband, William, came charging down the hall she filled him in on the news. "I think it's just awful, they are going to bankrupt the company. Then where will they be? The higher wage won't matter if the place is closed."

"You're right dear. I feel for Edward, but there isn't much we can do to help. The business world can be tough and doesn't always follow logic. I suppose this is going to force Edward to seriously consider a move," William said out loud what everyone else was afraid to utter.

Alice sure didn't want to think about that. She knew her younger sister Sarah would follow Edward wherever he went. She would too, but first she would have to convince her husband. William's business was doing well here and she couldn't jeopardize their future to follow Edward into the unknown.

I think William could see the distress on Alice's face, because I sure could. I knew she looked up to Edward as more than a brother. The words were unspoken between them, but they each were probably thinking the same thing. Would they endure a move to keep the whole family together? I'm sure William secretly hoped it wouldn't come to that. William loved Cambridge. We all did.

I left Edward's office feeling depressed. I recalled how close we came to shutting down permanently when we endured our first strike in 1885. Edward negotiated fairly and quickly with the union and thankfully we were back to work with shorter hours and more pay. The men surely felt they could strike again and get the same result. Could they live with the consequences if they lost?

Chapter 10

Edward demonstrated a great deal of respect for his workers and in return they soon gave him the respect he earned. Most were ready to give Edward a chance and soon the majority of them came around. They found a way to eventually fully appreciate his role in the company. They learned that Edward took their concerns and issues seriously and he worked hard to demonstrate that he wanted them all to work together and succeed together. It was the only way Edward thought was right.

Although everyone was now back to work, I found it extremely hard to concentrate today. I knew Edward's meeting with the board was soon at hand. The future of the company was on the line. I woke up in the night and began thinking back on our first trip to Toledo. The trip went way better than either of us expected. The town had much more to offer than even Edward realized.

I knew Edward's first thought about Toledo included Florence. She was definitely a lovely surprise. I laughed thinking of how clever George was and how satisfied he must have felt sensing the chemistry between the two. I had to tip my hat to him and agreed that what he did was a genius move. As Edward always said, "In business you should use every legal advantage to win!" George had certainly done that!

Setting Florence aside, Toledo did have other charms. It was situated in a fantastic location with access to the Great Lakes. Ports for shipping were accessible for bringing in supplies and sending out shipments. The railways also had a good foothold established. Gas was plentiful, and cheap. Further there were sand pits in nearby Monclova. These are the points Edward would have to rank against the other locations. If only the external factors weren't forcing the move, I lamented.

I knew Edward's preference would be to stay in Cambridge. He would rather stay in his hometown, than move anywhere. I thought of his father William and wished Edward was able to consult with him on this issue. Edward must know his father would also have had to face the fact that moving wasn't an option.

In order for the business to survive, Edward had to move where he could get his costs more in line with his competitors. It wasn't unusual for businesses to move around the country to save on costs, be closer to customers, better labor markets, or a host of other reasons. Now we all knew it was our time to move.

Edward was going out on the road again for one last trip before weighing all our options. The towns in Ohio were clamoring for businesses and Edward wanted to see them all in person. The first stop of this journey was Tiffin, Ohio.

Tiffin is about 60 miles south of Toledo. Tiffin was looking to make a name for itself and yearned to become a prosperous industrial city. It was connected by two railway lines and the abundance of natural gas was an attractive feature. These qualities made it appealing to many porcelain and glass manufacturers.

Findlay, Ohio which was near Fostoria was very aggressive in recruiting new businesses to grow its town. In the early 1880's the town had become known as the place to be for any glass company. The town boasted over 30 glass companies due to the abundance of natural gas that was found a few years earlier. The town quickly tripled in size. The charming Blanchard River that ran through the town was a big selling point. Townsfolk could always be found fishing along the river.

Fostoria, Ohio was a city located about 40 miles south of Toledo, Ohio. It was a growing city and also attracting attention from the glass industry. The city had recently discovered a huge gas supply and was offering it free to businesses that would locate there. The town quickly doubled in population as several glass companies decided to move in.

The bonus of free gas in Fostoria was enticing, but the town did not have the same cultural lures that were already established in larger towns like Toledo. This fact would be a big strike against Fostoria for Edward who wanted to offer his workers the same cultural advantages they had in nearby Boston.

Toledo, Ohio just about 50 miles north of Fostoria, was visited previously by Edward. Toledo's streets were muddy and the place was a bit of a swampy mess the folks in Fostoria reminded him. However, they didn't know that in Toledo Edward met with Mr. Pomeroy and his friends. That meeting, which I had the pleasure of attending with him, would have a long lasting appeal that seemed now like destiny.

Toledo's population was maybe 50,000 in 1882. This was nothing compared to a city like Boston that boasted 420,000 and growing. Boston had history, culture, flourishing businesses, prestige, and what did Toledo have? Well frogs for one thing. The marshy land, full of water everywhere you stepped, was a haven for frogs! The Maumee River was overflowing from the heavy spring rains and it made it almost impossible to keep your feet dry, as I discovered on my first visit!

Chapter 11

Decision day was finally here. Edward had poured over all the data he collected on the potential new locations for the business and knew what he wanted to do. He told me he had made up his mind. Now it was time to meet with the Board of Directors and get their support and agreement. I would be there for support and to answer any technical questions about such a move.

The board members filed into the conference room early that morning. The group knew each other well since they had worked together for years. "Gentlemen, good morning, how is everyone today?" Edward asked as he strode confidently into the room. They all greeted one another and chatted pleasantly while coffee was poured and they settled around the long conference table.

When it was time to get down to business Edward began, "We have a full agenda today. There is one important matter that we all know has come to a critical point. We must make a decision about the future of the company today." Edward had a feeling of where each of the members were on their preferences of the outcome of this decision. It would be debated loudly and vigorously over the next few hours. Each man took a turn to state his opinion and advice as Edward presented each option.

The choices included: West Virginia, Pittsburgh, Pennsylvania, and in Ohio the towns of Tiffin, Findlay, Fostoria and Toledo. Each location had some viable advantages. Edward knew in his head, and his heart, what he believed to be the best decision. But he listened intently to the others. For the ones who had a different view, Edward would listen objectively and try to understand their point of view. Then if disagreed, he would debate the issues and hope they would come to an agreement with him.

After exhausting all options it was finally time to vote. When the votes were tallied I saw Edward sigh in relief and knew the result before he spoke. The vote for Edward's number one choice won handily. Edward tried to contain his excitement, but he found that difficult. He was ecstatic they would be moving to Toledo, Ohio.

The fact that Edward would be moving to Toledo and would be closer to Florence was like the cherry on top of his sundae, the best part! This decision had been weighing on everyone, but especially on Edward for months, and it was a relief to finally have the decision made. The focus was now on the future and all the plans to set the change and move in motion. Now came the next hard part, he would have to tell the workforce.

Edward had the support of the Board of Directors but would he get the same from the workers? His first concern was about the artisans. The skilled group of a hundred men who made the product something that was so well regarded to the public was critical to his operation. These men were highly sought after for their skill and knowledge.

The learning and expertise the artisans had acquired to create glass masterpieces was a very long process, sometimes it took years to perfect. Naturally the talented men were highly sought after by the hundreds of other glass companies in the country. Most of the men in our employ had worked at the Company for many years and were very loyal to Edward's father.

Edward was convinced that some of the artisans thought he was too young to take the helm at 30 when his father suddenly passed away, but so far not one of them left the Company. They quickly learned to appreciate Edward as they saw how well he handled the sudden change in responsibility to fill his new role as the business leader. The men also had a great respect for me and with my encouragement they gave Edward the benefit of the doubt. They didn't let him have too much slack, but they soon grew to respect him and his style of management.

In quick order they found Edward to be more of a collegial, thoughtful leader. He respected his workers and gave them authority to manage themselves. Edward's first official meeting to the employees, when he had to break the news of his father's death to everyone, set the tone right away.

I was the first to know we were moving to Toledo. How you ask? I knew Edward too well and I could feel it when Edward wouldn't even dare admit it to himself. After our first trip to Toledo, Edward came back to tell hilariously, dreadful stories of a city that seemed plagued with frogs, that may have turned some off. But, he had an undeniable twinkle in his eye when he mentioned that beautiful lady he met, who was the realtor's daughter Florence.

Most people might not have picked up on this clue, but knowing Edward the way I did, this fact gave Toledo an unbelievable advantage. After all, Edward was constantly being hounded by his sisters to settle down. They were frequently trying to play matchmaker by having a young single lady "unexpectedly" drop by whenever they invited Edward over for dinner. Edward didn't want to admit it, but he was ready to find romance.

Society also dictated that someone of Edward's age should be married. Edward was always too wrapped up in the business though, especially since his father's death propelled him into the driver's seat at the company. Luckily he had friends like me and Mr. Pomeroy who could help him out.

Edward wouldn't be the first to base a decision on a beautiful young lady, and certainly not the last. I was glad to see that someone had finally caught Edward's eye. He deserved that kind of happiness in his life. We all did. Don't we all aspire to that?

Chapter 12

"Just pull the bandage off all at once and get it over with quickly," I counseled Edward.

That sentiment was usually Edward's viewpoint too. The best way to deal with disseminating bad news is quickly. Everyone knew this news was coming sooner or later anyway, although most didn't want to accept the real state of the business no matter how many times Edward tried to broach the subject.

The business had been around for almost seventy years so people took it for granted that it would just be around forever. People gossiped and rumors flew around about the challenges of the company, but they always found a way to survive before. Therefore the workers just brushed those fears and conversations aside. They said it was just talk, it didn't feel real to them.

A mandatory meeting in the packaging area at 8:00 a.m. had everyone nervous. We gathered around in the large open space. The others were all animated and chatted to each other but I stood by in silence. Several made wild guesses about what the urgent meeting was about, although for the most part they already knew. Rumors were rampant all morning. A few men said they saw some of the board members in the factory this morning which led others to speculate this was the "big news". I kept quiet, just observing and trying to anticipate the response to the news I knew was forthcoming.

I learned that while I was in the board of directors meeting earlier that morning the workforce was conducting its own "meetings" around the factory. There was even a betting pool going around to vote on where you thought the business was going to reside in the future.

The home town of Cambridge was favored by a distinct group of employees. This group consisted of mainly the older workers who couldn't seem to come to grips with the fact the factory could be located and operated anywhere else. They just couldn't be objective about the true challenges facing the company.

The younger workers were much more pessimistic about Cambridge's chances. Maybe it was their youth and inexperience in the business world, or maybe they were more open to change. For some reason they were more likely to vote for a move. Maybe they just romanticized the notion of packing up and heading west. From what I could hear, most of them still had wildly differing opinions on which town it would be. I was glad to hear some were receptive to moving, with hopes of increasing their pay and to try new adventures.

The workers debated back and forth all morning on the merits of the towns they suspected could be on the list. These were towns they really didn't know much about, but that didn't stop them from bragging up one town over another. The couple of employees who went around taking bets were quite busy. They tried to stay objective as people placed their bets and tried not to sway them with their opinions. They didn't comment openly to their choice, they just nodded their heads and moved on down the line. Not much work was getting done this day, there was just too much uncertainty and excitement buzzing in the air to concentrate on work.

Everyone was gathered around the packaging area and when Edward arrived they slowly stopped talking. Edward raised his arms straight up and waved his hands up and down as he entered. This was a signal for everyone to quiet down. Then Edward began, "Men, I wanted you to hear this directly from me. You may or may not know, but I just met with the board of directors. The topic, as you could guess, was about the future of this company. More specifically, how and where we can operate to compete in this challenging environment. I've been very open and transparent with you about the state of the business and the competitive disadvantages we face. For those reasons we have come to the difficult, but rousing decision that it is time to move westward. The factory will be moving to Toledo, Ohio," Edward paused to gauge the reaction of the crowd and let the words fully sink in.

Edward had been living with this issue much more intimately than anyone and had time to come to terms with it. He knew many of his men didn't want to believe this move was a real possibility. I knew his next words were important too, but I could tell many of the workers were just worrying about what this decision was going to mean to them and their families.

"There were several options on the table, but in the end the majority agreed, as did I, that Toledo was the best choice. I do sincerely hope each of you will join me in this grand adventure. I hope you talk this over with your families tonight and give me your decisions as soon as possible. I understand you all have kin to consider but please know that the schools, churches, and cultural opportunities there are all comparable to Cambridge. You may come to find, as I have, that there are many benefits to living in the smaller town of Toledo."

Edward cleared this throat, took a sip of water and continued, "The city of Toledo has been aggressively seeking glass businesses to locate in their town. You may have read about this or saw the advertisements over the past several months in our local newspaper. Our factory will be their first and will be built in a part of town they have named Glassboro. I also negotiated and acquired land for housing near the plant. We will all be close together living as neighbors near the plant. This will provide a great family like atmosphere for us all. If anyone has any specific questions you can ask me now, or stop by my office later. I hope you will see this as a great opportunity for the future of our Company and our families."

One gentlemen shouted, "Lucky Toledo!" and others looked at him. Edward stayed and answered questions that a few were brave enough to ask. When the questions ceased and the crowd dwindled down, Edward turned and headed back to his office. As Edward stepped away I could hear the confused workers talking amongst themselves.

The reality was finally starting to set in and some guys were elated and some were furious. Edward knew it would be a hard sell for those with big families that had lived here for generations. He knew some families would be more supportive about the news than others but he felt he didn't have a choice. Difficult choices had to be made in life and now the final decision was up to each of the men. "I hope they choose to follow me, Red. I want to keep as many as I can."

"I'm sure you're relieved the decision and announcement are finally completed. Now give the guys some time to think on it and you'll see them come around," I said hopefully.

Now Edward could begin the task of finalizing and approving the details of the new building. One benefit to moving to Toledo that wasn't mentioned to the workers, was that Toledo had a well-established and experienced fire department. This was another factor that helped sway the decision.

We had been lucky that we had not had a fire damage our factory, but it was an unfortunate reality for other glass companies. Firemen or not, Edward wasn't taking any chances. He was determined to make sure this new building was constructed with more fire resistant materials than the current factory. The city also had a good pool of laborers to help with the construction. He was assured the plant would be ready in a few months.

It was going to be a banner year for the workforce in Toledo. One crew would be building our plant while houses would be built by another crew at the same time. The businessmen who helped broker the deal were going to be heroes, I surmised.

I followed Edward to his office and he closed the door to have a moment alone with me. The conversation soon turned to Florence. "Red, how do think Florence will take the news? I'd never let on to anyone, especially her, how much her presence may have played in my decision. I don't even want to admit it to myself!"

"It's hard to keep that kind of secret Edward. I know you've only seen her a handful of times, when you made those few stops in town, but anyone with half a clue could see how smitten you are when you are around her!"

"Well, I do plan to make it a habit to see her more frequently now that we moving the plant. I just hope she will be happy about that," Edward said nervously.

"You know, as soon as you tell George, I suspect he will make a beeline to alert Maurice who would naturally tell his daughter Florence. Oh I wish I could be there to see the look on her face!" I said enjoying watching Edward squirm in embarrassment.

The move couldn't come soon enough to Edward. Now that the decision was made, he was ready to go. Well, there was still the pending discussion with his family and the mayor of Cambridge. Breaking the news to the mayor would be a difficult conversation and he felt it only right to deliver it personally. I didn't want to be the one to present that news, but Edward dragged me along. He didn't need me there, but I guess he didn't want to go it alone.

Edward had talked with the mayor several times over the past few months about his business prospects. I had met the mayor a few times and knew how concerned he was about the factory moving from his town. After all, our company had been in town since it opened in 1818 and we had grown to be the town's largest employer. We turned out a high quality product and the town was proud to have us there.

The mayor must have been dreading this day but he heard the rumors and must have known it was coming. He couldn't have missed seeing all the advertisements in *The Cambridge Chronicle*, pronouncing free land and free energy for anyone who would set up shop in various towns throughout Ohio and West Virginia. How could he compete with that?

When the mayor was advised by his secretary that Mr. Libbey was in the lobby, his shoulders slumped as he looked up anxiously from his office. "Show him in Mary, no sense keeping him waiting," the mayor said. "From the look on your face, I just know why you're here. We lost you didn't we?

"Mayor, how are you today?" Edward said as he extended his hand to shake.

"I'm afraid I'm not going to be doing as well in a few minutes." the mayor said as he motioned for Edward and me to take a seat.

"Mayor, my board met this morning to review our options. As you know, our finances have been terribly strained the past couple years. We had to take a serious look at our opportunities to try and stay in business. Unfortunately we have determined that the best decision for our future is in Toledo. You know I love Cambridge as much as you do, and if there was any way we could stay here we would. I know this will be a big change to the town, but for the chance at our long term survival we had to make this decision. I hope you can understand," Edward said thoughtfully.

"Mr. Libbey, I appreciate you coming to tell me this in person. I can't tell you how disappointed I am that you and your workers will be leaving our town, but I do understand. I just knew it was a matter of time before we would lose your business. I can't really blame you. I might have done the same if I was in your shoes. I truly do wish you the best of luck and hope that you do well in Toledo," the mayor said.

The mayor then took a few minutes filling us in on some of the upcoming projects he was working on. He said he knew the glass factory move was inevitable so he and the city council had begun looking at what they could do to attract other types of businesses. They were formalizing plans to try and lure more food manufacturers. They already had a couple snack manufacturers in town and thought they could entice more to come with their new strategy.

Edward thanked the mayor for all his hard work in making Cambridge a great place to live. We wished him well and headed back to the factory.

The meeting with the mayor was as unpleasant as I envisioned. Of course it's never a good feeling to break bad news to someone, but the mayor took it in stride. He probably realized some time ago that our glass factory was moving out his hometown. The mayor was a former businessman and he understood it was best for the business and nothing against the town.

Cambridge had been around since 1846 and I was confident it would bounce back from this setback. Cambridge had a lot to offer and the townsfolk would find other sources of employment. The proximity to the Charles River made it an attractive place and with Boston just up the road that certainly didn't hurt. They would be just fine, I kept telling myself to feel better.

Chapter 13

"It's a go!" Edward exclaimed happily to the architect Charles Hamilton, who was already set up in our conference room.

Edward had hired Charles to draw up the preliminary plans for the new factory. I was quite impressed with the blueprints Charles had sprawled out on the table. The new layout was more practical and the entrance was so much more elegant than our current building.

"Excellent, congratulations Mr. Libbey! Where will we be building the new factory?" Charles inquired. Charles seemed pleased to hear we were settled on Toledo. "I had a pretty good feeling that was going to be the location. I scoped out all the places you had under consideration, but the Toledo site was hands down my favorite too. That location has a lot of space to work with to build the factory and the extra outlying buildings."

Charles had a great deal of experience building factories for the glass industry. This new one for Mr. Libbey was going to rival them all he assured us. It would be like a palace compared to all the others he had built. Edward wasn't sparing any expense and wanted to ensure the building was built to last a century or more. Most of the owners of the other factories he built were more short-sighted and only looked for what they could get now Charles told us regretfully. "If only all my clients had half of the vision that you did sir. That is one of the qualities I admire most about you Mr. Libbey".

"I'd like to go over these latest drawings. I have a few new ideas to discuss with you," Edward said.

"Of course, I'd be happy to discuss and make any changes you like," Charles said eagerly.

Edward then pulled a notebook out of his left desk drawer. Edward had written out a few notes yesterday and wanted to review them with Charles. Oftentimes ideas would just pop into his head and he would jot them down throughout the day. Sometimes he would show them to me laughing while ripping the page out of the notebook, rolling it into a ball and tossing it in the garbage. Other times, he would be satisfied with his idea and we would banter back and forth about how to use it or add to it. I loved to antagonize him because it was so easy for me to set him off with a discouraging look or a shake of my head. I always enjoyed our fun, lively debates.

Many of the ideas Edward had were for new glass shapes. He wasn't an artist, but he had a great appreciation for those who had such talents. He was delighted if his sketches could be used by his artists for inspiration.

Finding the right name for his products was also something he relished. Glass products needed names so customers could order them. It's like naming a child he would say, you want to think about what special characteristic you want to attach to it. A special name was more memorable than just using an item number, he would often say. An item number was used internally as new products were developed. These numbers came in handy for internal reports too, but the name is what the customers would know and use to refer to a specific glass. So if a word popped into his head, he would jot it down on a list he kept and submit it to the marketing team for consideration. He always encouraged others to make suggestions too. I wasn't quite so imaginative, so I didn't participate.

Edward didn't expect his workers to approve just anything he presented. "If you have a better idea or a different opinion about a name, I want to hear it," Edward would often say.

Of course we had to be careful not to use a name that was already in use by a competitor. We sure didn't want any confusion about the origin of the product. Our company name or logo on the product also helped identify the source. Ultimately Edward was the boss and final approver of product names but he respected his employees and wanted them to be open and honest with him and not just agree with anything he suggested.

Edward turned to a blank page and began doodling. "Red, an idea came to me last night that I need to get down on paper. We must design a new product to commemorate our new hometown." Soon he had filled the page with sketches of a tumbler, vase and stemware that embodied a vision we saw all over Toledo.

He sat back in his chair and admired his work. He was certain his designers could shape this into a new product line that would be a gift to the citizens of Toledo. He held up the paper and smiled at me. "Well the sketches aren't that great, but the idea has potential. Don't you think the residents will appreciate this?"

"Definitely, and they will be especially thrilled that it doesn't have frogs on it."

Toledoans weren't exactly thrilled with the nickname of "Frogtown". It was so named because its swampy land was a fertile nesting ground for frogs. The business people hoped with our move to their town that Toledo would soon become known as the "Glass Capital of the World". I had to admit that name had a nice ring to it. I wondered how my co-workers were going to react to seeing all the frogs in their new surroundings. It is certainly a departure from the refinement of Cambridge!

The remainder of Edward's day was spent in meetings with various department managers. The agendas were similar and focused mainly on how to prepare for the upcoming move. The conference with the engineers from my area was more technology focused.

We reviewed designs of some new innovative machines that would be installed in the new factory. Some of my colleagues who were previously appointed to the construction project, were anxious to fill Edward in on their progress of scouting out necessary materials. As I glanced around at the engineering group, I suddenly felt a wave of fear wash over me. Sweat began pouring down my face. Terror was enveloping my thoughts, I had to get away. I jumped up from my chair and raced down the hall….

Chapter 14

Frantically I raced to the washroom and splashed water on my face. My hands were a sweaty, clammy mess. I haven't had a panic attack in years and felt a little foolish for letting my body work against me. "What's wrong with you?" I chided myself in the mirror, "Pull yourself together man, you knew this was coming."

I had been at the company for 26 years and had always lived in Cambridge. It was just me at home now so I didn't have to go discuss the move with family members like my co-workers were grumbling about doing. I would certainly discuss it with my son, but he was away at college, a grown man now and wasn't living at my home anymore.

I was so proud that my son had been offered the opportunity to go to college. This was such a luxury and not something I ever thought I'd be able to provide for my son. Robert was stunned when he was approached by the principal of his high school with some life-changing news when he was in his final year of school. The principal told him that due to his academic achievements, he was the recipient of a scholarship for college. *(My kindness to William all those years ago was being repaid. I didn't know it then, but William had set aside money for Robert's education when he was born. William never forgot my help when he needed it and wanted to see that my son got the education that alluded me.)*

Eventually I calmed down and went back to my workspace reflecting on the big change with mixed thoughts. I tried to concentrate on my work but it was hard. I could see others struggling with their quiet thoughts too. My main worry was about Robert. However, I knew my son had dreams of moving way out west when he completed school, so I didn't think Robert would have a big concern one way or the other of where his Dad lived.

The reality of the move also had me seriously contemplating early retirement. I wasn't that old but since my wife's passing last year, an early retirement was sounding more attractive. It would be an adjustment. I had been working practically all my life and I did enjoy keeping busy. Yet, a sudden jump to a new town made the thought of retirement more appealing now. On the other hand, maybe a change of scenery was just what I needed. It would be a long day if I kept pondering over this dilemma but I would have to say something to Edward about it this evening.

Edward insisted I join his family for dinner tonight. "I'd like you there to help me convince my sisters that this is the best decision," Edward said as more of a statement than a request. That was ok with me. I was rather intrigued to see how this news would sit with his family. I knew his sisters almost their whole lives and thought this would be hard for them to accept. If I could help ease Edward's burden I would.

As I arrived at Edward's home for dinner that night I immediately felt the jovial mood that wafted through the Libbey home. Edward's sister Sarah was buzzing with excitement in the kitchen when Edward and I arrived. Alice and her husband William were also expected any minute. Sarah greeted us at the door, "Oh Edward you look happy! Did you get your way? Of course you did, you could sell snow to an Eskimo!" Sarah exclaimed excitedly.

Sarah had picked up on the way Edward talked about Florence when he returned home the first time from his trip to Toledo. Edward held his feelings close to the vest, but Sarah had a keen sense about these things. She knew that moving to be closer to Florence would be good for Edward. Sarah wanted so much to see him settle down, marry and have a few children. She confided to me often, "Edward is such a caring young man and he would make an excellent father you know. Can't you help me find him a suitable lady?"

Edward tried to keep up his poker face as he greeted Sarah. "Oh, now remember I'm not going to discuss the matter until everyone is seated at the table. When is dinner going to be ready? I'm famished!"

I could tell he enjoyed making her wait just a little while longer. Although Sarah was fairly certain of the outcome, she still seemed eager to hear Edward finally say it. He always enjoyed dragging out a story and embellishing it with all kinds of flavor.

Edward gallantly walked over to the cupboard and pulled out a tumbler. He wanted to enjoy a drink and relax on the sofa while he waited for dinner. Before he could finish pouring the drink, Alice and William came in the front door. They were too excited to wait any longer and rushed over ahead of schedule. Edward waved them into the parlor.

"William, can I pour you a drink? How about you Alice? I think we have much to celebrate this evening." Edward said slyly as he winked at me.

On that note, Sarah rushed in from the kitchen. "Once everyone has a drink I'll say a toast," Edward said. We quickly all grabbed a glass and gathered around him. He looked at each of us, seeming to enjoy the look of anticipation on our faces.

"It's off to O – HI - O we go! Toledo to be exact!" Edward boasted loudly as he raised his glass. We all clinked our glasses together and cheered. Sarah gave a sly wink to Edward. She looked ecstatic that he got his way.

Sarah, like Edward, had been mulling this over in her mind for weeks. She grabbed my hand and whispered quietly, "I want so much for Edward to make a success of this business. You know, like I do, all the trying times Edward has been through, especially from the pressure placed upon his shoulders when our father suddenly passed away. I just wish Alice and I could do more to ease his burden."

Edward never expected to run such a major company at his age, but circumstances decided otherwise. Sarah wouldn't make him feel alone though. Sarah was the type who would do anything she could to help and support her brother.

Looking at Edward now, and how he confidently told them the news, I knew she would help make this move a success. Sarah expressed her admiration of her brother's determination and willpower. Poor Sarah was so young when they lost their mother and then their father. Naturally, she instinctively looked up to Edward as a substitute father figure. I was certain she would follow him anywhere.

The news quickly spread around town. As a result, my social calendar filled up more than usual. My night with the Libbey's was followed the next night with dinner with a couple old friends.

We met at Alexanders, one of my favorite restaurants. I hadn't been there for a while, because it was also my late wife's favorite and it brought back too many memories. It had been a year since Louise passed and there were a few places that reminded me so much of her that I just avoided them. It was finally time to put a more positive view on these matters and think of the good times we enjoyed I decided. That was what I had been telling myself since accepting the invitation from Jack.

Jack was a childhood friend of mine and I had known his wife a long time too. In fact, Jack was the best man at my wedding and I returned the favor the following year when Jack married Joanna. Jack was really trying his best to get me feeling good about life again. Getting me out of the house more was something Jack was determined to do. He worried about me spending so much time alone, especially knowing Robert was away at school. I told him I was just fine, but he persisted. He was a good friend. Jack was lucky to still have his wife and two daughters at home. A home with three ladies sure couldn't ever be quiet or lonely.

We were joined by our mutual friend Connor James. Connor and I worked at the factory together for many years and had much in common. Connor was a whiz with machines, loved music and was a widower like me. Unlike me, he didn't have any children. This important fact made his decision about the move much easier.

"Red, I say we have a great chance to start over in a new town. You told me Ed found quite a beautiful lady there, so maybe we have a chance too?" Connor said with a laugh as we made our way to our table.

"Sounds like a good enough reason to give it a go, I'd say!" Jack chimed in supportively.

I ignored their comments and quickly grabbed the menu to peruse. I didn't need to read it though. Ever since I accepted the invitation I was looking forward to my favorite dish, clam chowder. The clams were always accompanied with large potato chunks and a creamy sauce, and irresistible homemade biscuits. The fresh seafood around town was something I knew I would miss. But I heard Toledo had some good fishing too and was a popular spot for walleye. I have never eaten walleye before but I was willing to give it a try.

Although Jack didn't work at Libbey with us, he already heard the news and probably knew more than we did about everyone's reaction. Even in a town this size, news spread quickly. Everybody seemed to know somebody who worked there. "So is this going to turn into a farewell dinner, boys?" Jack asked me, almost certain that I would never leave our hometown.

"Let's not start that talk. I haven't made up my mind yet." I said. "Let's enjoy the evening. Do you both want to start with a drink? I could go for a shot of whiskey."

I didn't drink often, but tonight, with thoughts of Louise and the pending move on my mind, I thought it would calm my nerves. I hadn't realized how nervous I was feeling until I had a chance to sit down at the table with my friends. We enjoyed dinner and conversation, and avoided the topic of Ohio until dessert.

"You have been good sports, evading the topic, but I would now like to get your thoughts and advice. You've both been great friends for many years and you know how difficult the past couple years have been with Louise's illness and passing." I said looking thoughtfully to my friends.

Jack started with his opinion on what he would do if he was in my position. Jack focused on convincing me to go as he could see Connor had already made up his mind. When Jack finished Connor gave his viewpoint and asked me several questions to ponder. We spent a couple hours enjoying each other's company before deciding it was time to end the evening. I thanked them both for their advice and said I would let them know my decision soon.

I knew what I had to do.

Chapter 15

I accompanied an unusually quiet Edward to Pittsburgh in February to meet with his architect Charles. He wanted to personally meet with Charles again and pour over each and every detail of the new factory. There were valid reasons for Edward to be so absorbed in the project. Most importantly, Edward's reputation was on the line. Additionally, all the money he had, and more that he was able to scrape together to borrow from family and the bank, was riding on a winning outcome.

Edward's love of art and European architecture also played a starring role in his motives for success. He wanted the building that was going to bear his name to be of the finest style, quality and workmanship. Edward did love the ornate features of Victorian architecture but eventually settled on something a little less baroque for the factory.

"Perhaps you can build a home in the Victorian style someday. I bet that is something Florence would like," I teased him.

Edward brushed off my suggestion, "Red, it is foolish to have those thoughts now. We have serious business to focus on."

Edward tried to hide the smile creeping on his face while he turned his attention back to the sketches. Charles didn't seem to notice, as he was too wrapped up in pointing out some of the updates he had incorporated since their last discussions.

"This is really shaping up to what I envisioned, Charles," Edward said enthusiastically. They were both standing back a bit from the drawing table to drink in the scope of the full design. Charles was pleased that Edward liked the revisions. I could see that Charles was eager to begin his masterpiece.

"Edward, as soon as you give the final approval, I can firm up the details with my team and guarantee the necessary materials are sent to Toledo on time. The railroad that runs adjacent to the property is going to be a real advantage to us. We'll have shipments coming up practically to the doorstep and timed to arrive when the men need them. It will really speed up the process. I can have the groundbreaking on March 1st if that is ok with you?" Charles said firmly.

Actually seeing the two dimensional drawings take shape was motivating to me. I could see the architect took great pride in his work and put in those extra touches that made his creations take on a special personality. I had the chance to see and admire his work on a prior visit. He took great pride in his work and assured us he would oversee every aspect of the building process, just as he did with all his projects. That is one of the reasons he had such a great reputation. People paid for his full involvement and they got it.

Charles also had great connections with material suppliers. Residing in the city known for steel was an advantage he coveted. Charles knew all the owners of the steel factories (including Andrew Carnegie) and Edward was confident he would negotiate a fair deal for this project.

When I observed Edward pull out his pocket watch for the third time I figured he was anxious to get back to Cambridge. Our train didn't leave until later tonight so there nothing we could do to get back sooner. This trip to Pittsburgh wasn't the best timed, but necessary. There was still a whole heap of discourse among the workers at the plant and much uncertainty as to who was actually coming to Toledo.

Since we had time on our hands, we decided to accept Charles' invitation to the theatre that evening. Edward always enjoyed the theatre and often attended shows in Boston. I wasn't much of a fan of the theatre but it beat staying in the hotel room.

"We may as well enjoy this while we can, Red. A fancy nightlife is one thing I'm going to really miss about Cambridge."

We met Charles for dinner at the Italian restaurant that Edward had been to once before. He enjoyed the cuisine and was pleased when Charles suggested it. The maître d settled us into a table adjacent to a flowing fountain.

"Edward, I'm glad to see you found this place again. I hope you don't mind, I brought Bradley with me. Brad has been working non-stop on the final plans for the construction. He will be leading the construction crew for me as I told you," Charles said.

The restaurant almost looked like a city street, it had ornate windows near the ceiling and below that was a walkway bordered by a rail of iron fencing. Plants and flowers draped down from the iron fence. It was a nice scene. Edward gave me a pleasing look when he noticed our glassware prominently on the table. Edward knew the restaurateur had used our products but it was always nice to see it in person. When the owner made his rounds to thank us for coming in Edward stood up, introduced himself, and thanked him profusely for his fine taste in glassware.

The owner smiled broadly, "But of course Mr. Libbey, everything in my restaurant is top quality. My customers would expect nothing less. I appreciate you coming into my establishment again, I recall your last visit very well. You are in good hands here with Charles, he is the best in his industry too!"

Charles and the owner were long time acquaintances. Charles bragged that he always brought his clients here for an introductory lunch or celebratory meal. The clients always raved about the food and the service and he expected we would too.

The four of us enjoyed a wonderful meal and conversation. Charles told Edward about the play we were going to see at the Drury Theatre after dinner. Charles remembered that Edward liked the theatre and he hoped that the Pittsburgh actors would live up to the quality of actors he was used to seeing in Boston.

Charles entertained us with some funny stories of his foray into the theatre. "I tried out for a play in high school because of a girl I liked. The girl was a beautiful red head named Sally that was way out of my league I don't mind admitting now. I was so smitten with her that I would do anything to be around her. When I found out Sally was going to be in the school play I knew I had to join her. She was a natural on the stage and showed no fear of standing in front of an audience. I however didn't have that same confidence, especially in my awkward teenage years."

He had us in stitches laughing heartily at himself as he described how his stage fright got the best of him during rehearsal one day that he stumbled backward, knocked over the tall wall and table behind him and fell face first into a potted plant.

"I would have been humiliated," I admitted cautiously.

Charles chuckled as he described wanting to die, knowing Sally was looking at him, and trying to stand and nimbly walk off the stage with a face full of dirt. He claimed he was embarrassed but not deterred.

"I later spoke with the teacher directing the play and begged her to let me be part of the show. She decided a backstage position would be more suitable for me. I was relieved to continue on through the rehearsal and production keeping very close to Sally. She never did go out with me, but we did become friends after that incident."

We told some stories about our first crushes but none were as colorful as Charles' story.

We eagerly made our way to the train station early the next morning. The evening with Charles and Brad was entertaining and insightful but it was time to get back. Edward was itching to tell his management team about the final plans. He also had some pressing work to address to finance the project.

"Red, I originally didn't want to offer stock in the company, but I think it is the best approach. If I get some of the men at the company to purchase some stock in the company, it would prove they were also committed to the company and the move. Don't you agree?"

"This is not my area of expertise, but your logic does make sense. I have a good feeling that you can explain this to the employees and it will have the desired effect."

I thought about how the last several weeks had been rough on everyone as we all weighed the decision to move over with our families. I spent the rest of the train ride staring out the window and thinking through my plans. Edward also took time to reflect and then shared his thoughts with me.

"Red, you know I wouldn't be here if it wasn't for my father. I just hope he would be proud of what I'm doing with his company. You remember that all I wanted was to be a minister growing up? My dad dreamed I would come to work with him and learn about his business. If I didn't have the chance to spend time with you I don't know what I would have done. I didn't fully appreciate the factory and what it was all about until I saw you working on those machines. You sparked my interest and made me take a wider look at all the wonders around the plant. I'm so determined to make this business the best, not just for myself, but for all those men and their families that depend on me. I also want to leave something lasting as a tribute to my father's legacy."

"You will make your father proud, just like always," I reminded him.

Edward was pleased when the train pulled into our hometown station. We stepped off to find a pleasant and not so chilly day. Winters could be brutally cold in Cambridge, but not today. Edward's brother in law, William Walbridge, warmly greeted us on the platform.

"Edward, Red, over here! How was your trip?" William asked.

We got caught up as we headed for the carriage that would take us home.

William, at his wife Alice's encouragement, had decided to invest in the glass business. Ever since William loaned Edward money he was more inquisitive to know all the minutest business details. The Walbridge's were also thinking about making the move to Toledo. This was mainly due to Alice's persistence. She was not eager to leave Cambridge, but she would do anything she could to ensure the glass factory didn't fail. She knew their younger sister Sarah was already poised to move with Edward. Family was important and she wanted to live close by them both. William would do just about anything to please Alice so he was pondering how to move his business to Toledo too.

March came roaring in like a lion that fateful year of 1888 across most of the country. The cold March winds had set up several parts of the country for a snow disaster. Strong gusts were blasting all sections of the northern parts of the country. Edward, myself and small group of our workers were in Toledo to oversee the building of the factory. Unfortunately, due to the storm, groundbreaking day on the Toledo site was canceled. Well, not indefinitely, but at least for a while.

A full blown blizzard was hitting everywhere from the northwest and all up the eastern coast. The biggest ever recorded blizzard, which the papers were called the "Great White Hurricane," was wreaking havoc on most of the country. The blizzard knocked out communication and even shut down railroad stations. Thirty to fifty mile per hour winds helped knock down several structures causing untold damage. The blasting wind whipped the snow all over the towns for days. I heard of some snow drifts that reached fifteen feet and stranded people in their homes for days. I felt awful for those people.

Fortunately, Toledo wasn't impacted too much by the blizzard. We braced for the large storm as much as we could, and luckily the brunt of the storm passed us by. However, the town was indirectly affected as the railroads weren't moving and couldn't bring in supplies or passengers. The groundbreaking would have to wait until the storm subsided.

Edward's main focus now was ensuring his family and workers were okay. "Red, can you help me check on our friends? I want to make sure everyone is safe and has food."

I jumped into action without hesitation. We braved the cold and wind and snow and managed to get to several people to check on their well-being. We delivered food and supplies to those in need and were soon joined by a handful of other employees who willingly volunteered to help. As much as we might disagree on some matters, Edward and I knew the crew would always pull together when it really counted.

It took more than a few days for the eastern states to recover from the storm of the century. I was shocked to read about all the destruction the storm left behind. Trees had fallen onto homes and some businesses fared no better. Citizens united and worked together to get trees removed and began the difficult task of rebuilding. Unfortunately, there was grim news that some people were found dead in their homes, likely frozen to death when they went too long in the cold without heat. It was a sad reality for many.

A few days later I took some comfort in knowing that my friends back home would cheer each other up by celebrating St. Patrick's Day. Cambridge had many immigrants from Ireland and the traditions of St. Patrick's Day were carried with them to America. Even those that weren't Irish were welcomed to join in the festivities and often did. Having spent several days stuck in their homes due to the blizzard, the people would be eager and ready this year to get out and celebrate. I knew the storm wouldn't keep everyone from gathering along the streets to cheer on the bands, the military and the politicians in the annual parade. Shamrocks were always on full display in the shop windows that lined the downtown streets throughout March. I wished to be there, but I was comforted to find that Toledo also had many Irish immigrants and many of the same traditions.

We had another special reason to celebrate St. Patrick's Day this year. Our groundbreaking was back on. This wasn't originally the planned start date, but I took this news as a lucky sign. Many of the employees that were of Irish decent like me found it good luck that the factory would start to take shape on this important holiday.

Prominent businessmen of Toledo gathered at the swampy site to witness and celebrate Libbey's factory, finally, officially break ground. When the first shovel of dirt was flung we all jubilantly congratulated each other on making Glassboro a reality. "The Glass Capital of the World is on its way, all hail the King of Glass!" several cheered happily.

Another glass company that specialized in making windows was already operating near our property. This company would be kept extra busy now making windows for our factory and our worker's new homes. They stopped momentarily to witness and celebrate the historical moment.

I felt surprisingly proud to be a part of Toledo now, and felt I was in the right place for the first time. It was strange, but as I stood there watching the dirt flying in the air and seeing the look of satisfaction on Edward's face, I had a sense that this building was going to stand a long, long time after we were gone.

Chapter 16

The weeks leading up to the move were hectic for everyone. There was so much to do, so much to prepare, so many goodbyes to say. Edward remained really downhearted that he was forced to leave his hometown. Last year he would never would have dreamed he would be moving to Ohio to secure his future.

Unfortunately this was the hand that fate had dealt. Edward resolved to make the most of it. "Red, you can't imagine the weight on my shoulders. I have the future of so many families riding on my decision. I know it was the right decision but I still feel I'm betraying my hometown and this is keeping me up at night."

The ones that elected to stay behind would struggle to find new employment. Some of the smaller businesses that benefited from the patronage of our workers would also have to grapple and adjust with less customers. Edward felt enormous stress in making the decision. At his young age it was not something he was prepared for, but he figured, nobody ever feels prepared for scary, big life altering changes. I was just glad I didn't have to impose this change on so many people.

"GLASSBREAKERS FAREWELL PARTY" read the large sign that Mr. Jim O'Toole hung upon the outside of his building.

"EVERYONE WELCOME SATURDAY AT 4 P.M." was written in smaller lettering underneath.

Mr. O'Toole wanted to give the glass workers a proper send off. As the owner of the local restaurant that was located nearest to the factory he had gotten to know most of the employees pretty well over the years. Although he liked us, and the free glasses we were always bringing him to sample, he would not be following us to Ohio.

Several of his regulars had asked him more than once, "C'mon Jim, you know we can't get along without your cheese biscuits and ham steaks." His biscuits were a favorite among his patrons, so much so, that it was pretty much a given that they were ordered at every table.

"I'm sure you'll have a many new delicacies awaiting you in Toledo. I hear their hometown specialty is frog legs!" Jim would say to the great dismay of some and boundless laughter of others.

I heard more than a couple scowls from the moms when the kids would groan, "EEWW, Mom, do we really have to eat frogs?!"

"MMM, ribbit, ribbit" O'Toole would reply laughing as he walked away.

I was delighted that O'Toole was going to give us all a proper Cambridge farewell. He knew many in the town were upset that we were leaving and heard some call Libbey a no good traitor, but he would put them in their place by saying, "Who can blame a guy for following his instinct and leaving for a better life? The fact that so many are joining him is a testament that they also believe in his vision."

When people complained that the loss was going to be so devastating to the town Mr. O'Toole told them, "Be grateful that the company was here in the town for its first seventy years. We should remember and celebrate all that the factory brought us in that time and wish them the best of the luck. They deserve our gratitude and I'm going to give them a fine sendoff!"

O'Toole soon had one side of the restaurant decorated with all the great things about Cambridge. He had pictures of the factory of course, and the ball team, the Charles River, Boston harbor and just photos of regular people that made the town special. He placed a large banner across the back wall that read "Good luck in Toledo! From your forever friends in Cambridge!" O'Toole had been encouraging everyone all week to write on the banner their own sentiments and farewell wishes. He told me he planned to present it to Edward as a remembrance on the day of the party. It was a way Edward could take a part of Cambridge with him and cherish.

The other side of the restaurant was plastered with Toledo memorabilia. A picture of the Toledo Pirates, the Maumee River, the downtown area, and several of frogs. It was a great way for us to remember the past while looking forward to the future.

Mr. O'Toole asked Connor James last month if the Libbey Glassbreakers band would play one more time. Connor and his bandmates, including me, were honored but also a little sad about it. Realizing it would be our final concert at O'Toole's made us all a little weepy.

Connor was the leader of our group, currently at twenty two, and we got together whenever we could to play music. Most of us had learned to play an instrument when we were youngsters. Several of us admittedly hated taking classes and practicing at some point in our life, but when we got away from it for a while we realized how much we truly missed it.

Our band formed a few years back when Connor complained to another fellow at work how he missed playing his drums and soon the idea was formed to start a band. Connor hastily wrote up a flyer that day and posted it in the lunchroom. It read: "WANTED: Anyone who can play an instrument. Meet at O'Toole's Wednesday at 7 p.m. Bring your instrument."

Connor didn't know what to expect but was pleasantly surprised when thirty guys, including myself, showed up at the restaurant. I hadn't played my trumpet in many years but now I couldn't resist. After I saw his poster I went home that night and dragged my old trumpet out from the back of the closet. My uncle had taught me how to play on this old instrument when I was a child and although I had not touched it in many years I surprised myself as my fingers seemed to remember what to do.

O'Toole's large, unused basement became our band's hangout thanks to Connor. O'Toole loved listening to live bands and told Connor that first night if we were any good we could play on Saturday nights. He figured the live band would be a good draw for business. After some practice we soon became a regular feature and had a small fan base.

Sadly tonight our band would play for the last time in Beantown.

Chapter 17

By August of 1888, with construction nearly complete, it was finally time for everyone to permanently make the journey to our new home. It was bittersweet as the train was loaded that day. One hundred workers and their families were leaving Cambridge to follow their jobs to Ohio. Some were more eager to go than others. A new opportunity lay ahead for so many of us. It was scary and exhilarating. Many were uprooting their families from the only place they knew. They all believed in Edward and were putting their lives in his hands. It was more incredible for us to find out that some of the people of Toledo had generously pledged money to make the deal happen.

Edward had wanted to make the move as easy as he could for us. He knew everyone was making sacrifices and he was concerned about everyone and everything people were leaving behind. One huge bonus about the move was the fact that we would be moving into new homes, in a neighborhood surrounding our factory. He figured if we all lived in a close community together it would help. That was one of the reasons he structured the deal with extra land for housing.

Many from the town of Cambridge turned out to say farewell. The train station was filled with well-wishers waving frantically at loved ones. There were tears of joy and some of sadness of not knowing when they would see each other again.

The workers put on brave faces for their wives and told their children this would be the first grand adventure of their lives.

I laughed to myself as I heard them say things to their kids like, "We're like the pilgrims who left their countries in search of a new world," or, "Just think of all the new things you'll see and do." Most of the kids looked wildly excited and eager to take a train ride to anywhere or nowhere in particular. I caught their enthusiasm and hopped aboard the train without looking back.

The countryside, especially as we entered into Pennsylvania and Ohio, seemed a never ending row of cornfields. Miles and miles of cornfields filled the landscape of the train windows hour after hour. The kids were asking constantly if there was anything else out there. Every now and then we would roll through one small town or another and actually see buildings and homes to the delight of the children.

Edward and I sat daydreaming and staring out the window for what seemed like hours. The cornstalks were tall and mesmerizing as the train chugged along the tracks. The agriculture business was currently one of the big businesses in Toledo I recalled from our first visit.

As that thought occurred to me I turned to see Edward pull out his sketchbook. As he slowly flipped through dozens of pages of doodles he had sketched out I tried to get a peek at what could be new products someday. Edward noticed my interest and said, "I've been mulling over ideas for months for a way to commemorate our new town and the people that live there."

"I do recall some ideas you showed me a few months back. You do have some interesting ideas there, but I kind of fancy this one," I said as I pointed to one of the sketches.

"You know, I think you're right. This idea was the first one that popped into my mind on our first visit, even before I seriously considered moving there."

I could see that he still had some work to do on it to bring it to life so I turned my attention to my book as he got to work. I quietly looked up from my book now and then and admired how he brilliantly sketched out a pitcher that was shaped like an ear of corn. The husks opened up around the bottom of the glass and the top half was cut out to look like the corn kernels. We could use this design on tumblers, bowls, and vases, just about any of the items I realized.

I watched with interest as Edward got up from his seat looking for Joseph, one of our best designers. "Come with me Joseph, I'd like to show you something," he said excitedly as he stepped near Joseph's seat.

"Certainly, Edward, if you can show me anything but all this corn I've been staring at for hours I'll gladly look," Joseph said not knowing he wouldn't exactly get his wish.

Edward led Joseph back to the empty seat across from me and sat down. "Joseph, I'm sorry to tell you this but all this corn gave me a great idea for a new product," Edward said as he opened his sketchbook and showed Joseph the few pages he had drawn. Joseph couldn't help but laugh, "Not more corn, are you serious?"

However, the more Joseph looked at it he said he couldn't help but like it. Edward explained that he had been trying to come up with something to honor their new hometown. He had wanted to manufacture a new glassware line especially for Toledo. Since Toledo was already well established as an agricultural site this just made perfect sense to him.

Joseph took the drawing and added some features and character to it. Edward was pleased, "Joseph, it looks like you have your first assignment when we arrive." He knew that Joseph would finalize the design and have the product made to his satisfaction. "I'd like it to have the design complete and the molds made up as soon as possible," Edward said.

"How about calling it the Maize Art line?" I asked hopefully. I didn't usually suggest pattern names to Edward but this one seemed so obvious it just rolled off my tongue.

Joseph took the concept and ran with it. Before we rolled in to Toledo he already sketched out a salt and pepper shaker that had a corn design on the jars and showed them resting on a small plate shaped like a corn husk. He also added a dome in the shape of corn husks, a cruet set and a vase.

"Aw, shucks Edward, I don't know why I didn't think of it. Inspiration for new art comes in strange places sometimes. I can't wait to see these take shape inside the mold. These could be a winner in more than just Toledo."

"There's a kernel of truth!" I said laughing at my own corny joke.

Chapter 18

"Here they come! Here they come!" an exuberant member of the crowd yelled.

Everyone in the train looked excitedly at the enormous crowd that had gathered at the station. The mass of people must have begun gathering at Toledo's Union Station hours ago. "My, would you look at that?" I said as I shook Edward hand vigorously. He grabbed me up in a triumphant hug with the biggest smile on his face.

Rumors of the Libbey group coming to Toledo had been the topic of conversation around town for months. There couldn't have been anyone in town who didn't know about it. It was featured constantly in the news for months. It was hard for me to believe this day had finally arrived. It was August 18, 1888, and Toledo's persistence in luring a large company to town was at long last coming true.

The mayor and hordes of well-wishers were in a jubilant mood. They appeared eager to embrace Mr. Libbey and his employees and families with a royal welcome. I didn't feel worthy, but I was excited to see my coworkers getting the kudos they deserved. So much was riding on that train track that day. The hopes and dreams for a bright and lively future for many new Toledoans was riding into town to greet the dreamers of Toledo. The train riders couldn't have been in higher spirits as we saw the future of our Toledo life in our view.

Someone at the back of the car started singing the Star Spangled Banner and everyone quickly joined in. As the train approached Edward said a few words of thanks to all of us for putting our faith in his hands and agreeing to move eastward to a new town and a new beginning. About half of the workforce believed in Libbey enough to uproot their families and head west with him and meant everything to Edward.

"It's not going to be easy," he said, "but if ever a finer group of people existed with the will and heart to make this dream come true, I'd like to meet them. I know all the sacrifices you have made to take this journey and I am humbled and grateful for your trust in me. May Toledo be a blessing to you all!"

"Cheers to Mr. Libbey!" someone shouted and everyone began cheering, clapping and hugging each other.

As the view of the crowd came more into focus the group inside the train was astonished. Most of my colleagues had never been to Toledo and they knew it was a much smaller town than Cambridge, but by the looks of the crowd, everyone in Ohio must be have been outside that station!

As we creeped the final hundred feet the cheering from the crowd outside was louder and more animated than anything we could have ever imagined. "I think the whole state of Ohio and possibly even Michigan know we are here, folks!" Edward exclaimed with the widest smile across his face.

Then Edward breathed deep, closed his eyes, and like me he must have taken a moment to engrain the image and noise into his head. I wanted to capture that excitement forever in my mind and heart. This was much more than even he could have hoped for as a reception for his people. "Red, there is no doubt the decision to pick Toledo was the right one."

Edward stood at the door as the train came to stop in front of the crowd. The mayor of Toledo raced up to the platform and shook Mr. Libbey's hand as the crowd yelled, "Welcome to Toledo, King Libbey!" Edward sure looked like royalty that day. A king couldn't have attracted a bigger or friendlier crowd. Of course the most important face in the crowd that Edward wanted to see, I spotted right away. Florence, looking elegant as always, was in the second row waving a large sign that said "Welcome to Toledo, the new Glass City".

It took a little while for all the passengers to disembark from the train, but nobody minded. The crowd of well-wishers were shaking everyone's hands and trying to brag to us all about the great town of Toledo. Most of the crowd even followed along as Libbey's employees and family members started the long march of the four miles from the train station to the factory site on Buckeye Street. After being cooped up on the train for over thirty hours I know I was certainly ready to get out and stretch my legs.

We all felt like royalty parading down the street, with so many waving and cheering at us. Some well-wishers carried banners saying "From Bean Town to Boss Town" and "Toledo: Our new home". Seeing our new factory in the distance made the reality of the day officially set in for me. The factory was state of the art construction and was a stunning site to see.

Our parade was met by about fifty Toledoans who would be joining us to work at the factory. They were excitedly greeting and shaking hands with their new fellow workers. They didn't have any experience in a glass factory but they looked like an eager, willing group. When Edward had confirmation that some of our Cambridge workers wouldn't move to Toledo, he had placed an ad in the Toledo paper. Four times as many eager applicants applied than we needed. These people felt overjoyed that they had made the cut and it showed on their beaming faces.

I was well behind Edward who was leading the parade. Edward, the Mayor, and Mr. Ketchum stood on the back of a carriage that was decorated in American flags. The team of horses expertly made their way down the street with a huge crowd behind them. Edward looked rather pleased and proud as he looked out at the dozens and dozens of people that believed in his dream and followed him here. It was quite a humbling site to me.

I watched from midway back as Edward stood there waving and looking down on the crowd of his new and old employees. Out of the blue he suddenly decided he needed to be down next to us. Edward surprised and delighted everyone when he hopped down from the carriage and stood alongside his workers. "If you are all going to walk to the new Promised Land I'm going to take each step with you."

Following behind us was an impressive group from the local high school marching band. If only my trumpet wasn't packed away I would have played along with them! I could see the excitement of the Toledo kids was not lost on the Cambridge youngsters. It would make opening day at school more comfortable seeing how happy they were to have new schoolmates I thought confidently.

Edward remarked that everyone in town must have been out lining the four mile stretch between the railroad station and the plant but he was wrong. Dozens more were at the factory grounds to greet us on our final steps. There were also several stationed at various tents cooking up enough food for an army. The aroma that filled the air was intoxicating to the crowd who now realized how hungry they were. The picnic set up was something the town wanted to do to surprise us and it was such a nice gesture that wouldn't be forgotten.

Chapter 19

"I can't think of anything that could have made our first day better. The welcome from this town is heartwarming," Edward remarked as we followed Maurice Scott and his family to the front table.

I secretly knew that Florence's presence there made it extra special. Edward made sure Florence and Maurice and Mary were made comfortable as we were joined by George Ketchum and Charles Hamilton. George and I exchanged a knowing glance, proud to see the young couple reunited again.

"Our Toledoans know how much you all have given up to make the move across the country and they wanted to show you how happy they are that you have chosen to relocate here," Maurice remarked.

I glanced around taking in the breathtaking sight. All the tables set up in front of the factory, full of my friends and their families. The townspeople really went all out with the large spread of food and drinks. Our workforce, treated like heads of state, were on cloud nine.

The kids thought Toledo was majestic. Several partook in the games set up for them on the large lawn. Before long many of the children were jumping and playing leapfrog with their soon to be new classmates. I was pleased to see the bonds of friendship forming so quickly.

Florence came up to Edward after watching him gazing at the kids with a contented smile on his face. "The kids will adjust quickly, they are resilient at that age. I'm sure they will find this is a nice place to grow up just as I did," Florence said.

As the two talked I spotted young Tommy Thorne sneaking up behind Edward holding a large frog. I held my tongue as I was a little curious to watch this play out. Tommy giggled as he got right behind them. Edward turned to see him there ready to try and scare Florence with it.

"I wouldn't do that if I were you, Tommy. Ms. Scott would not appreciate - "

Edward went silent as the slippery frog pulled away from Tommy's grip and leaped in the air toward Florence.

Florence caught the frog as it landed on her shoulder. She then turned to the shocked little boy and said sweetly, "Now this, Tommy, is one of our finest friends around here. You hold them like this."

Tommy smiled shyly as he took the frog back from Florence. His brother, who stood by in the distance, looked relieved.

"I don't think he expected that reaction from you! I just hope these kids all grow up here as happy and smart as you," Edward stated. Florence blushed and turned away.

"Oh, don't forget, my father expects you to join us for dinner tonight. He has a special evening planned. A few of his friends are joining us too," Florence reminded him and then turned to me, "Of course you must be there too, Red."

"I wouldn't miss it," Edward replied as I nodded my head.

I hoped, for Edward's sake, this would be one of many dinners in Florence's company. As the two sat down to partake in the nice lunch, I excused myself to give them some time alone. I then made the rounds to make sure everyone was enjoying themselves.

Some of the men had gathered at one end of a row of tables and were engrossed in a game of cards. "Care to join us, Red?" one of them asked as I approached.

"Thanks but I'm afraid I'd lose my shirt to you fellows and I've grown quite accustomed to it," I said as they laughed knowingly. A couple of these guys were quite adept at making bets and they seldom lost. It was a good way to pass the time and helped supplement their income they confessed.

"Mr. Libbey what's back there? Is that yours too?" I heard a young boy ask Edward as he pointed toward some trees on the right side of the building.

"Oh, that's a little extra land in case we want to expand the plant someday. I'm afraid right now it's a bit of a damp, marshy mess. Best to stay out of there. I don't think your mom would want you, or any of you, traipsing out there and getting lost," Edward said pointing and looking each of them seriously in the eye to ensure they understood.

Edward and I stepped away from the kids as we looked out at the land and deliberated over all the possibilities. He promised me we would prosper and make quality products for the world. I had no doubt in his convictions. I knew he had hired some of the finest cut glassmen in the world. They even faithfully followed him here and brought their families. I was confident we could put American glass up against any of the finest in the world.

The fresh start in Toledo seemed to give Edward a renewed energy to grow this company. His move to Toledo was looked upon as a courageous, but crazy move by some, and he was determined to show the people of Toledo their vision in him was not misplaced.

When everyone had eaten their fill, Edward held up a large envelope and addressed the crowd. "My fellow friends, the people of Toledo have blessed us with a great lunch which I know you all enjoyed."

The crowd clapped and hollered, "Yeah."

"They were also busy these past months building you new homes to live in and raise your families. They wanted you to live in one big neighborhood together and have made this Glassboro community for you. How would you like to see your new homes?"

The crowd cheered in excited anticipation. We had been eyeing the houses from afar as we ate and chatted about who might live where. All of the houses looked bright and cheery and welcoming.

Edward continued, "Follow me and we will walk together up Ash and Buckeye Streets and I will drop each of you off at your new home."

The group eagerly jumped up, called to their children and gathered around Edward. The townsfolk also gathered around waving and cheering as they followed the glassworkers up the street. Edward looked like a young Santa Claus, minus the big belly and beard.

When Edward arrived at the front of the first house he looked down at his map as everyone waited to hear the new owner's name. "Mr. & Mrs. Hammesjahr, Kathryn and Herman, welcome home! Here is the key to your new house." Mrs. Hammesjahr was in tears as she stepped onto the porch and waved at the crowd. She continued waving until Edward arrived at the next house and called out Mr. and Mrs. Bronson's names.

Mrs. Hammesjahr then turned to her husband and said, "This is wonderful. A new home and right next to my friend Betsy." Mr. Hammesjahr smiled, looking relieved that his wife seemed happy with their new home. He told me recently how he had found her crying several times at night and suspected she was not happy about the move, although she would never say it to him directly. She was a very obedient wife and always deferred big decisions to her husband. She felt it was the husband's role to decide such things, which normally Mr. Hammesjahr preferred, but he confided to me this was one decision he wished she had been more vocal about.

This reflection made me wonder how my wife would have reacted to the news. I think she might have put up a bit of a fight, especially leaving Robert so far away. I'm glad I didn't have to put her through that, but I did wish she was here more than anything.

"Red, come on in, I want you to join us as we look around."

I quietly stepped through the crowd and joined Herman on the porch shaking his hand, "I feel honored to be the first guest in your home," I said sincerely.

I was impressed with the woodwork trim around the windows and floor boards which shined like new, which of course they were. Kathryn had never lived in a brand new house and she asked Herman to pinch her to make sure it was real. "Oh Herman, this is so much more than I wished for," she said with tears swelling in her eyes.

The kitchen was roomy enough that a small table could be placed in it for small intimate meals. To Kathryn's delight there was a small enclosed porch off the kitchen. It had large windows on three sides and a door leading to the backyard. It would be a great place to house her plants, she surmised. Kathryn enjoyed growing her own herbs to use for meals and suspected this room would do quite nicely. From the porch she could also view the small yard.

"Well look at that," Kathryn said as she stepped out the back steps to find a small garden full of flowers. She wasn't quite sure what kind of flowers they were, and I couldn't tell her either, but she appreciated the extra care someone had taken to plant them there.

Herman came up and patted me on the shoulder. We didn't have to speak, but I'm sure he knew what I was thinking. We stood quietly, both smiling to see Kathryn so happy. "Well, I best be getting back out there," I said hastily as I turned to leave. I didn't want my sudden sadness to ruin their happy moment. I couldn't help thinking what a joy it would have been to see Louise's face if I was able to provide her with a new home like this.

I was soon distracted from my sadness, when I rejoined the crowd and saw Edward. Watching the men take the key to their new homes filled Edward with pride, which was contagious. He knew for many of them this was a very special occasion.

I caught up to Edward as he whispered to me, "I'm so glad we stuck firm to our demand for extra land. I expect over time, more companies will set up shop in Glassboro and add to the neighborhood." That was what the business committee anticipated as well.

The crowd dwindled down as we got to the last house. The last man was overly excited and jumping up and down hooting and hollering, which Edward pretended not to notice. When we all arrived, Edward turned to the small crowd and said this last and final house was his. The crowd started to cheer but was interrupted when a man stepped forward looking a little upset and confused and said, "What about me, Mr. Libbey?"

"Oh dear, I don't see you on my list. I'm sorry about the mistake. Perhaps you could stay with Mr. Thorne and I can see if we could build another home for you?"

At this point the man, trying to comprehend this new development and probably trying to think of a polite way to tell his boss that living with Mr. Thorne and his two feisty boys was not exactly what he had signed up for, looked a little miffed to say the least.

Some in the audience like myself, knew that Edward wasn't taking one of the homes. He had already expressed his plans to stay at the hotel for now. A few started whispering to those around them that Edward was playing a joke on the man. Before the man got too upset Edward let out a big laugh and let everyone in on the joke.

"Larry Andrews, since Mrs. Thorne probably wouldn't take kindly to a long term guest in her new home, I guess I will give you my home here." Larry looked a little relieved, but still concerned before Edward continued. "Don't worry Larry, I was just joking with you. This is your home. I'm staying elsewhere as planned out before. Welcome to your home."

Larry, with the cheering crowd behind him, walked up the steps of his new home. Edward shook his hand and whispered, not too quietly for me to hear, "I wanted you to have this best house. You can see the Maumee River from here and it may help you attract a wife."

Larry smiled and caught the eye of a lovely young lady whom he'd been admiring all afternoon. She smiled broadly at him upon hearing that he was unattached. The smile she gave him likely washed away any misgivings he had about moving here. I had a feeling more good things were coming Larry's way and they would in time.

Edward and I and the small group of townsfolk turned back toward the factory. We were cheered and greeted by the new homeowners as we walked up the street. "This ought to make your heart sing, eh Ed?" I said patting his shoulder.

We arrived at the factory grounds to see most everything picked up. Edward checked his watch and noted that we still had a couple hours before the dinner party. He wanted to stop in his office to attend to a few matters before dinner. At first I thought I would run over to my new home to relax, but then I figured I should stop into the office too.

"Looks like you need to make another speech." I said as I spotted a reporter from the local newspaper waiting near the factory door. Edward and I recognized Mr. David Locke as Edward had a few interviews with him over the past few months about his decision to move to town. In fact, Mr. Locke was the owner of the Toledo Blade. He was also one of the businessmen that had worked on the deal to entice the glass company's move.

"Mr. Libbey, might I get a statement from you for the papers? My readers would be most interested in your impressions on your first official day in town."

Edward smiled and said, "Really, I think everyone from town was here today to see it for themselves. However, if there was someone that happened to miss it I'd just like to thank everyone on behalf of myself and my associates. The city opened their hearts to us and we are all very grateful. We hope that we will be here a long time and help in the prosperity of the town for everyone here."

David thanked Edward for his time and reminded him that a copy of the paper, with the Libbey move on the front page, would be delivered to everyone in Glassboro in the morning. I would be sure to get an extra copy to send to Robert. Maybe something about seeing the story in print would help him decide to move here after graduation. A father could always wish.

"I'll bet seeing Florence again was a big highlight of your day!" I said changing the subject as we entered the factory.

"She was exactly as I remembered. She was as enchanting as ever today, even when confronted with a frog! Just between us, I can't wait to see her again tonight."

Edward soon called me into his new office where he was poring over some reports from the engineering team. A group of us had been in and out of town the last few months to oversee the construction. We were also charged with starting up the furnaces last week. Furnaces always took several days to reach the right temperature before they could be used for manufacturing. Our optimal furnace temperature was around 2,400 degrees Fahrenheit.

Once the furnaces heated up to the precise temperature, the testing phase could begin. We had prudently decided to purchase some of the raw materials, like soda lime and silica from different vendors now that we were in Ohio. Soda-lime was an important ingredient used to aid in the hardiness of the glass. Silica, along with other minor additives, was used to obtain clarity of the glass. Since we made changes in our suppliers of these important materials we wanted to take additional time to carefully test their quality to ensure the clarity and purity of our products would still be the same.

Sand was also a vital ingredient of glass making. We found there were ample sandpits in Monclova which was not far from Toledo. Edward was tempted to use that sand someday, but for now he had committed to stay with his current long standing supplier from back East. The additional shipping charge to Toledo would be an extra cost he decided he would have to absorb for now. He didn't want to take chances on changing everything at once. There was a great deal to consider when changing batch ingredients and he decided to take it slow, one step at a time, so as not to negatively affect the quality.

At 5:00 p.m. Edward went back to his hotel room to freshen up for dinner and I dashed to my house. "I'll meet you at the hotel shortly, I just need to clean up."

I arrived at Edward's hotel room to find him looking quite nervous. He was fussing over his clothes more than usual. I knew he had a very important reason for that. Florence was a very fashionable dresser and he clearly wanted to show he was up on the latest fashions as well. I smiled to myself as I saw him splash on cologne and carefully put on the special cufflinks that belonged to his father. I noticed he had selected the red and blue striped tie that his mother had given him. I wondered if he consciously knew that he was bringing his parents with him that night.

We showed up to the Scott's house promptly at 6:00 p.m. Edward greeted Mrs. Scott with a bouquet of flowers and a nice bottle of wine. I could see Florence was impressed as she took the flowers from her mother and offered to put them in a vase. Mr. Scott was waiting for us in the parlor with some of the other guests. We knew the businessmen from the prior meetings but we didn't know all their wives. After introductions were made Maurice offered everyone a drink. The men carried on about local politics while the women made their way to the dining room.

It was very evident to me that Maurice was growing very fond of Edward. Edward was the youngest of the businessmen here, but he was just as well educated in business and country affairs as the rest of them. Edward was also well versed in the intricacies of local politics, having dealt with a number of them to get his permits and construction completed. The rest he would learn quickly from his new friends.

I couldn't seem to shake this feeling I had about Florence. She was just as I remembered and more. I just knew these two were destined for each other. Although I'm sure Edward would have preferred the company of her alone, he didn't seem to mind having an audience this evening. At least this made their re-acquaintance more casual and less awkward. I was thoroughly enjoying seeing the two interact.

Edward had never before expressed interest in taking a bride. However these last few months, since he had met Florence, had revealed he may have found the one that changed his opinion about the topic. Edward had pleaded with me to keep his feelings under wraps, likely concerned of unwanted rumors floating about town. In particular, he warned me to be discreet around his sister Sarah who was already quite suspicious about the matter. I really didn't need to say a word though. Anyone observing them for a minute could see the love blooming between them.

"Red, could you help me in the kitchen?" Mrs. Mary Scott said more as a statement than a question.

I happily followed Mary into the kitchen. She quickly confided to me her feelings. "I must tell you Red, as I can tell you feel the same way as Maurice and I do about Edward. We find Edward to be a most charming young man. Over the past few years I feared Florence wouldn't find a gentleman that could match her in wit, intellect and caring, and then along came Edward."

I listened as Mary said she could see Edward's admiration and infatuation with her daughter right away, even if her husband was too daft to see it. I realized then that Maurice may have been holding back his hopes from his wife. Perhaps he didn't want to get his wife's hopes up, as he plotted a way to get the couple together.

I couldn't get a word in edge wise as she spilled out all these thoughts she must have had bottled up inside for some time. She claimed that Edward's real interest in coming to Toledo versus Findlay, where gas was offered for free, had much to do with her daughter, and she looked to me for confirmation. As I thought about what I should and shouldn't reveal, she assured me that she whole heartedly approved the match.

"It's just a matter of time I figure. I can be patient a little longer, but anything you can do to help this along with Edward I would sincerely appreciate," she stated and then left me in the kitchen as Florence stepped in.

"Mother what are you thinking? You've got a strange smile on your face," Florence asked.

Mary just replied, "Never you mind dear. I see something wonderful coming and I can wait a little longer."

See what, Florence seemed to ask as she looked quizzically at me and back to the door where her mother quickly vanished. I didn't know what say so I just returned her puzzled look and shrugged my shoulders. Your mother's wish is to have you happily married to Edward and then bless her with a few grandchildren, were words I couldn't bring myself to utter aloud.

I returned to the dining room to see Edward enjoying himself immensely with his new circle of friends. They were all so charming and enjoyable to be around. These new friends would surely make Edward feel content with his decision. I hoped all of our team would find such great new friends here.

"That was such a wonderful reception we received today from the residents. I know it meant a lot to my staff too. I'm hoping they will soon find comfort in calling Toledo home," Edward said.

"To new friends," Maurice proposed as he held up his glass and encouraged the rest of us to follow suit. "May you all find health and happiness here in the new Glass Capital of the World." The rest of the group agreed and smiled thankfully at Edward.

The dinner was marvelous. It started with a cream of broccoli soup followed by salad. Soon we were treated to a lovely cooked roast, potatoes and asparagus. The food was made all the more memorable as Mary proudly told everyone how long Florence had been in the kitchen that day insisting on preparing everything herself. Edward smiled at Florence and I secretly enjoyed seeing her look of embarrassment. She didn't care for cooking and dreaded doing it normally, her mother informed everyone in spite of Florence's attempts to stop her from talking. She was saved as Edward broke in, promptly noticing her discomfort, to ask if anyone had been to London recently.

He went on to tell stories about this latest visit and his encounter with an intriguing man who was always presenting him with odd treasures to buy. The man had heard that Edward was a collector of antiquities and would seek him out whenever he heard he was in town. Edward said he never knew how this man would know he was there. He suspected the antiquity world had a small number of serious buyers and the sellers kept tabs on where to find potential buyers when they had their hands on the latest rare treasures.

Edward soon had everyone hanging on his every word. He told his stories with such vigor and when he saw he had his audience's attention, he would throw out some outlandish points, just to see their reactions. This night he was telling of being led down a dark staircase, below a shop, to find the most wondrous treasure. He told the group that his collection consisted mainly of paintings and ancient artifacts like jewelry and pottery but this man insisted he had a rare treasure that he must take off his hands.

When everyone was chattering and blurting out their guesses to what it could be Edward just kept telling them they were wrong and encouraging them to keep guessing. This man had showed him a most magnificent winged creature. "A parrot?" "A sparrow?" some offered in jest before Edward revealed it was a tiny dragon. At that moment, he had them all practically rolling on the floor in hysterics.

"You are a great weaver of tales, my friend," Maurice said recovering from the laughter this image provoked.

"Who knew you had such an imagination," Mary said.

Edward tried heartily to keep a straight, serious face as he tried to convince Maurice it was true, but when he started laughing he gave it away. The other men tried taking turns to tell a more outlandish tale, but they soon hailed Edward as the best storyteller of the evening. If only it were true I thought wistfully to myself. What a souvenir that would be!

Ever since Edward was a young lad I had encouraged him to read stories of the winged dragons who wreaked havoc in faraway lands. They were the kinds of stories I loved as a child. I thought of dragons as mystical and magical and seeing one for real would have made the young impressionable young boy in me scream in delight. As Edward was telling his story, I couldn't help but see the amusement in Florence's eyes. I was glad to see she enjoyed his sense of humor and adventure.

It was sad to see the evening coming to an end, but it was getting late. Edward rose and said, "Dear Scott family, I have enjoyed myself enormously. I do hope this is the first of many dinners together."

We thanked our hosts and other guests and left for home. Home. That word had a strange feeling to me. This was our first day here and it already felt like a place that would be my home for a long, long time. I was pleased with how comfortable I was with that thought.

As we headed down the street I turned to Edward and said, "A dragon? Our first dinner at the Scotts, and you subject them to your wild imagination?" I snickered as we walked the rest of the way in silence. The walk was refreshing, the night quiet and calm, but now all I had was dragons on my mind.

Chapter 20

I found myself feeling quite melancholy at the end of my first official night in Toledo. When all the excitement of the day wore off, I was there alone inside my big, quiet new house. I thought of Louise and wondered how she would have liked the day. The fanfare and hoopla would have rendered her speechless. She would have enjoyed the spectacular sight I was certain. It was a day I'd never forget. I couldn't wait until I could tell Robert all about it.

I sat reflectively on the back porch thinking about all the work that lie ahead. The house was beautiful and shiny new, but it had a ways to go before it looked like a home. Louise would have been prancing about, measuring the windows and rooms and trying to decide what should go where. She would have complained there was so much to do, while secretly reveling in the challenge.

The look of the big, empty house was intimidating to me. Setting up the household was not something I was skilled at doing. So instead I started thinking about the factory. There was so much to do there as well. However, this was a challenge I was looking forward to most. I enjoyed my work, and creating things with my hands and my imagination was what I loved most.

I had some ideas for a machine that would make the glassblowing process easier, but I had much to work through in my head before I could begin committing it to paper. I also wanted to make some improvements to the side lever press machine. That was a wonderful invention a couple decades ago but I thought I could tweak to make it work better and faster. The press machine opened to allow a gob of glass to be dropped inside the mold. Then the operator pulled the handle down and the glass would form into the shape of the mold. Press molds were a great invention because it allowed us to make different patterns in the glass. The machine could make decorative glasses many times faster than we used to do by hand.

If there was anything that needed fixing I was the guy who could do it, I reminded myself. Some of my friends swore I could fix anything and I usually could. Whatever broken thing they brought me, I would find a way to repair it. This was something that came natural to me. I sighed admitting out loud, "I reckon this house is likely to stay barren for some time. I have more pressing matters to focus on first."

"Red, are you awake too?" Connor yelled from his back porch across the way. "Want a beer?"

I didn't want to be un-neighborly and I couldn't refuse a free beer. I made my way over to Connor's porch. "Having trouble sleeping, Connor?"

"I'm too excited to sleep. I feel like the luckiest guy in the world. Look at this new house and its mine. I feel like my luck is changing for the better."

"You deserve it Connor. I'm glad you were so excited about this move. You really helped me that night we had dinner with Jack. I have no doubt you will make the most of this new opportunity."

We sat sipping beer and reminiscing about our lives. Connor said he'd been smiling to himself all day as he unpacked. He was glad to leave behind the sadness he felt in Cambridge lately. The loneliness without his wife there was something we had in common. We also admitted that there were a few people that we were glad to have left behind.

"Some of my old friends made the last several months a little unpleasant as they fought with Edward about changes that needed to be made. The last strike was promised to end the factory, but a few of those guys wouldn't listen to anyone, including me. When Edward said he would close down the factory and move it, they still wouldn't listen. Well, I guess Edward called their bluff didn't he, Red?"

"He sure did. I know you tried your best. I could understand some of their issues, but what's done is done. To the future!" I said as I held up my glass triumphantly.

Connor named some friends that he was glad had the sense to journey here with us. "I'll get to know the others that came here soon enough as we are all neighbors now."

I noticed Connor had several boxes still unopened in the kitchen. I offered to help him with the chore of unpacking his belongings. He didn't bring much with him so it didn't take long. "I wanted a fresh start and so much of what I owned I left to my sister and her family back in Cambridge. I'm just a simple man with simple tastes and figured anything I needed I could surely find here."

Now looking at the sparse rooms I could see he was regretting that decision a little. Well, at least he had the sense to bring his bed with him or he'd be sitting and sleeping on the floor. Tomorrow he'd better find out where the furniture store is, he is going to need it I thought to myself.

It seemed that most of the citizens of Glassboro weren't going to sleep much that first night. As I left Connor's place and headed back to my house, I could see a number of lights on in the houses on my street. The long train ride, parade and festivities should have knocked us all out early. However, the excitement and reality of our new lives was probably keeping all our minds spinning. We have a big, hard day ahead of us tomorrow, but I think a restful sleep is not coming for most of tonight. If they were like me, they would be running on adrenaline for several days before getting a full night's rest.

Early the next morning, about half the households were illuminated as the start of the first official day approached. As the men and women converged on the street cheerful greetings were exchanged. I admit it was a bit strange to be part of a procession walking together down the street and into the factory. It was a much smaller parade then yesterday, without all the family members and townspeople and marching band, but it was still loud and full of spirit.

Some women and children were left behind to tend to the unglamorous chore of unpacking and getting their homes in order.

Most of the children quickly gathered with their friends outside and waved to us as we passed by. I'm sure their moms wanted them to go out to play as they could likely get more done without the children underfoot. I chuckled as I heard the moms sending the children out with the same warnings, "S*tay out of the street, don't go wandering off to the river, don't go near the factory or else…*"

Chapter 21

Edward was waiting at the front door of the plant to greet us. He told us that he was covering our lunch today in the cafeteria. Actually he said the town was treating us to lunch, perhaps for the whole week with the amount of food left over from the picnic. I could see the men were looking forward to lunch, but they were also eager to get to work.

We all followed Edward through the plant as he dropped each gang off at their new work areas. The fresh cleanness of the factory would be enjoyed while it lasted. Soon enough the grease and grime would take some of the shine off the place. Truthfully that's how most of the men preferred it, including me. It just felt like you were working harder, if there was dirt and broken glass pieces around.

We all knew it would take some time to get the furnaces running at full tilt and to get good product coming out. We were all anxious to get started. The urgency took on new meaning when the groups started bragging about who would produce the first, best batch of glasses. With the challenge thrown down, the race was on.

Edward got everyone settled in to their new areas and headed to his office. He turned and called to me, "Red, can I see you in my office?"

"In trouble already, eh Red?" Some wisecracker yelled.

I lowered and shook my head which received a few laughs. I didn't know what Edward wanted but I thought it might be about our dinner last night. It had been awhile since I had laid eyes on Florence but I could tell she was still interested in Edward. It seemed that both her parents were also plotting to get the couple together.

"Red, thanks for attending the dinner last night. I think everything went well, didn't you? Florence was even more beautiful than I remembered."

"So when will you be seeing her again?"

"I do not have any formal plans to see her again. Stop - I know what you're thinking. Don't think I didn't see you and Maurice whispering and laughing together. So tell me, why are you older gentlemen always looking to find matches for the young? Does misery truly love company or do you want others to experience your wedded bliss?" Edward said curiously and then looked guilty. "Sorry, I didn't mean to be insensitive."

"It's fine, really. Truthfully I think everyone should marry once and you are long overdue Edward."

"Florence is wonderful, but I have so much to do to get the factory going in full gear and a new romance would be quite a distraction."

I left his office convinced he was trying to find excuses not to court Florence because he was scared. In Florence he had finally met someone that could be the one. Maurice and I wouldn't have to nudge him too much to ask her out. He wouldn't be able to hold himself back for long.

The first shift ended and left the workers feeling a little down. We didn't feel we had made as much progress as we all expected. "Don't worry, we'll get there. Go home and enjoy dinner with your families," Edward called out to them as they left.

I hoped that made them feel better. I watched as several of them waved and hollered to the night crew. "Good luck men! Good night!" I sensed a new bond forming as I stared at them walking together down the street and towards their new homes.

Once the next shift was settled into their stations, Edward and I left for the evening. He left the foreman in charge and told him to get him if there were any problems. Edward left by trolley to his hotel as I strolled back to my house. I couldn't help looking back with pride at the factory and the new possibilities in front of us. I thought of Florence and wondered if Edward would call on her tonight. Realizing the lateness of the hour, I knew that wouldn't happen tonight. Perhaps tomorrow he would find his courage I laughed aloud as I prepared for bed.

I tried to sleep but after a couple hours I gave up. I just had too much on my mind to sleep. I took out my notebook and began jotting down some of my thoughts. I reflected on some of the struggles the men were having today in several areas. I knew most of the problems led back to the batch formula.

Using gas for heating the furnaces was still new for us and also proving challenging. It was difficult to control the furnace and the batches were inconsistent and the glasses weren't as easy to form as before. This slowdown in quality was frustrating to everyone. We had the sales orders flying in, but not enough quality products to answer the call. I knew Edward would be working hard to create new batch formulas to try tomorrow. Just writing these thoughts down allowed my mind to relax. I slumped down in my chair and was asleep in no time.

Edward showed up early the next day to a growing list of problems. Some of the snags started early yesterday and Edward had hoped they would have been resolved overnight. Unfortunately that was not the case. Most distressful was finding that the furnaces were running but the gobs of molten glass coming out were not the right consistency. Luckily the next shift arrived refreshed and ready to tackle the problem.

It took some time but by the end of the day crew three had produced the first good glass. The crew was happy they won the bet, but the others were just as glad that things were finally starting to run right. Edward complimented the men and then walked towards his office. Just as he arrived his assistant learned Mr. Scott was at the gate.

"Wonderful, have them send him down, I'll meet him at the front door," Edward said.

"Edward, I can go get him. You wait here," I said helpfully. I made my way down the stairs and stopped at the bottom to straighten the glasses in the display case. I turned as I heard the door opening and went over to welcome Mr. Scott.

"Welcome Maurice. What a pleasure to see you."

Maurice shook my hand and said, "Thank you. I do hope I'm not disturbing you or Edward."

Smiling broadly I replied, "No, not at all, you are welcome here anytime. We've had a bit of a bumpy start but we are just working past it. How is that lovely wife and daughter of yours?"

"Fine, fine. Wonderful in fact. By the way, did you see the way Florence looked at Edward last night? I think a romance is blooming!"

"It's about time," I said to Maurice.

"Between us Red, Florence has pushed away every man that has looked her way. I was starting to fear I'd never see her get married. I worried all the travel and education we lavished on her had spoiled her for the men around here. Most seem pretty intimidated when she speaks of the worldly things she has seen and done."

"Well, Edward seems to have her same love of Europe and art and books. Sometimes you just have to wait for the right one to come along," I said. "So what exactly brings you by?" I asked as I led Maurice to Edward's office.

"I just wanted to check and see that everything is running smoothly. It's the least I can do as a member of the Business Men's Association," Maurice said trying to convince me that his motives had everything to do with business.

"And your colleagues, is everything satisfactory with their new homes?" Maurice inquired as we walked together down the hall.

"Yes, we are most grateful and happy to be living in new homes that are close together and so nearby the factory."

"Well, I know you are still getting settled in and that Edward is staying at the hotel, so I'd like to invitc you to dinner Friday night." Maurice said more as a statement than an inquiry.

Edward replied, "That sounds great, and that's very generous of you. I hope that Mrs. Scott won't tire of seeing me again so soon."

Maurice told Edward that his wife loved to entertain and truthfully probably preferred Edward's company to his own. His stories were old and worn and Mrs. Scott thoroughly enjoyed hearing Edward's funny stories and tales of adventure. I excused myself and let the two men get caught up on business affairs and assured Maurice that I would escort Edward to their home on Friday.

The rest of the day ran along with a few glitches but nothing glass shattering to report. I was now just looking forward to Friday when Edward would see Florence again. If this dinner went well, I expected he'd get the courage to ask her out on a formal date. I knew she liked the theater and would suggest he ask to escort her there.

As I headed back into the manufacturing area I was stopped by the quality manager. "Red, we have a problem. The first batch that came out didn't anneal properly. The glasses are all breaking or showing signs of cracks."

I knew Edward's good mood would fade with this news as I asked, "When did you find this? Is it the whole run?"

The manager replied, "Yes, I'm afraid so. We'll have to toss the whole run. We made some adjustments and I expect the next batch to fare better. We'd didn't start packing anything, so there is no need to quarantine anything in shipping. Do you think Edward will want to release the department? They won't have anything to do for quite a while."

I knew Edward would hate the thought of sending home the shipping department but there was no sense having them standing around doing nothing.

"I will break the news to Edward. You can tell the men to go home." So much for a turnaround today I thought as I headed back to Edward's office to break the news.

The men were glad to go home early, but they knew they'd make up for it the next day as they were falling way behind schedule and orders were piling up. We had plenty of product in inventory, but it never seemed like it was for the items we needed most. Some regular customers were already agitated because our new location was expected to cause some delay in delivery. The east coast companies, who previously enjoyed very minimal freight charges, now were concerned about paying higher shipping charges.

Increasing prices was something Edward was careful to avoid. He was so concerned about losing his larger customers that he had agreed to keep freight charges the same for one year. He had a loyal customer base and didn't want to jeopardize losing their business at this juncture. In fact, this news was taken as a great win to his customers. His customers knew they wouldn't have found better pricing anyway, as most glass companies had already moved out of the east coast region.

I kept myself extremely busy that first week in Toledo. There were numerous problems with our machines and I found myself being called from one to another all day long. I preferred keeping busy, and I didn't have anyone at home waiting for me, so I didn't even mind staying late.

My main concern was the delay in production that each problem caused. Idle machines meant money was being lost. I prided myself on my ingenuity and I was determined to make sure everything was up and running as quick as possible. I soon noticed we were using much more gas than what was originally planned. If my calculations were correct, we wouldn't be saving nearly as much money as Edward expected.

If we could tinker with the furnace some more and improve the efficiency it should help. No, it would help, I promised myself. Everything was riding it. If the costs didn't come down as Edward had expected and planned, I knew the factory would close down for good. The town put on quite a welcome for us and I was determined not to let them down.

Friday took it's time arriving, I thought. As I dressed for dinner, I realized how much I was looking forward to the evening at the Scotts. As far as I knew, this would be a more intimate affair with just the elder Scotts and their daughter. This way Edward would have more time to talk with Florence.

As we turned down Monroe Street I spotted Maurice waving to us from his porch. Edward soon joined him in the open rocking chair and inquired about Mr. Scott's business. I half-listened as I stood admiring the rose bushes in full bloom. Mr. Scott was an astute businessman and each time he talked Edward found some useful tidbit that he tucked away to use in his affairs later. He was also impressed with all the land the Scotts owned. He listened a little jealously as Maurice talked of all his plans for the city. Edward only wished to follow in his footsteps one day.

Edward dreamed he would have the opportunity to leave a great legacy to his new hometown. As I was reminded of that, I thought about Edward's promise to his father at his funeral. Looking down at his dad in the coffin, taken so suddenly in the prime of his life, Edward vowed to turn around the business he had put his name on and make him proud that he brought his only son into his glass company.

Edward was not disappointed that he had accepted this dinner invitation. Florence looked smashingly beautiful and the food was delicious as always. The three of them had so much in common and the conversations were so natural. They were gracious to me as well and I was glad to be included. Dinner was happily followed with drinks in the parlor.

I had a hunch that Edward would talk all night if it would prolong the dinner party. Florence was much more relaxed this evening. She sighed as she told Edward about a couple pieces of art she had her eye on that she had spotted earlier that week. I could see that he was taking it all in and I wouldn't be shocked if he surprised her with a gift of one of those paintings someday.

Edward and I could easily see how much Florence loved and respected her parents. It was one of the reasons she stayed in Toledo, eventually returning after having been schooled and educated in larger cities. It was one of the things Edward really admired about her. He also was very close with his family.

Edward's family bonds were so tight that his sister Sarah had agreed to move to Toledo with him. He knew moving was the right thing for the business, but he would have been heartbroken if his sister had stayed behind. As it was, he felt guilty enough that Sarah had to move away their other sister Alice whose family remained in Cambridge. He hoped in time that Alice may change her mind and relocate. He knew Sarah was missing her niece and nephew already just as much as he did.

Since the night went so well Edward was determined to set the next date. This time it would be just the two of them. If Florence would agree that is. When Mrs. Scott went to take the glasses to the kitchen, Mr. Scott shot up quickly to help her and I jumped up to help them as well.

Edward realized he was finally alone with Florence and as I headed down the hall I smiled as I heard Edward say, "Florence, I was wondering if you'd do me the pleasure of attending the theater with me next Saturday. I saw that *The Proposal* is in town. I hope you haven't seen it yet."

"Oh it is my favorite play. I would love to attend again with you!" Florence replied joyfully.

Edward figured he best be going before the happiness wears off and she comes to her senses. We bid farewell to the

Scotts and left feeling pleased. Edward got more out of the evening than he had wished. And this time, he knew exactly when he'd see Florence again. I was pleased to see him so giddy.

"What do you know, Ed and Flo, going to a show…." I sung quietly under my breath.

Chapter 22

Orders for glassware were coming in more regularly now but that didn't slow Edward down. This week would be filled with travel for Edward. He found it harder to leave Toledo than he expected. A week away from Florence was one reason. Leaving the factory was another. Edward felt confident things would be running up to his high standards soon, but he was still apprehensive.

A couple of the more challenging workers stayed behind in Cambridge but Edward had to manage expectations of a new reality. Moving a factory was more expensive than originally thought. He had left in some money for unknown expenses, but they had blown past that projection. Unexpected delays and costs were a constant source of worry.

The potential new customers Edward was meeting this week were critical if we were going to hit our sales projections for the year. His first meeting was with the head of a small but growing hotel. The hotel was adding 150 rooms and another restaurant. Edward's goal was to win the installation of his Pomona line for the restaurant. Barware and glasses should be in each room he surmised.

Edward had a good feeling about his pitch and expected a good outcome. He had worked with the owner for years and he always told Edward that Libbey products were the best. Edward would offer an attractive deal to get the full installation. He expected the hotelier would expand outside the city someday and he planned to be there with him every step of the way.

Edward wanted more than just a one-time win. Edward wanted to build partnerships with other businessmen and grow their businesses together. Delivering quality products at a fair price and on time was his goal with every customer. His name was on each product and that was a reminder of his promise to his customer.

Once the customer issue was resolved, Edward was scheduled to meet with Fritz in Wheeling. Fritz was an experienced manager and Edward needed someone with his background to assist with training the new hires. Some of our new guys were not being trained too well by the older workers and Edward needed someone who wasn't afraid to stand up to them and keep them in line. The men were fine when Edward was around, but sometimes a few would slack off when he wasn't there.

When Edward returned from his travels he stopped into check on my latest project. "Red, you know I went to West Virginia to meet with Fritz and that meeting went fairly well, but strangely as I was leaving my hotel the next morning to head home I was approached by this young man by the name of Michael Owens."

"Wait, what happened with Fritz? Is he onboard?" I asked anxiously.

Edward ignored my questions and continued on. "Michael boldly introduced himself and proceeded to tell me that he should be hired to manage my business. I was little taken aback by his boldness, but also a little impressed. Michael went on and on about his years of experience, but I was already set on Fritz."

"I don't know this Michael Owens guy, but Fritz does have experience and seems well suited for the position," I offered.

"I just left Michael standing there as I stepped away. He thanked me for talking to him and looked rather disappointed but there's something about him-" Edward stopped in mid-sentence as if lost in some thought.

I presumed that would be the last I'd hear about Mr. Owens. Little did I know then how wrong that assumption would turn out to be. A few days later Edward received a letter from Michael Owens. Michael's letter stated that he would do just about anything to work for the famous Mr. Libbey and if the manager position wasn't available he would be happy to work as a glassblower for him. Edward told me he found Michael's persistence endearing and irresistible and he would write to him and advise him to get to Toledo as soon as possible.

When Michael arrived a couple weeks later he gushed with excitement about leaving Wheeling for Toledo. He was ecstatic to finally be working for the best glass company in the country, he said to a beaming Edward. By the time he arrived at the factory, things were at their worst. Fritz had taken the manager job and he was terrible.

It wasn't long before Michael heard everyone complaining about Fritz. Since Michael had known Fritz well from their work days together in Wheeling he tried to give him a break. Michael caught up with him after work one day and asked to join him for a drink. I was at the pub sitting alone at the counter and couldn't help overhear some of their conversation.

Michael proceeded to carefully tell Fritz that his management style wasn't working on these northerners and that he needed to try another tactic to get the workers on his side. I could see Fritz didn't take kindly to Michael's advice because he slammed down his glass and stormed out of the bar.

I realized if Michael played his cards right, he would soon get what he wanted. I liked Michael from the start. Michael likely knew it wouldn't be long before Fritz would be gone, one way or another.

Michael bided his time and when Fritz threatened to call it quits a few days later, Michael barged right into Edward's office while I was standing there.

"Mr. Libbey, you have a situation on your hands with those workers out there. They are disgruntled and feel disrespected about the way Fritz yells at them. I've witnessed fights that started over the arcane rules he is trying to implement. Fritz is always talking down to them like he is better than them. He is so arrogant and telling them how to do their job, a job he doesn't have the skill to do himself. I have a much better temperament and can get your worker's attitudes turned around and get them focused again. I'm one of them, I know how to make glass, I know the hard work and discipline it takes, and I can lead them to get the job done. What do you have to lose? Let me show you what I can do," Michael said adamantly. He was determined to get this job and Edward could see that he had made the mistake in hiring Jacobs in the first place.

"Michael, I must say, I've been impressed with your tenacity and I agree you are a very skilled craftsman. Your willingness to come in and tell me to my face that I've made mistakes shows you have great courage, or stupidity, or both," Edward chuckled. "Michael, I would very much like you to take on this management role, effective immediately!"

Michael looked at Edward with a serious look and said, "Sir, you will not be disappointed." And with that he immediately left the office and gave the news to the men.

For the most part, the men seemed relieved. They were glad to hear Fritz was gone and they were willing to give Michael a chance. Although Michael hadn't been there too long, they all liked him immensely.

The New Inner Circle 1888-89

Edward and I got together with a group of businessmen for dinner at the Bavarian Inn restaurant that night. Mike Owens was already there when we showed up. "Hi Mike, how are you this evening?"

"Doing well boss, and yourself?" Mike asked.

"Can't complain, well if I did, nobody would listen would they?" Edward said laughing. The three of us ordered a drink and grabbed a bar stool. Edward was glad we had a few minutes before the others arrived. He wanted to talk about the issues on the lines that were causing problems that morning.

Mike assured Edward it was a minor setback and that everything was under control. Actually Mike complained it wasn't the machines as much as it was the workers. There were several of the Cambridge employees who had traveled here with Edward that were causing trouble for the new employees.

A few of the guys that came from Cambridge seemed resentful of anyone new joining the company and were allegedly not training them properly, according to the newer hires. Mike told Edward that he had some experienced workers in West Virginia and he could entice them to come here if he would just give the approval.

Edward was apprehensive about hiring more employees, but he also had to recognize the homesick flu that was going around. A few people had already left Toledo to go back home to Cambridge and we knew others were likely to follow. He told Mike he would keep the proposal in mind and get back with him shortly with an answer.

Edward looked relieved when we were joined by our friends, John Willys, George Pomeroy and Dave Locke. "Remember, Dave, everything tonight is off the record. We don't want to see it in the paper tomorrow!" Edward said jokingly as the others nodded and laughed in agreement.

Dave was used to this sort of ribbing from his friends. It was just part of the territory of being in the newspaper business. "I can't guarantee it, if something earth, err glass, shattering happens then I'm obliged to report it," Dave replied.

The waitress appeared and escorted us to a table. As we walked to our seats, several other patrons looked our way and waved. The excitement wasn't over me, I deduced. The men I was with tonight were very well known in Toledo and seemed to garner attention wherever they went. The waitress took our drink orders as we settled into our chairs.

It wasn't long before we were all laughing and catching up on each other's lives. By the time dinner arrived someone from the group, there would be many arguments later on who exactly first broached the idea, suggested they should open their own club. A businessman's club with a formal membership was suddenly the hot topic.

The men talked through a list of what this club would do, where it should be, who should be a member, and other details as dinner progressed. Edward was a member of such a club in Cambridge and since he'd been in Toledo he realized how much he missed it. It was interesting to hear the excited chatter of the men as they formulated the plan.

By the time dinner ended David revealed they already had a similar such a club in Toledo. He knew because was one of its founding members. His organization was called the "Draconian Club". The word came from Draco, a seventh century B.C. legislator who wrote a written code of law.

"What we need is our own clubhouse. A place that will be an architectural gem, a place we can relax, entertain and celebrate." David concluded.

The men agreed to meet again on Thursday to continue planning the creation of their Draconian Club's own facility. *(The Club's name would later be changed to The Toledo Club and is still in existence).*

Chapter 23

Shortly after everyone settled into their new homes and new workplace, Edward was restless to continue expanding his product line and its reach across the world. He soon told me that he was leaving for Europe to drum up new business. Knowing Edward the way I did, I knew there would also be time for a little treasure hunting.

Edward loved fine art and there was no better place to find it than in Europe. He always came back from his trips with a new painting or artifact. His collection was growing quite large and I said in jest, "If you keep this hobby up, soon you'll need a bigger house, or a museum to hold everything!"

I chuckled at the thought and blurted out, "Yeah, can you see this swampy city with a museum, that's just crazy!" *(Little did I know then that is exactly what would happen. Toledo would one day soon have a world-renowned museum thanks to my boss. And Red's great, great grandson would admire the works Libbey collected a century later.)*

I didn't find out until several days later just how special the European trip was for Edward. Edward didn't tell me before he left, but I eventually found out that that he wasn't exactly alone on his trip. The Scotts were in London on a family vacation. I'm sure Edward had planned to "accidently" run into Florence and her parents on the trip. "That sly dog!" I said laughing to myself. "I wonder if Florence will be surprised."

Florence had the same love and passion for art as Edward. It was one of the interests they shared that initially drew them together. Florence had also spent a good deal of time pursuing her quest for fine art and ceramics over the years. She was especially fond of Rembrandt, Monet and van Gogh. Edward was lucky he could share his hobby with his new love interest. *(As they grew older they would spend more and more time traveling to exotic lands in search of fine art and antiquities.)*

Edward was gone for a few weeks when I received a mysterious telegraph from him. "Meet me at the train station on Friday evening, 11:00 p.m. Stop. URGENT. Stop. DON'T BE LATE."

"What in the world? Why would Edward need me to meet him at the train station? Why couldn't he just stop by my house the next morning?" I stammered out loud as I re-read the telegraph. It was highly unusual for Edward to contact anyone, let alone me, during one of his trips. The situation was ever more intriguing because I knew about the Scotts, but there is no way Edward would know I discovered that detail. Could this have something to do with Florence? I sure hoped everything was okay. Now I had three days to fret and ponder over this mystery.

I knew it must be quite an urgent matter for Edward to send that telegraph. The message sounded as if I had no choice in the matter, but he didn't know if I'd even be available or if this could be a problem for me. This was unusual behavior from Edward as he was normally so well-mannered.

The next couple days, I found it difficult to focus on any task. My mind kept racing with all kinds of crazy thoughts. What could have happened in Europe to put Edward in such a state? What did Edward really think I could do about it? Why was it so urgent that he couldn't wait until business hours the next day to tell me?

Whatever it was, I had to just wait it out as there was no way for me to reach him. I told myself to stop thinking about it and concentrate on my work. Getting involved in my project would help distract me, just get to work I told myself. I did my best to avoid looking at the clock the rest of the day.

I was at the station an hour before Edward's train arrived. There were a few others waiting there as well, anxious to see their loved ones I assumed. There was a slight chill in the air, but the wind was calm. I was glad I had brought my heavy coat. I hope the ship wasn't late and that he was able to board the train for Toledo.

I walked briskly over to the attendant's window, "Excuse me sir, can you tell me if the train from Chicago is coming in on time tonight?"

"I sure hope so mister, I'm ready to knock off for the night! I haven't heard any news so I bet it will be on time. Are you waiting for a lady friend?" he said curiously.

"No, it's nothing like that." I said as I walked away and found a bench to sit on.

Right about 11:00 p.m. the train came chugging up the tracks. I could see many people now waving excitedly from the windows to the people near the front of the station. This scene always made me chuckle to myself. Did people really think their friend or family member could actually pick them out from the crowd and see that they were being waved at so joyously? Some things people did always amused me.

"Red, Red," I heard a familiar voice yell.

I went towards the front of the line and saw Edward frantically waving me over. Then I noticed Florence just behind him. That nifty fellow I thought, I knew he must have planned to see Florence in Europe, but I didn't realize they'd be coming back on the same train. I wonder how much of this trip was devoted to business. The sight of Florence had me even more curious as to why Edward wanted me to meet him here. I do hope they are both okay.

I walked up and exchanged pleasantries with Ms. Scott, such as "How was the trip? Did you have a great time?" and other such questions. Ms. Scott was so animated in responding and trying to explain that they didn't travel there together and that they just happened to run into each over there. She looked worried like I wouldn't believe her and was quick to point out for my knowledge the fact that her parents were there too as they came up the platform towards her.

Edward excused us from Florence for just a moment, he promised. He looked around and saw a small alcove area and ushered me to go there with him. His face looked mischievous and a little hesitant at the same time. "Red, I have a come across something in my travels and it is of monumental importance that I get your word you will not breathe a word of this to anyone."

Before I could respond he went on, "Once I came upon this, this souvenir, let's call it, I immediately knew I had to have it. There are so many possibilities of its use that flashed before me when I saw it, I couldn't go home without it."

Well Edward sure had my attention, but I still couldn't fathom what in the world could possess him like this.

Edward continued, "Once I was able to secure its purchase, I thought long and hard about who I trusted most, who would understand my vision, and be able to help me put my plan into place and pull it off. Red, your name was first and foremost on my mind. Actually, you know, I didn't even consider anyone else. Your loyalty to me over the years and our dear friendship, well, there is really nobody else I could think of that I would want to confide this secret. Not even Florence is aware of it." He stopped for a moment and grabbed my arms.

"Please tell me I have your word you will keep this under glass. You can't utter a word of what I'm about to share with you," said Edward pleaded.

I had no idea what I was getting myself into that night on the deck, but this was Edward Libbey, and I never had a truer friend, confidant, "little brother", and boss. There is nothing I wouldn't do to help him, so without a moment's hesitation I said, "You got it, Boss Man."

What Edward told me next wasn't the most incredible thing I ever heard. I guess looking back on that night, the way he slowly confided in me was probably the best course of action. If he had blurted out the full secret, right there, in the dark of the night, huddled in the alcove, on the pier with Florence waiting patiently nearby, I probably would have laughed too loud, decked him or even pushed him off the platform, thinking how wicked it was that he was messing with me this way.

"We can't talk here, it isn't safe. I have the souvenir in a box that you must take home with you tonight. Please do not do anything to disturb it. Whatever happens, do not open it until I arrive at your home. I will be over as soon as I get Florence home." Florence didn't know anything about the package and he intended to keep it that way for now.

Edward pulled the claim ticket from his breast pocket and told me where to pick it up from the porter. They were holding it in my name. He again swore me to secrecy and we parted ways.

Picking up the package went off without a hitch. The only trouble I had now was that my curiosity was killing me. "Edward better get here soon," I kept repeating while pacing back and forth across my kitchen floor.

A long strange day was going to turn into a long, long night. I sighed. While waiting for Edward I started a kettle to boil hot water. A cup of tea would warm me up after the long night at the station. I didn't worry that the tea would make me sleepy. There was no way I could imagine falling asleep tonight. I sat, sipping tea, and staring at the package for what seemed like forever before Edward showed up.

Before Edward could knock a second time I was throwing open the door. "Get in here and tell me what in the devil is going on friend!" I yelled to Edward.

Edward smiled and thanked me profusely for all my inconvenience. "You are a great friend, Red, I knew I could trust you with this secret, I trust you with my life," he said as he looked at the table and saw the package was resting neatly, with no wrapping disturbed.

"Red you wouldn't guess in a million years what is in that package. It is something I didn't even know was really possible. It is going to change both our lives! It's a really long and complicated story how I came about acquiring it, and I will save all those details for another time as I'm sure you're anxious to have the box opened."

He was right about that. I am a very patient guy, and normally not opening a package wouldn't have bothered me in the least, but all the mystery surrounding this night, led me to believe, without a doubt, inside this box was something extraordinary.

Edward looked at me with such gravity as he whispered, "Please keep an open mind and keep quiet, don't utter a sound."

I stood there frozen with my eyes glued on the box. Edward cut across the top and slowly opened the box. I heard a faint, strange sound, but I didn't say a word. I couldn't discern what animal would make such a sound, it was like nothing I had ever heard before.

Edward turned around and pulled the item out of the box with his back to me and then slowly turned around as he opened his hands. In the palm of his left hand was a small creature. I stared at it in utter disbelief. Edward beamed as he saw me struggling to register that what I was seeing was actually real.

I stood staring for what seemed like hours, and finally in a shaky voice I said, "How is this even possiblc?"

Chapter 24

"I own a dragon!" Edward said proudly, like he was a new father to a baby boy.

"HOLY TOLEDO!" was the first thing that popped out of my mouth. I couldn't believe my ears or my eyes. There is no such thing as real dragons, but there it was right in front of me. It looked just as I remembered the descriptions in all the legends and stories I heard as a boy. Although, I never imagined a baby one could be so adorable. It sat timidly in Edward's hand and looked inquisitively at me and back at Edward.

I had to sit down before I fainted. I thought everyone in town could hear my heart thumping. "What on Earth, but how, but what, but why??" I stammered and shook my head in amazement as Edward let out a huge laugh.

The creature was glorious! It was a soft shade of orange, scaly like a lizard, and about the size of a small apple. It looked at me curiously and spread it wings to show its might. I held in my laughter, knowing that someday soon this act of spreading his wings to intimate would work handsomely, but for now it was just quaint, but alluring. The scales on his back went all the way down his tail which he was swinging wildly back and forth. Edward pulled the cage out of the box and set the dragon back inside of it and sat it in front of me in the middle of the table.

"I've just solved our money problems, Red!" said Edward happily.

He went on and on, in great detail about how this dragon would be trained, by me no less, to work in the factory and produce fire to keep our furnaces burning. The cheaply priced gas that was one of the lures to bring us to Toledo, was not turning out to be as inexpensive as Edward had been led to believe. He also lectured me about how gas prices naturally would fluctuate over time and the way he could keep costs under control was staring at us right in the face! Edward apparently had some time to mull this over and while I tried really hard to listen to what he had to say it proved nearly impossible. I just sat, memorized by the wondrous creature in front of me.

I did manage to nod my head in agreement to some foolhardy things he was saying before I fully realized what he said. When his words started sinking in, I sat back in my chair and said, "Whoa, did you actually say that you are keeping this thing and I'm going to train it to work for us? Are you crazy? This is the silliest thing I've ever heard!"

"Just take a moment to think about it, I already have, and its genius really, you'll see. This is the best investment I've ever made. This is going to be one remarkable adventure, Red."

"It's a completely mad idea!" I exclaimed more than once as Edward chatted away. Yet the more the idea festered in my head the more I found myself unable to stop thinking about the possibilities.

"Oh, Red, don't worry so much! Your mind is as sharp as a shard of glass, and I know you'll work it out!" Edward exclaimed while patting me on the back.

I don't know what it is about Edward, but when he starts talking, he has this magic way of pulling you in and you can't help but fall under his spell and agree to anything he says. Before the sun broke above the horizon that morning, it was settled. Our confidential "Project Ignite" was a go and soon to be officially underway.

Our first step was to get the dragon something to eat. Edward filled me on the types of bugs and insects that made up his diet. Edward had some food in the box to get him through a few days before we'd have to set up a steady recurring supply. Edward was warned the dragon would grow quickly and his appetite would increase accordingly.

Edward taught me some of the basic commands that the previous owner had trained him to do. Today would be spent getting him comfortable with me and used to my voice. Dragons are like dogs, they are very loyal and eager to please their masters. These qualities should make him easy to train according to Edward.

Edward said he was going to the plant ahead of me and would get the lab set up for our experiments with "Project Ignite". He reminded me, "Red, you are under strict confidentiality and no one can discover the dragon or what we are attempting to do until I decide it is prudent to do so. It is simply too dangerous to let this secret be discovered, especially for the dragon."

Most people have grown up hearing too many horror stories about dragons and have many incorrect misconceptions about them. Unfortunately, history has shown us that sometimes people are quick to try an animal that they fear and don't understand. Of course, there was also the bigger issue that people don't believe dragons are real either. The fact that there is one here in front of me proves that wrong, but this information in the wrong hands, could prove dangerously unlucky for their kind I quickly realized.

The reality of the situation began sinking in shortly after Edward left me alone in my house with a dragon on my kitchen table. I figured I should treat it just as I used to treat my old dog, Rex, which I was lucky enough to have for twelve great years. I came across Rex, wandering in an alley when he was just a scrawny pup. He was a mutt, a Shephard, Collie mix from what I could tell. And he turned out to be wonderful companion for many years. I missed Rex. I wondered how he would have taken to a new pet in the house!

"Well, how do you, little fella? I'm Red, and we're going to be spending a lot of time together for a while. I hope that's ok with you," I said in a voice that some may call baby talk. I don't know how you're supposed to talk with a dragon, but his small stature just reminded me of a baby.

Wait, I don't think Edward told me the dragon's name. He must have a name. I looked at him, and he looked up at me. "What shall we call you?" I said to him and wondered, what is a good name for such a magical creature? "I don't know what Edward was going to call you, but for now you will be Spark. Yes, I think that's an appropriate name for you." I took Spark's silence as acceptance of his new name.

Over the next hour as I got ready for work I found myself talking to Spark about my life. I found Spark to be a great listener, just as old Rex used to be. I moved Spark and his cage around the house as I went about my morning rituals. It was lucky that I lived alone at this time and didn't have to worry about anyone walking in on us.

As I got ready my mind was flowing with many thoughts about how we were going to be able to pull off this event at work. I'm often working in the laboratory by myself so that was helpful, but there was the issue of getting to and from the lab which was located near the back of the factory. At least Spark's small size would make it fairly easy at this time to hide him inside my lunch box. The metal box should keep any noises he may make to a minimum. I would just walk quickly through and appear to be in a great hurry so I wouldn't be expected to stop and chat with my co-workers as would typically happen most mornings.

We would have to take it one day at a time and see how it goes. I can't imagine how long we can expect to keep this secret from the hundreds of employees at the factory but I would do everything in my power to try. I had no choice. I looked at Spark and realized the gravity of the situation and how his life depended on me.

"I won't let you down, or Edward. Failure is not for us!"

After giving Edward what I thought was enough time to set up, I decided it was time to make the journey to the plant with my new companion. Luckily I lived just down the street from the factory on Champlain Street in one of the fifty houses that were built on lots that were part of the deal to bring our factory to town. This made the commute to and from work a breeze. This proximity would prove even more important now that I also had to contend with Spark.

Looking out the window I noticed the weather looked a little cloudy and gray, which I was finding was not unusual for Toledo. "Ready or not Edward, here we come!"

As I suspected, a few people looked up when I walked through the main aisle of the plant. I stayed calm, made a quick wave and said I was late for an appointment. That was certainly understandable and didn't raise any suspicions. I let out a big sigh of relief when I reached the lab and was able to close and lock the door.

There were a couple of small windows in the lab that looked out towards the packaging line. I went to the windows and pulled the curtains closed. As I was figuring out where to put Spark I saw the door handle turning. I moved quickly in front of Spark and put the box down over the cage. No, this can't be happening I fretted. Then I felt relieved as I saw it was just Edward stepping into the lab.

"Wonderful, you're here and just in time. I have everything situated here and have his food set up near the back counter on the floor. I told the plant manager that you were working on a special, urgent assignment for me and you were not to be disturbed the rest of the day. That will give us some time to adjust and figure out how to get started on this project. So, have you given it any thought yet?" Edward inquired.

Are you kidding me? I thought to myself but then responded, "Well, in the few hours I've had to contemplate this venture of yours, in a word, NO, I haven't the foggiest idea how to get Spark to start firing up our furnace!"

"Spark? Is that what you're calling him? I guess that's suitable enough," he snorted. "I was so busy figuring out what we would do with him I hadn't even thought to give him a name," said Edward regretfully. "Well Spark, what do you think of your new home?" Edward said as he waved his hands around pointing out the room.

"Red, I will make sure you are not disturbed. I will check back with you as soon as I can. You can take this time to begin drafting a detailed plan of our objectives, risks, and ultimate goals for "Project Ignite". Edward turned before I could respond and was out the door. He knew my specialty was planning and developing ways to take his ideas and make them work.

Edward didn't get bogged down in the tedious details, he was more of a visionary kind of guy. The fact that he told you the goal and gave you the freedom to manage and develop it on your own was one of the best features of having Edward as a boss. He was the best boss I ever worked for, although his dad wasn't so bad either.

Edward's passion and dreams were so uplifting it would inspire you to push yourself to try new ways to accomplish your goals. Don't get me wrong, it wasn't always easy and sometimes it was downright impossible, but was also invigorating. I think that special quality Edward possessed is what made so many people follow him from their homes in Cambridge to Toledo.

I sat down at my desk and begin writing down our goals and objectives for this project. Then, with my limited knowledge of dragons, *because really who had much knowledge of them*, I began contemplating and imagining what we could train him to do and how it could possibly work.

One important goal I did not write down, but I vowed to myself it would not be forgotten. My ultimate goal was to someday unite Spark with his kind.

I smiled at Spark and patted his head gently and whispered, "There must be more dragons out there and we will find them for you someday."

Chapter 25

I spent the next couple hours developing a plan of action. First and foremost I outlined what I needed to learn about Spark and his kind. That got me thinking, were there others of his breed? Of course there must be, he had to have been born to a mother dragon. Were dragons a multiple birth? Could Spark have siblings out there?

Well this line of thinking wasn't getting me anywhere. These questions were important and intriguing of course, but not likely to be answered by me anytime soon. Edward had not revealed much information on how he came upon this discovery and how he was able to purchase it and this weighed heavily on me. At this point I resolved to just deal with the situation that fell into my lap, or more accurately, my kitchen table.

My attention was quickly diverted as Spark began walking back and forth in his cage. "Good day Sparky," I said, "look around, you're going to be spending a lot of time here with me. I hope you will feel at home here soon enough. It didn't take me too long to get used to this place. I know people were really reluctant to leave Cambridge, but they are starting to find Toledo charming. It may not be everyone's cup of tea, but it has some special qualities you'll see."

The people of Toledo couldn't be friendlier or more helpful. Most have really gone out of their way to welcome us to town, and are constantly treating us to free meals when they find out we're from Libbey. It was a nice feeling and nothing I had experienced before.

Some of my co-workers were homesick, but with each day I was beginning to think of Toledo as my permanent new home. Now if only I could entice my son, Robert, to move here when he finished college that would make it perfect. Boy, how quickly he'd come if he knew I was rooming with a dragon!

"Spark, someday I hope to introduce you to my son. Oh, you would just love him. My wife Louise and I were only were only blessed with one child, although I had secretly always wished for a home full of children, it apparently wasn't in the cards for us. Oh don't get me wrong, Robert was our pride and joy and we couldn't be happier. He was just in his freshman year of college when we got the news of Louise's illness. There was nothing the doctors could do and she passed away shortly thereafter."

That memory stopped me for a moment. I sat and took a breath remembering what a difficult time that was for me. I was suddenly alone in the house we had shared for so long. With Robert away at school, the house had such an empty, hollow feeling. I allowed a tear to well up in my eye, and quickly brushed it away. I wasn't going to dwell on the sadness. Just think happy thoughts I told myself.

Robert, the wonderful son that he was, offered to come back home and go to a local college, but I wouldn't hear of it, no matter how much I missed him. It was important to me that Robert follow his own path, no matter where he ended up. And who knows, with Toledo's growth potential, he could find opportunities here after graduation in a couple years. I quickly put that secret wish out of my mind. I couldn't allow myself to dwell on it now. Thanks to Spark I had a new challenge to focus on which needs all my attention.

I went back to my desk and stared at the draft of my plan. I scribbled out some sections and began again. By lunchtime I had a better outline with several objectives and the start of a plan of attack to get where I was sure Edward wanted to go with this project.

It was fun to create this plan without any blueprints, journals, or "how to" books to look over. I was pretty sure even if I took the time to try and research this, even if I traveled throughout Europe, there would be nothing to find. I liked the opportunity to be creative. I was honored that Edward had entrusted me with his most treasured find. This project was exhilarating and beyond my wildest imagination.

It just goes to show, you just never know when life is going to throw you a curve ball. After enduring my wife's death, I thought most of my happy days were behind me, and now look at me. I wasn't always adventurous, but this year I took a big risk, moved 700 miles from the only town I ever knew, got settled into a new home, and then a dragon drops into my life! My work and home life would never be dull again. Life sure could be wondrous and mysterious when you least expected it!

I lost myself in my work as I daydreamed ways to capture this potential new energy source and also keep its identity hidden from the others. I knew I would need to be extra careful about my comings and goings in the plant to avoid the detection of Spark. At this point, Spark's small stature would make him fairly easy to conceal. But how long would that last? How fast does a dragon take to grow to an adult size and what size would that be? Although, maybe we wouldn't have to worry about that if I couldn't figure out how to employ his gifts. "I'm not going to let that happen Spark. We're going to be together a good long time, don't worry yourself about that."

I was suddenly famished. I figured Spark was too. I thought it would be a nice change to have a companion to dine with in my office. However, watching Spark eat his meal of crickets and worms rapidly diminished my own appetite.

By the time Edward showed up at 3:30 p.m. I had a good outline of a plan for Project Ignite to share. Edward pulled Spark out of the cage to let him move around the room as he half listened to my plans. Spark's tiny wings gave us confidence that he wasn't ready to take flight anytime soon. They didn't look strong enough to hold him. I wondered without his mom to guide him, would he know how to use his wings? I'm sure some things like that are part of the instincts all creatures seem to be born with, but time will tell.

Edward trusted me with this project and was very agreeable to the plans I drafted. He was so thrilled with his little acquisition, but he didn't need to be mired down in all the nitty gritty details. "Let me know what you need for any of these experiments and I'll see that you get it. Thank you again for agreeing to be his, eh, guardian at this time. You know there is no way I could take this to my hotel room where the maid or Florence could discover it. Florence likes pets, but I don't know how she would feel about this, and I'm not ready to find out."

Chapter 26

I was not surprised how quickly I became attached to Spark. The little guy was hard to resist. He was getting more comfortable with me and his new surroundings each day. I settled into the routine of hanging out with him in the evenings in my home.

After a few days, I started letting Spark out of his cage more and more. I worked quietly in at my kitchen table each night, and Spark would often lay by my feet, after taking some time to explore the room. It was like having a pet dog – well, almost. I didn't normally get many visitors to my home when I lived in Cambridge, and here in Toledo it was even less. This lack of visitors suited me just fine, especially given my new roommate.

I found Toledo to have an excellent library with an extensive collection of medieval books. After my third visit to check out books that were all about dragons the librarian took notice. "My, you seem to have quite an appetite for dragons, have you always been interested in the topic?" the librarian inquired.

I was more than a little embarrassed of her question. Of course, the last time I probably checked out such books was in grade school. I was around nine or ten when I first learned about dragons and searched out every book I could find. Back at that time though, the topic was pure fictional, fantasy reading for me. I could have day dreamed about seeing a real dragon but never visualized I would grow up and actually befriend one!

To throw off any suspicions the librarian may have, although I wasn't sure her interest to be anything more than curiosity, I brushed off her comment. I didn't really think that she could ever guess I was doing research on a real-life subject. Then I nervously blurted out, "Really, are you sure? Hmm, that's strange, I didn't even realize my prior selections were so similar."

From now on, I told myself, I would mix in other "monsters" into the pile of books I was borrowing. *(I was so preoccupied with the feeling of panic at the thought of my secret being exposed that I didn't realize until I later relayed the incident to Edward that there was a simple explanation for her inquiry. Edward said the librarian surely had found me attractive, noticed I didn't have on a wedding band, and that she was trying to strike up a friendly conversation to get to know me. I quickly dismissed that explanation, but it made me smile a little inside.)*

The exchange with the librarian just left me determined to be more careful. I realized that seemingly innocent, normal, everyday actions, like checking out a book from the library, could be interpreted by others in all kinds of ways. I thought of the strange looks I felt I was getting lately from a few nosy neighbors. I don't know if I was paranoid but I vowed that I would have to be more careful around everyone.

After all that extra stress from the library trip I didn't even find many of the books I checked out very useful. The authors had several things wrong about dragons, at least from my admittedly limited, but now experienced, point of view. Frankly, I could tell the authors had probably never met a dragon, and were relying on information that they had heard or read about over the years, or what others had made up and passed along. I continued to read every book, and jotted down notes on anything I thought could be true, so I could be more prepared for our project.

It's been a few months since Spark came to Toledo now. Spark was developing a playful and feisty attitude. He learned commands very well. He knew the basics like sit, lay down and no and stop. He seemed eager to please and would look for items to fetch without any prompting. This would usually result in me getting things brought to me that I didn't need. That was ok. However, I also learned to be more careful to move some critical items out of Spark's reach. Unfortunately his fire breathing trait was uncontrolled and he managed to singe some items as he went to drop them. Luckily, no serious mishaps had occurred so far.

"How do I teach you to breathe fire on command?" I asked Spark who responded by looking at me with a curiously, confused look on his face as he scampered away. I pulled out my notebook with my ideas and theories and decided it was time to begin experimenting with different techniques to get Spark to breathe fire on command.

We mainly used natural gas at the factory now which wasn't perfect. The problem with using natural gas was that temperature control was more or less a judgement call. We found out quickly that natural gas required a lot of trial and error. If the gas was controlled and vented correctly, the carbon would combine with the lead and cause a cloudy look to the glass. If I could control Spark's energy he could solve more than just the financial problem for us.

"Let's show Edward when he returns from his trip, how much you've learned," I said to Spark. I knew he couldn't talk back, but I felt in time he would understand some of my words.

Since our dragon friend was starting to practice his fire breathing skill now, it was an even more breathtaking time. I was hopeful but my early experiments were proving to be mostly hits and misses. I was patient though and kept at it. I was sure results would come with time and practice

Spark was growing so quickly during this time too. At the rate he was going he could be a couple hundred pounds in a few more months. When I wasn't busy training Spark, I was spending time making preparations for bigger accommodations. Soon it wouldn't be practical to bring Spark to and from my house. I was going to have to keep him at the factory full time. I had grown very fond of Spark and I was not looking forward to that day.

The factory was a four story building situated on four acres of land. The first floor was home to all the offices and the mold shop. The offices were occupied by the owner, finance, sales, purchasing and other clerical functions. The second floor contained the forming operations, packaging and shipping area. The third floor was used by the carton department. Most of that space was for materials and one area was used by those making the boxes. Boxes of every size variation were cut and built right on site. All boxes were now made of cardboard, with the company name and description of the product printed on them.

Each glass style had a name, for identification purposes, and each product could be packed in a different size box depending on the customer's preferences. The most popular sizes held one or three dozen glasses. If the glasses were going to be sold at a department store, like Sears or Macy's, they would be further packed in a smaller, fancier box, with drawings of what the glass looked like or how it could be used.

We convinced some stores to display our glass out of the box and directly on a shelf. The brilliant cut glass products would shimmer and sparkle under the light and attract more attention than if they were packed away in a box. If a customer could see the glass, they would be more likely to appreciate it and purchase it, Edward always said.

The basement of the factory contained the furnaces and water pipes, gas tanks, and storage space for extra materials. Most people didn't know it, but the building was constructed with a sub-basement too. It was dark and secluded and not a place most people would want or need to go.

Actually as I remembered this space I realized this would be the perfect home for Spark. If Edward had this in mind he had not yet verbalized it to me. While the description of this location may sound dark and slightly depressing to you, it was utterly perfect for a dragon. It reminded me of a cave, since it was far underground, a little cool and didn't have any natural light beaming through.

The fact was, the dragons lived in caves for safety and shelter for many centuries. I decided to make my way down there and walk around. I immediately found the solitude down there to be very relaxing. There is much less risk of having someone discovering Spark down here than in my current office.

"This just might work. I could get so much more work done without so many interruptions if I worked down here, too," I said out loud with no fear that anyone could hear me. The new challenge I would have address either way is keeping Spark safe when I wasn't around. I was going to have to have a serious talk tonight with Edward about the new arrangements.

Edward stopped by my home that evening just as he promised. I was like a proud father, showing off all the new commands I taught Spark. Spark didn't disappoint me and aced every command. "I started by offering him a treat after each correct response. I took a little work, but he's picked up a few of the basics rather well, don't you think?"

"He sure has. You're doing a great job with him Red," Edward said and then turned his attention away from Spark as he grabbed a cookie and sat down on the couch. "Now, what's on your mind Red. You seemed so distracted at work today."

I felt a little guilty laying this out now, knowing how much Edward had going on back at the factory. As I filled Edward in on my daily struggles with sneaking Spark in and out of the plant, and feeling a little trapped at home afraid to leave him alone for long, Edward stopped me and put me at ease.

"Red, you're right. This hasn't been fair to you. I brought home this great creature and dropped him into your life. I'm sorry,

I've been so pre-occupied trying to get everything running I didn't stop to consider,"

"No, Edward, it's quite alright. I don't mind, really, I don't. Spark is the most amazing gift. I'm just concerned about him being discovered. However, I think I have a solution and I wanted to run it by you."

Edward looked relieved as I unveiled my proposal and agreed it was a perfect solution.

Chapter 27

One night Edward showed up at my door unexpectedly around midnight. I don't know if he figured I would be up but he said he wouldn't have knocked if he had not seen my lights on. A problem at the factory had him out late this night. Although it wasn't unusual to find him at the factory at all hours of the night several times a month.

Whenever Edward had trouble sleeping he'd make the rounds at the factory. The factory was a 24 hour, seven day a week operation. The men that worked the late night shifts always appreciated it when the Boss Man showed up to say hello and chat with them, even if it was only for a few minutes. They knew how important and busy he was, but he always made the effort to get to know everyone by name and treat them in a friendly manner. Edward never forgot where he started when he first came to work for his father. He worked in many of the different positions over the years learning every part of the business alongside these men. The fellas had tremendous respect for Edward and the feeling was mutual.

Edward sat down on the couch and filled me in on the new problem at the factory. One of the machines had broken down and an important order was in danger of not shipping out the next morning. Edward had worked through some alternatives with the client as the engineers worked diligently to repair the machine. This was a very important client, as they all were, and

Edward always took the time to talk with the client directly instead of just relying on the Sales Manager to handle it.

Edward started to relax and perk up after petting Spark. It was hard to stay in a foul mood with Spark around. He was as playful and frisky as a puppy at this stage. Edward picked up the pilsner and took a few sips of his drink.

"You have really impressed me with how well you've trained Spark," he laughed and said, shaking his head, "I'll never forget the look on your face when I opened that box and showed you Spark! I thought you were going to faint! Your face turned whiter than I've ever seen."

I laughed in spite of myself remembering that night too. "This was the last thing I would have guessed was in that box. And to think I foolishly brought it home and obediently waited for you to arrive. I didn't even think of peeking, but I'm glad I didn't shake it trying to figure out what was inside!"

"Edward, I know this may not be any of my business, but I'm really quite curious about how you got Spark. If you're not ready to tell me that's okay. I figure you haven't told me everything because it your way of protecting me and trying not to put me in any further danger."

"Well, the best purchase I ever made came about by pure luck. I really just went to Europe on a business trip. I was hoping to secure some new orders of our Corinthian line. I was really worried about all the extra costs we incurred moving to Toledo and was determined to turn our finances around. You know the board was behind me on the decision to move, but they were all anxious to see a return on the investment," Edward stated.

"I'm glad I don't have those big-wigs to worry about, but you know I'd do anything to help you make this business successful," I said truthfully.

"Of course I didn't realize Florence and her parents were there as well. It was pure luck, or fate, that I ran into Florence on the street outside her hotel with her parents on my second day. I couldn't resist asking Florence out since I wanted to spend some time showing her all my favorite places in the city, which of course would entail some antique shops," Edward revealed and then took a big swig of beer.

He smiled as he began speaking again, "We were on the same ship back to town and two days before we were due to return home we happened upon a shop I had never seen before. It had a beautiful oil painting, The Architect's Dream by Thomas Cole, in the window. The painting caught Florence's attention so she went right in to look at it up close. You know Florence has quite an art collection herself and she is always looking for new pieces.

"'I *think my father would really like this painting. It has such appeal. It really draws you in. The rich tapestry framing it makes you feel like you are looking out a real window and into this gorgeous Greek city. Just look at the way he has the light reflecting on the river and the light shining through the windows of the church, just amazing,'* Florence said to me almost in a trance as she stared into the painting."

As Florence was busy near the window, Edward said he started walking towards the back of the shop. A strange noise caught his attention, and the shopkeeper looked up and scurried to the back behind a curtain. I could just imagine the sound he was referring to as I recalled Spark made a very strange squealing sound when he first arrived.

"A few moments later he poked his head out and hissed at me," Edward stopped to clear his throat and then continued, imitating the shopkeeper, saying "Pssst, pssst….are you in the market for a work of magic?"

"What the devil do you have in there? I asked the strange shopkeeper."

Edward's voice was starting to get more animated and loud as he recalled this peculiar encounter. "The shopkeeper motioned for me to come closer and because the way he was acting was quite intriguing and amusing to me I followed him behind the curtain. I don't even think Florence had noticed as she was still busy at the front of the store and there were no other customers in the store."

"And you didn't find it odd that he wanted you to go back behind a curtain? I don't know that I would have done that," I admitted.

"No, because when I got closer to the shopkeeper for the first time I recognized him. Don't I know you? I started to ask, and he nodded and smiled, almost a little embarrassedly and said, something like, '*I know who you are Mr. Libbey. And I know what I have is exactly what you can't live without. When I came upon this treasure you were the first person I thought of that may appreciate it. In fact, it is destiny that you have appeared here at my shop at this time. I was trying to figure out how to reach you. I sent you a letter recently but it was returned to me.'*"

"You're putting me on Ed! This is too strange, even for you!" I laughed and started feeling foolish for getting sucked into Edward's story.

"No really. I couldn't believe it either but then he started rifling through a drawer in his desk, mumbling something like, *I know I have it here somewhere, and I prove to you.*"

"I started getting a little less skeptical and told him I did recently move. Then I asked him why on Earth he would go to all this trouble to seek me out instead of just selling the item to someone else?"

My thoughts exactly. I sat back intrigued by the story, but trying to repress my cynicism.

"He said, '*Oh Mr. Libbey, this is not something that I would entrust to just anyone, no, only someone with your integrity and ingenuity would be worthy of this special object d'art. You may recall I'm very particular about who I allow to buy any of my artefacts. I always take great care to ensure they reach a proper home and are cared for and respected just as I would do myself. Most of my objects have great historical significance, but not everyone can be trusted to care for things properly, to protect and preserve them,*' the shopkeeper who I recalled as Mr. Lee said with the most serious look on his face."

Edward went on to tell me that the shopkeeper seemed to quiz him for about a half an hour. Edward was so swept up in the strange conversation in the back of the room that he almost forgot Florence was in the shop. When he realized the time, he excused himself and went to check on Florence. He spotted her across the room and told her he was looking over some items in the back room. She told him to take his time because she found many pieces of artwork to admire, although she warned him the longer he took, the more she would find to buy.

"I went back to the rear of the shop and told Mr. Lee I answered enough of his questions, and said I couldn't wait any longer and he must show me his artefact."

Edward sat quietly in a daze, making me wait it seemed, just like he was made to wait by Mr. Lee.

Finally he continued, "Mr. Lee looked me intently in the eye and whispered to me what I was about to see was an ancient artefact, of sorts. It was not something he wanted to part with but he was afraid he would not be able to keep it much longer, without it being discovered. He worried that keeping the artefact could put it at great risk of being damaged beyond repair, which he cried would be devastating and a great tragedy."

Edward couldn't comprehend what in the world was about to happen, but he revealed that it did feel like his life was about to change in a very profound way, one that you could never expect or plan for. The energy of the room seemed to take on an auspicious feeling. What he saw next was breathtaking beyond words.

The most exquisite little creature he could ever imagine, Spark, was resting in Mr. Lee's hand. This wonderfully, perfect little dragon, laying so quiet and still. It was so tranquil that at first Edward thought it was a joke and that it was a small statue, but even though it should be impossible to be staring a real live dragon, he knew without a doubt, he was doing just that.

Edward said he just couldn't stop staring at the creature in Mr. Lee's hand. Everything in his mind was saying, this has to be some kind of joke, dragons aren't real. His mind was racing through all the typical questions, how, why, where, etc. but he didn't have to say anything. Mr. Lee just kept talking and answered all the questions he assumed Mr. Libbey had on his mind. Most importantly, he implored to Mr. Libbey that the dragon was in danger and that he only trusted him to take him and shield him from the world. He wanted the dragon taken, far, far away for its safety.

Mr. Lee was the one that put the idea in Edward's head that the dragon would pull his own weight and could be a valuable asset to his company by supplying him with much needed fire. Mr. Lee explained that this was a fire-breathing dragon and would be a loyal companion if Edward cared for him properly. He told Edward about some former acquaintances who were lurking around the neighborhood, asking questions and were making him suspicious that they knew about the dragon.

The shopkeeper may have been a little paranoid but he told Edward he was more concerned with each passing day. He worried that these individuals would stop at nothing to take the dragon if they were able to discern the truth of its existence and location. Mr. Lee implored to Mr. Libbey's good heart and said he had the opportunity, and duty, to preserve the dragon for future generations.

I don't imagine it took much to convince Edward to purchase that charming creature. Who wouldn't want to own a dragon? How much he paid for it, he never did tell, nor did I dare ask. Asking someone what they paid for anything in those days was considered inappropriate and horribly rude. Although I often wondered what value could be put on a priceless, mythical creature?

The shopkeeper somehow knew the dragon would be safe with Mr. Libbey. Mr. Lee must have thought his options through some time ago and that's why he had written to Mr. Libbey. His letter told Mr. Libbey to contact him about a rare and wonderful "antique". But surely, Mr. Lee must have realized that this discovery may be hard to grasp when it was just sprung upon Edward unexpectedly like this.

"Mr. Lee walked back to his desk and pulled a small leather bound book out of his bottom desk drawer and handed it to me. He said the book contained information about the dragon, its origin, family history, and what the creatures are like. He told me to take the book home and read it over carefully. If I was willing to purchase the dragon, I should return to the shop at 7:30 a.m. the next morning." Edward relayed as my eyes wandered over to the book.

He didn't need to stress to Edward that the book should be guarded with his life and not shown to anyone. While Mr. Lee was nervous about letting the book out of his sight, he thought it was only fair to give Mr. Libbey the opportunity to know exactly what he was getting into if he decided to make this acquisition.

Edward confessed he was reluctant to leave the back office, as he was sure it would leave him feeling like he woke from a dream and all of this was somehow just in his wild imagination. He laughed inwardly as he pinched himself just to make doubly sure he really was awake! It was hard to compose himself. He took a moment to analyze the situation and prepared himself to return to the store front as if the most wonderful thing in the world had not just revealed itself to him.

Edward was used to keeping many secrets and confidential information in his business life and he would just file this away as one of those affairs. In his mind he had already resolved to return at 7:00 a.m. sharp for his date with destiny. (He was always early for appointments.)

"The words Mr. Lee had spoken about the dragon being an asset to my company were already dancing around in my head and I knew this was going to be a fantastic new adventure! Red, my mind was racing with all kinds of ideas and ways to use this dragon to our advantage."

"How did you ever manage to keep this from Florence?" I asked.

"I almost skipped out to Florence, I was in such a jovial mood, but I kept it inside and maintained a poker face outwardly."

I know how dignified and regal Edward always appeared, especially in public, but this must have been a truly exceptional performance to pretend you didn't just meet the most incredible thing and not be able to talk about it.

'Florence had settled upon purchasing the painting *The Architect's Dream*, for her father, so this made the perfect excuse for my return. I told the shopkeeper to get it packaged up and I would return tomorrow to pick it up. I winked at him, without Florence noticing, and he nodded back shrewdly."

"Well that was fortunate for you."

"I'm sure Florence was so giddy with excitement over the thought of her newly found treasure she didn't inquire much about yours, huh?"

"Florence wanted to go back to the room for a spell before we went out for dinner. I was glad to take a break from her so that I could get to my hotel room and begin reading the journal. The journal looked pretty well worn but cherished. I wondered if I was the first one to read it besides the author. It was possible since Mr. Lee's insistence that I was his first choice as a buyer did have an air of truth to it."

Edward continued, "So after I picked up the purchases in the morning, I had to secure their safe and timely arrival to the ship. I arranged for a courier to deliver the painting, but the second package was not going to leave my sight. I would make room for it in my carrying case. Mr. Lee assured me the box he was putting it in was nearly sound proof, and if he wasn't concerned, I wouldn't be either."

I could see that Edward was amazed that he had made such an impression on Mr. Lee all those years ago and that he was putting all his faith in Edward to take on his most valued treasure. Although I'm sure he did get quite a fortune out of Edward in return.

Were there not other worthy businesses in all of Europe? Did he just think it was safer out of this continent or did he truly think Edward would be able to harness this energy and make something out it? These were questions that turned quietly in my head.

There is a difference between treasure hunters and collectors and not everyone is interested in being both. A hunter is one who searches for something that he knows others want and once acquired he tries to find a buyer to get the most profit out it. Mr. Lee understands that collectors are a special breed and they will put almost anything above preserving their treasure. A collector understands the significance and importance of protecting special things for future generations to be able to appreciate. They do it not only for their own enjoyment, but they also feel a sense of purpose to safeguard a part of history.

Edward asked me how much I had read of the journal so far. I pulled out the journal and set it on the table in front of him. I had to admit that the information it contained was not quite what I was expecting but spectacularly so much more. It began with a history about dragons and how they were feared and hunted to near extinction. The few people that understood and cared about the mythical beasts formed a secretive group whose mission was to find and protect these creatures. They were the preservationists and they were a small but mighty and determined group.

The preservationists were led by one the most powerful man in the land, named Fallon. Although he was very prominent and powerful, his power to protect the dragons was in danger of failure. He was conspired against by an unworthy opponent who rallied several townsfolk against him. Fortunately, he did have some very loyal friends who joined together to work in secret to protect the few dragons they could save. If it was ever found out what they were doing, it would be the end of them and the dragons. They were bound together in their resolve to preserve this mighty beast for the planet.

The prominent Fallon owned a vast amount of land in the countryside. It was on this land where he would be able to hide and contain the dragons. His land had a small thicket of untamed forest land. Not many had traveled into the forest as the property had been held in his family's hands for generations. Inside this forest was a large cave. It was hidden deep in the forest and partially covered by a blanket of thick trees. The cave descended down several hundred feet. Actually, it could be much deeper but that was as far as his family had hiked down it. The location would be the perfect place to hide the dragons and anything else that should be protected from danger.

The journal also contained an old map. Sadly, it was a pretty crude rendering and was missing key landmarks. It was also tattered and faded. Nothing on it looked even slightly familiar to Edward. The location on the map did hold some interest to Edward, but the dragon that came from it was the real prize, which he now owned.

"Oh, Red, you know my imagination was going wild as I absorbed every word I read in the journal that day. Do you think any of these people could still be alive? How could this dragon have been taken from them along with the journal?"

"So you kept it all secret from Florence and she never had a clue?" I asked.

"I must admit, looking back now, I must have acted a little peculiar that night. I was scheduled to take Florence to a wonderful restaurant that I frequented whenever I was in town. My mind wasn't fully on my date, as it should have been, but back on what I saw in that strange back room earlier that day. It was ironic, that the restaurant we went to was situated in what was once a small castle."

Edward described that he felt like he was being transported back in time as they walked up the winding path on a small hill to the building. With every step he took over the small bridge that led to the front door he felt an eerie presence of a dragon looking down on them from one of the tower windows, but it was only the foreboding gargoyle statues.

"The place was well kept up for its age. Huge urns full of flowers adorned each side of the double-sided entrance door. Florence appreciated flowers and was captivated with the arrangements. The doorman opened the door just as we arrived near it and held it open for us as we stepped inside. The owner whom I had gotten to know over the years was waiting to greet us. The room was buzzing with laughter and joy and was filled with guests."

"This sounds like a place my Louise would have adored!" I said thinking of the last time I treated her out to a fancy meal in Boston.

"Oh yes, she would have loved it. The table setting was remarkable, of course the most wonderful thing to my eyes were the glassware pieces, made at our factory no less. The table was glittering with the candlelight setting off the brilliant cut glass of the stemware, water glass and small vase on the table. I felt a sense of pride when I looked around the room and saw people celebrating and enjoying themselves and seeing that our products were right there with them. I think Florence was a little impressed."

"I think I recall Florence telling me she boasted to a few patrons that the glass in their hand was made at your factory!"

"She sure did! Florence was proud that a company from her home town had products on full display in the castle."

One of the perks of making glassware for the table is that Edward got to spend a lot of time visiting restaurants around the world. However, all this constant fine dining would eventually wreak havoc on his waistline I warned him. Edward brushed off that thought as something that was well off in the future. He would worry about that if and when the time came. Besides with the way Florence felt about him, a few extra pounds wouldn't diminish that, would it? Of course not, I knew.

"I tried to enjoy the dinner and the company. But I must confess, I couldn't wait to get back to my hotel room. I walked back as briskly as I could without arousing Florence's suspicions. I didn't stop to think that she may have thought I was in a rush to get away from her. Normally on a stroll like this after dinner I would be gushing about all the architecture of the historic buildings we passed. Usually I would stop to admire a particular detail about a building up close and take to my sketch book to jot down a few features that I wanted to remember."

I knew that since Edward was a small boy he always carried a small book with him. In this book he would scribble down notes, names of people he met, something personal they had told him, or scratch out a rough drawing of something special that caught his eye. He thought it was important to remember what people took the time to tell him about their personal life. He would look over his notes nearly every evening before he went to bed. He told me this would help him recall the day and commit all the most important details to memory. And if someday his memory failed him, he need only look back to his notes. I thought it was clever, but I never picked up the same habit.

"Well, this certainly was not a typical night for you."

"No truer words were ever spoken, Red," Edward said as he poured himself a little more to drink. "As we strolled along I found my mind wandering to the day's events. Well not actually all the events, just that one unbelievable one in particular. My thoughts kept going back to replay that moment Mr. Lee turned around and showed me that glorious creature. The thoughts of how I was going back home with such an amazing treasure filled my head to the point I thought it would burst. There was just an enormous amount of things to think about since that fateful stop in Mr. Lee's shop. Florence must have been wrapped up in her own thoughts about her journey and travels home because if she noticed anything amiss with my demeanor she didn't mention it."

Edward returned Florence to her room and reluctantly turned down Maurice's invitation to join them for a nightcap. He made up an excuse about needing to pack and got away. He had a journal he had to get back to that would keep him up all night.

Edward was a bit of a dreamer, but he also had the tenacity to follow his dreams and make them come true. Nothing was more invigorating to him than solving a problem that vexed him, except maybe dreaming up something new. While Edward was not a master craftsman and could not easily make the glass pieces that his most skilled workers could do so effortlessly, he did have an eye for art. He would come up with designs for glass pieces, sketch them out in his notebook, and then stand in awe as his craftsman created his vision before his eyes.

"I locked the door behind me and raced to the cabinet where I had stashed the journal that Mr. Lee had given me. As I read, and re-read, all the notes about the dragon I was more content about my plan. It was as clear as glass to me. I knew I was given a great opportunity that would help my business and also help my new pet. A pet, which was another reason not to reveal this to Florence just yet. She had a heart of gold, but never fancied herself a pet person. She would fuss over someone's cat or dog briefly when she visited someone who owned a pet, but it never put a thought in her head to bring one home for herself. She was truly not ready for a pet dragon - who was really?"

"You need to continue keeping this secret from her. I realize you don't want to keep a secret from the woman you love, but it is simply too dangerous at this point. We need to learn all we can first and guarantee she would be safe before you can even consider an introduction between those two," I said sternly to Edward what he already knew in his heart.

"I don't think I slept a wink that night, so around 6:00 a.m. I quietly left the hotel. Not many people were up moving about at this hour, as most people were there on holiday and tended to sleep in until mid-morning. I was glad I didn't get stopped to make idle chit chat with anyone. Normally I would love to talk with strangers about this or that, but today I was only focused on my acquisition. I walked hurriedly to the shop that was holding my treasure.

"Mr. Lee was already there re-arranging his window display since one of his large paintings was just packed up for Ms. Scott. Mr. Lee opened the door and said something like, *'I had a feeling you would be here early. Your package is waiting for you in the back, please follow me and I will explain what you need to do to get this home safely without discovery.'"*

"I bet he wasn't surprised that you had read through the journal. I can just see you there, peppering him with additional questions."

"So true. Mr. Lee told me everything he could. I described my intentions, my assurances of the dragon's safety, and made Mr. Lee feel that he had made the right choice for the dragon's future. While Mr. Lee would be enormously sad to see him go, he knew it was the best thing for him, for his survival."

"How did you remain calm, carrying that treasure back to your hotel? I would have been a nervous wreck," I admitted.

"As I walked down the road I felt people looking at me more intently but I didn't know if I was just being paranoid. I felt a tall, gangly man behind me who was beginning to follow me a little too closely. I tightened my grip on the case. The nearly soundproof, but breathable box, was meant to keep the dragon out of sight. At least that was my hope. Wow, I thought to myself, I've never been a paranoid person but I think Mr. Lee's concerns were getting to me. What if someone had been watching Mr. Lee's store and figured out what I was doing there? Would they really kill me over a dragon? The thought made me shudder, of course they would. If the threat to Mr. Lee was real why wouldn't that now extend to me?"

We sat quietly for a time. Both lost in thought about what kind of dangers could have followed him over the ocean and back to Toledo.

"What have I gotten myself into? And you into, now?" Edward asked.

"Don't you worry about me. I can take care of myself," I said stiffening up, "so what did you do next?"

"Well, I decided to break up my walk and I ducked into the first place I saw open. I stood just behind the door and watched the stranger that had been following behind me. The man didn't seem to particularly notice or look concerned that I wasn't in front of him any longer. He kept his head forward and continued along the street, without making a move to follow me into the shop. I was now feeling a little foolish for being so paranoid, but I got a good look at the man's face, just in case."

As Edward sat there, quietly swirling his drink, the enormity of our new life was starting to sink in. We would both have to be much more watchful of who was around us and what we said. There was no point in taking unnecessary chances. Whether Mr. Lee was truly in danger Edward really didn't know, but this was the first time we were really starting to feel what that could be like.

"So, once I caught my breath, I returned to the street. I quickly scanned each person on each side of the street. I took a little longer to return to the hotel as I zig-zagged around the streets. I didn't want to follow the same path I took to get to the shop. Who knew if I was being watched when I left the hotel. At that time I really wasn't paying any attention, I was just on a direct path to the shop. Someone could have overheard me talking with Mr. Lee yesterday and followed us back to the hotel. I wouldn't have any idea, as I had no reason to feel threatened."

Sure Mr. Lee told Edward he was in danger, but apparently he didn't really take him seriously. Edward thought he was just playing up the danger angle a little to get his attention and help facilitate the sale. Edward guessed that if he had stopped to really contemplate what Mr. Lee was saying, he didn't know now if he would have gotten involved and taken the item. Well, what is done is done, there is no turning back now Edward surmised. He promised to be extra careful and made me swear it as well.

"When I was safely aboard the ship, I had plenty of time to think through who I was going to have help me with this plan. But you know I really only had one person in mind, you, Redmond

Wynston." I smiled and he continued, "Red, I just knew you had the skills and knowledge that could figure out how to implement this plan. And most of all you have always been a true friend and confidante."

"I bet once the ship set sail for America you must have felt a bit relieved. Hopefully leaving those people Mr. Lee warned you about behind," I said sighing a bit as I straightened up in my chair.

"The long trip left me thinking more and more about the people Mr. Lee said were trying to find out about the dragon. I knew that just leaving the country would not be enough. I would need to be extra careful to keep this secret under wraps for as long as it is in my possession."

At this point, I saw no chance of him selling it ever. Once Edward made a purchase it was with the intent to hold onto it for life. He was not like some people who just wanted to make a quick return on their acquisitions. He was an art lover and thus far all the antiquities he had purchased over the years were proudly on display in his home.

Edward always enjoyed entertaining friends and family and at some point in those evenings he was easily cajoled into telling one of his fascinating stories about one of his acquisitions. Even if the guests heard the story before, they still encouraged him and got wrapped up in the story as if hearing it for the first time. He was a natural storyteller and could drag a story on for hours. He did so enjoy an audience.

Many days sailing the ocean gave Edward time to prepare himself for the new life at home. While he had the dragon with him now, it was kept very well hidden, and he didn't dare take it out of the cage for long. When he returned home, and got the dragon settled with me, he promised the dragon that he would have a good life.

"I believe that Mr. Lee would not have been able to keep him for long and feared that he would have been killed at an early age. That was likely the fate of any of his kind. After all, nobody has reported seeing a dragon that I recall. If there happened to be any others they were likely hunted and killed in infancy. Sadly, there aren't a lot of places to hide a dragon are there?"

"Well, your factory is large enough to keep it hidden from the world for a century or more!" I chuckled. "You know, your story reminds me of the one you told at the Libbey's that night, remember? You told them of a dragon – was that a coincidence or a premonition?" I muttered as I looked intently from Edward to Spark.

Our dragon was a subdued shade of copper. Edward informed me that from his readings of mythology that dragon's personalities were linked to their color. While feeding and talking with the dragon Edward told me that he laughed out loud as he remembered what copper dragons were known for. They were always the fun loving pranksters and jokesters of their group.

"Well, we'll have to keep a listen for that won't we?" I jested to the dragon. I looked at the dragon intently, half expecting a response, then laughing in spite of myself, as the dragon just glanced up and then returned to eating his meal.

As I watched the dragon eat I studied his features. The creature was scaly like a lizard, but the skin was not too rough. I wondered if it would harden or change as he grew. I also noticed the dragon had five toes.

"What is the significance of five toes?" I asked.

Edward had taken a Mythology class back in college and read many books on the subject just for fun. Just as skin color had meaning he knew the number of toes also meant something. He would have to look that up when he returned home.

"You know Red, this little guy also gave me a great idea for a glass design. Look at these sketches I doodled while on that ship home."

I took the notebook and studied the drawings he had made. A tumbler shape took on a look like fire flames coming up the sidewalls. I knew instantly this would be a great addition to the product lines if the glass artists could craft it. I looked over to the dragon and imagined seeing flames coming from his mouth. When that day comes, things would be smoking at the factory, I laughed to myself.

The copper coloring of the dragon's scales had given Edward another brilliant idea. What if they could make a glass with that coloring? Shades of light copper to red moving from the top to the bottom of the glass would be exquisite. The glass would dance like fire as it sparkled in the light. "The glass will look like embers. Embers, embers, Amber, Amberina. That's it, I will call the new glassware line Amberina. Only we will know that my inspiration came you little friend," Edward say joyfully as he petted the dragon.

So within less than a day Edward's new friend had given him ideas for new products. Will he also be able to help with fueling the furnace? Edward was sure we, or rather I, would find a way. I wondered if anyone else had ever thought to try and tame a dragon the way we were contemplating. Edward felt he was probably the first and that excited him enormously. He liked creating and doing things few people could or would do.

The only thing that saddened us about this venture was that we would have to keep it secret. That would be a challenge for Edward, who so enjoyed sharing his views, thoughts and products with the world. However, the implications of this getting out was not an option. Edward knew this could not be shared and he would have to be content keeping it top secret. I just hoped that the dangerous men would remain at bay.

Chapter 28

The 1880's were a booming time in America. The country was experiencing an industrial revolution. Mass transportation allowed more travel and cities were flush with expansion. It was the time in which women were just beginning to step outside the home to work. Any inventions that could speed up chores would be welcome by housewives. Edward was unwavering in his belief that most women would still find a way to use glassware products daily and maintain that lovely table setting. All he had to do was convince them that a table wasn't complete without Libbey.

As a middle class was growing in America, their taste for more consumer goods also grew. The market had an appetite for more products and our company was ready to fulfill their hunger. Table settings included many "must have" items that could be made by our skilled craftsmen including napkin holders, creamers, sugar bowls, plates, water and wine glasses and even knife rests and the ever popular dinner bell. Formal table settings were common and expected for all classes of families.

How did people hear about products for sale? Big department stores were just coming into prominence during this time. Some stores you may have heard of that sold our products were Sears & Roebuck, Montgomery Wards, among others. This was also the time when magazines were becoming popular as well.

So many products were being created and sold in the late 1800's that magazines like Ladies Home Journal and Good Housekeeping were flush with advertisements of our products and others. Our ads described the high quality of the glass. The exquisite craftsmanship was evident and made the items highly prized possessions for purchasers or for gift giving.

Our name was getting out in all these new modes of communications as soon as they were implemented. It seemed like our name and products were everywhere. The quality of our craftsmanship was second to none. Little did anyone know that all the extra special sparkle these products embodied was thanks to our secret.

1889 was going by fast and our company's move to Toledo would mark its first year anniversary in a couple months. Edward had worked so hard the last year he almost didn't realize the anniversary approaching until Florence broached the subject. "What are you planning to do for your first anniversary?" Florence asked Edward innocently. "Do you have something big and festive planned?"

"Oh, I've been so busy I really hadn't given it much thought," Edward replied as he now wondered why this momentous occasion had slipped his mind. "The company still isn't doing so well so I'm not sure a big celebration is really in order," Edward further said as he thought of all the debt he still owed on the business.

"But think of how hard all your employees have been working, how much they have sacrificed during this past year. Surely you want to take the time to thank them properly?" Florence said with a bit of concern in her voice. She knew many of the families by now and had become friends with many of them. Several were still having trouble adjusting to their new lives. A little time to stop and celebrate would show how they are all appreciated she told Edward.

Edward didn't need to tell her about their struggles, she knew how hard it was for them. He'd been doing everything he could think of to help them get over their homesickness fearing he'd soon be the only one left. Quite a few families had already given up and moved back east. That was part of the reason we were struggling more than we had planned. Edward knew it would take some time to get the business up and running, but he didn't anticipate losing experienced workers month after month.

"Maybe you're right Florence. We should do something special to mark the occasion. Do you have any suggestions?" Edward inquired, now convinced that he should do something.

"How about a day at Cedar Point for all the workers and their families? I used to love going there with my family. The children would really enjoy it too. There is plenty for adults to do as well. What do you think?" Florence asked eagerly.

Cedar Point in Sandusky had been around for decades and was a favorite get away for Florence and her family over the years. Edward had been there a couple times since moving here. He went once with Florence and returned alone to do a little business at the park late last summer. He was able to sell some souvenir glasses with the park's name on them. As they talked, I recalled how pleasant it was to stroll along the shoreline. It wasn't far from Toledo but it felt like a world away when you could enjoy walking along the beach.

"Or is returning there too scary for you?" Florence teased. Florence re-enacted her version of him and the way he jumped in surprise when they visited last year and went through the haunted house. She even threw in a little scream.

I couldn't help but stand next to Florence and reenact my interpretation of Edward screaming. He pretended to get a little miffed at the two of us ganging up on him.

"Now, now, that is not the way I remember it all. And there is no way I let out any kind of scream. As I recall I was protecting you when you jumped back in fright," he said trying to re-invent the actual facts of the event.

"I can't imagine Florence being afraid of anything," I said smiling helpfully towards Florence.

"That was such a fun day. I recall how much money you spent trying to win that stuffed bear for me. You must have thrown a hundred balls trying to get them to land in one of those glass bowls," Florence said as she smiled at Edward.

"What do you mean tried? I did win that bear for you, fair and square," Edward responded triumphantly.

"No, I quite remember the man felt so sorry for you because you wouldn't give up and after you had spent ten times what the bear would have cost at the store, he felt sorry for you and gave it to you!" Florence said gleefully winking at me.

"You do have such a faulty memory, that is such a shame," Edward replied having to have the last word. Florence smiled knowingly at him and pretended to let him win this argument.

"Would you like to help plan this party? You are so good at organizing these things. You can stop in and talk with my secretary to get flyers written up so we can get the word out. It would be nice if we could do it on August 8th, is that enough time for you?" Edward asked knowing full well Florence would enjoy the challenge of getting everything together in the short time frame.

"Consider it done. I will talk with your secretary right away and make the arrangements at the park. Edward your employees will really appreciate this kind gesture," Florence said excitedly as she waved goodbye to us.

Florence spent the morning writing down the details of the party. She stopped at my office later that day with a draft of the announcement of the event. "Can you take this to Ms. Halpin this afternoon? I'd like to distribute these around the plant as soon as possible. I'm heading home to contact the park to reserve a pavilion for the families to have a lunch together. I also want to get some items together to provide for some raffle prizes. I know the families really enjoy going to the ballpark and I'm sure I can get the park manager to donate some tickets."

Before I could get in a word, Florence rambled on about a big collection of art supplies she had and that she could set up a table for the small children to use them at the park. The park certainly had many things to keep everyone busy but she knew the kids would get antsy and want to run to the rides when the parents would want to take a break and enjoy their lunch. The art supplies would keep the kids in the pavilion area and within the watchful eyes of their parents during that time she explained.

Florence was getting excited just thinking about the day and her mood was contagious. She was glad Edward had allowed her to be a part of it. She didn't work at the factory, but she felt like a part of the Libbey family anyway. Maybe it was because of her fondness of Edward. Ever since that first chance encounter, I knew she was always in his thoughts. They had such fun together and got along so well. She knew he worried about his business and his workers and if she could do anything to help them she would. A day away at the park would put everyone in a good mood. It always worked for her, so why not for these former Bostonians?

Some of the workers were more excited than others to read about the anniversary party. However, those reluctant ones, who may have dreaded riding the scary rides, were forced to come around to the idea when they told their families about it. The children were overjoyed at the thought of going to the park for the day. This made the mothers happy and the men were content that they were able to provide this benefit to their families.

The morning of the anniversary party started out with gray skies in Toledo. The overcast skies didn't dampen the moods of the fairgoers at all. They were too excited to let the potential of a few raindrops spoil their outing. Besides, Cedar Point was all the way in Sandusky and the skies could be cleared up by the time they arrived over there. Rain or shine, there was still plenty to do and enjoy. Just having the day off work was a pleasant bonus!

Most of the families arrived together. While the parents were turning in their tickets at the gates, the children were looking with amazement at the first rides they could see from the park entrance. You could hear the excitement in the air as the children were pointing excitedly and yelling out where they wanted to go first. The parents would have to run to keep up with the little ones as they got through the gate and went running in every direction.

Edward was there well ahead of everyone. Florence was happily by his side. She wanted Edward to stand near the entrance and welcome the slew of his guests as they arrived. The families proudly wore a pin with the Libbey logo on it. The pin wasn't necessary for Edward to recognize them. He knew everyone personally and their family members. He made it a point to get to know everyone that he employed. Edward greeted them and reminded them to be at the pavilion at 1:00 p.m. for a group lunch. They were free to enjoy the park until then. The parents responded appreciatively to Edward but the kids were running by too fast to stop for anyone.

Florence got a kick out of watching the excitement on the children's faces. She was so glad Edward had agreed to this idea. A few of the mother's greeted Florence and thanked her for her help in planning the event. Ms. Halpin had let it be known that the party was all Florence's idea.

Once everyone was inside and scattered around the park, Edward thanked Florence. "I must admit this was a splendid idea. All those smiling faces are thanks to you. Now what would you like to do first?"

"I really could use another bear!" Florence said in jest as she recalled the frustration on Edward's face last year when he tried so hard to win her one.

"Oh, I've got to see this!" I said laughing loudly.

Edward, never one to back down from a challenge, surprised her by saying, "I will absolutely guarantee I will win you a bear, my lady," he said as he bowed before her like she was royalty.

"Oh, what makes you so certain? I recall a mighty long struggle the last time you tried that game," Florence replied.

"Ma'am, did you forget you are talking to the King of Glass. I assembled a bunch of my glass jars in a similar configuration in a corner of my warehouse and I've been practicing for weeks," Edward proudly boasted.

"So you are a swindler?" Florence said in a pretend gasp.

Edward replied, "Of course not. I see it as a game of skill, and like any game of skill, it just takes practice and tenacity to master it."

"I see, that is true enough. But is it fair? I mean, not everyone has a factory load of glasses at their disposal to use for practice," Florence responded challenging Edward's defenses.

"If there is a will, there is always a way, is the way I see it. I see others that have won at that game and I suppose they have found their own way to practice and hone their skills. I have done no less. Further, I have the make shift game set up in an area so that any of my workers could practice too. So we may see several ladies dragging giant cuddly bears around the park today!" Edward said.

Florence knew better than to try and win an argument with Edward. Besides she did want to see him win the bear this time so she didn't want to discourage his tactics.

Chapter 29

By the end of 1889, The Draconian Club was constructed and the name changed to The Toledo Club. The building took up residency on 14th and Madison Avenues downtown. The building was designed by their friend David and the membership was expected to grow dramatically after it was opened.

The opening night was advertised in the paper as the new exclusive club in town. Getting publicity for the club was easy since one of the five founding members was the editor of the local paper. The five founders had enacted a set of rules and would scrutinize an abundance of applicants in the first weeks of the opening.

The grand dining room was decked out in all it splendor for its opening act. A grand piano was in the corner and music was playing throughout the night. Edward and the other hosts were in the foyer and greeted all their guests as they arrived. The crowd marveled at the glorious carved woodwork and oak paneling throughout the interior.

The tall ceilings gave a feel of stepping into an old castle, which was something totally unexpected to the Toledo residents. The opulent stairway in the lobby was covered with red carpeting. At the foot of the stairs, on each side, was a podium with large vases of flowers. The cut glass of the vases sparkled brilliantly from all the candles hanging on the walls.

The artwork on the walls consisted of paintings Edward had collected in his travels and donated for display. Edward couldn't resist buying fine artwork when it struck his fancy, but his small hotel room wasn't a good place to display them. The rooms here were perfect for them and the view was stunning. The portraits dazzled in the glow of beautiful chandeliers. My breath was taken away by the opulent sconces around the room that made all the glass objects situated throughout glimmer.

Once you climbed the staircase you were greeted with more paintings along the hallway on the second floor. You could also take advantage of the balcony to look down on the lobby. There were several smaller rooms that were decorated in different themes. The owners each had their favorite that seemed to show off their personal tastes.

Edward's favorite place was the Red Room. He had ordered it to be designed in the Italian Renaissance style that he admired. He put his most favorite paintings in the room. He also selected unique glass objects to display in the room. The room was capped off with a stunning crystal chandelier which drew your eyes upon the hand stenciled ceiling. Edward expected to spend a lot of time in this room over the years. I hoped to as well.

Edward also had a room designed that he thought Florence would appreciate. It was a surprise to her and he couldn't wait to show it to her. When Edward saw his chance, he grabbed Florence's hand and pulled her away from the pack and motioned for me to follow. "Where are we going?" Florence asked as she happily followed Edward down the hall.

Edward, with a twinkle in his eye replied, "I had a room decorated especially for you. I hope you like it. Now close your eyes," Edward commanded as they reached the door of the room.

"Did you know about this Red?" She asked, already knowing the answer.

Florence was intrigued and happy to play along. She lifted both hands over her eyes and said, "Ready."

"No peeking now," Edward teased, as he took her by the elbow and led her inside the Garden Room. He directed Florence to the middle of the room and stepped back.

"Ok, you can open your eyes," Edward said and Florence quickly dropped her hands and looked straight ahead. She stood in complete silence for a moment, just looking up and down, drinking in every detail as she twirled around to get the full view.

"Well?" Edward said expectantly. She didn't have to say anything. We could tell by the expression on her face that she loved the room.

"This is absolutely stunning Edward," she finally blurted out. "The latticework on the ceiling and the mirror, I can't stop staring at it. Can I live here?" Florence jested.

Edward was pleased to see that look on her face. He would let the designer know he had hit the mark. Florence could have stayed in that room all night but she knew they had many guests waiting elsewhere.

"Let's keep this room a secret for a while. I'd like to surprise my mother and friends with this by having a luncheon here next week," Florence said as she walked up to closely inspect the artwork hanging on the walls. Edward was happy to oblige to Florence's wishes. Since this room was on the fifth floor and the festivities tonight were in the main dining room on the second floor he didn't expect many to make their way up here tonight.

"Florence, where are you?" We heard from down the hall.

"Oh no, it's my mother!" Florence sighed.

"Quick everyone out. Close the door, Red!"

Chapter 30

"Tonight is the night, Red!" Edward exclaimed as he pulled me into his office and shut the door.

Immediately I knew without another word, what he meant. Edward had been quietly contemplating an official engagement for quite a spell.

"It's been on our minds for some time now. Neither one us would say it out loud for fear of scaring the other one away," Edward said truthfully.

I knew that Edward was really hesitant because he wanted to be sure he felt worthy of Florence. She came from a very prosperous family. Even though he owned his own business, he was still struggling to build it into the empire he dreamed it could be someday.

Edward was confident that he had the best craftsmen and designers and that one day his would be the biggest glass manufacturer in the whole world! Europe had many fine glass companies competing for that crown too, but now they had one very determined competitor in the United States. If Florence was at Edward's side, he would have even more reason to fulfill his vision.

Edward knew he didn't need Maurice's blessing or permission to ask for Florence's hand in marriage, but it was important to him to have it anyway. If her father agreed to the union he would feel more confident in its success. He had decided he would talk to Maurice about it tonight. He was taking Florence out that evening and he would talk with Maurice before or after. The timing would depend on his courage when he arrived that night. He figured if he did it right away then it wouldn't be on his mind all night haunting him. However, if Maurice had any reservations or came out and said no, the night would be a nightmare. What to do, he fretted as he prepared for the evening. I had never seen him so tense about anything.

He was expected at 6:00 p.m. and so he had another hour to bump off. I didn't know why he was so nervous. I think part of him was sad as he realized this was a talk he never got to have with his own father. True, his stepmother was here and they were very close, but it wasn't quite the same.

As he sat thinking of his father, I assured him William was looking down at him with approval. I reminded him how his father had talked to me many times about the importance of marriage. "Your father had a talk with me when I asked him for advice about proposing to Louise. I was so nervous about marriage and I didn't have anyone else really to talk to about those things. William was so kind and I'll never forget his advice. He said if Louise is the lady who makes you feel like you couldn't live another moment without her in your life then grab her quick before someone else does. He also said it was important that Louise and I had common interests which I appreciated more as time wore on. Edward, you know how easy it is to fall for someone with outward beauty, but to build a long, happy life you need a companion, someone that wants the same things in life as you do. If you don't have that, marriage can be a very long, lonely ride. I think you struck gold with Florence, she's the full package!"

As Edward thought back on those words that his father had told me he poured himself a cup of coffee. As he held the drink in his hand and took a sip he began to relax. Edward told me stories about the way his father doted on his mother. This was the way I remembered it too. I reminded him that I met his father when he was running an errand to surprise his wife. No matter the ups and downs they went through, up until the end, they cared for and loved one another. It was the same with his father's second wife.

Edward recalled the day he had to go home and tell his stepmother that her husband, his father, had a heart attack and died at work. It was a day I could never forget either. "The utter sadness in my stepmother's eyes is something I will never get over. She pulled herself together and put on a brave front as we went and told my sisters, but I knew how devastating the loss was to mom. She told me that she didn't regret one minute that they had together and was lucky that they had so many wonderful years together."

"I will never forget the day Louise died either, but I have many years of happiness to look back on too. Nobody knows how much time you have on Earth, so grab happiness when you can," I said.

Edward reflected and said, "Red, this feels right. I'm ready for the kind of love my parents had. I know I will have that with

Florence. From the first time I laid eyes on her, I knew she was the one."

I think the conversation about his father bolstered his confidence. "I don't need to wish you good luck. I already know Florence's answer," I said with a wide grin on my face.

"Thanks Red. I'll see you tomorrow," Edward said setting down the glass and giving me a big hug.

The next couple of days Edward was swamped at work. He hardly had time to think about his upcoming proposal which was heartily approved by Maurice. He was set to take Florence to dinner Saturday at his new Club, The Toledo Club. He planned to propose to her there. The Club had just opened last month and was already one of their most favorite places.

The Club offered an elegant ambience that was hard to describe. You just felt like you were someplace special from the moment you walked in the door. The staff was wonderful and always ready to attend to your every request before you even thought to ask it. Florence loved the double winding staircase in the foyer. She also loved the main dining room. Everything from the grand piano to the grand paintings on the wall to the fine china on the tables were exquisite. Her favorite table was a small intimate table near the large bay window.

The celebration would be shared with their families and a few close friends. We were invited to dine at the club that evening for a special event. Maurice and I knew the real reason, but I wasn't sure if Edward had kept it from all the others. His sister Sarah was rather clever, and no doubt had figured out the true meaning of the evening. We were scattered around the room, just out view of Florence's table.

When Florence and Edward were escorted to their table, I saw him excuse himself abruptly. When I noticed him head towards his waiter I knew the plan was underway. I watched eagerly as the waiter returned quickly with two glasses of champagne and sat them on their table. When he stepped away Florence looked down and seemed to notice something in her glass.

Just then Edward got down on one knee, took Florence's hands in his and said, "Would you do me the favor of making me the happiest man in the world? Would you be my wife?"

With tears suddenly streaming down her face, Florence said, "Yes, yes of course!"

"With this glass, I give you my heart," Edward said as she pulled the ring from the glass and put it on her finger. Florence stared down at the sparkling ring. The gold band contained a one caret pear shaped diamond. Florence looked overjoyed.

Edward embraced Florence as we heard the waiter clink a glass in his hand with a spoon he was holding. The ringing sound got people's attention and the waiter proudly yelled out, "She said yes!"

The crowd of diners, many whom they knew like me, joined the waiter in clapping their approval. If Florence was embarrassed, she didn't show it. She looked happily around the room and said thank you. From the far side of the room her parents and Edward's sister rushed towards her. The realization that they were here put an even bigger smile on her face.

"You knew?" Florence said pretending to be upset by their sneakiness as they drew near.

"Oh darling, congratulations!" said her mother and then she turned to her husband, "So this is why you insisted on coming tonight? I didn't know anything about this, but I had a feeling these two were up to something. Is this what you two were talking about so secretly in the parlor the other night?"

Maurice smiled and said, "I can't reveal a confidence," and then he turned to Edward, "Congratulations my boy. Oh that has a nice sound to it," he said and Edward certainly agreed.

Edward directed us all to a table in the other corner that was ready and waiting to hold us all for a celebration dinner. The happy couple spent the dinner answering all kinds of questions about the wedding. Florence seemed well prepared for the interrogation with a complete list of all her ideas for a lovely June wedding.

Edward just wanted one more thing from Florence tonight. He asked if they could stop by and tell his stepmom. She wasn't feeling well these past couple weeks and he didn't want her trying to get out tonight or he would have had her here to witness it too. Florence was more than agreeable. She was looking forward to telling everyone about the engagement who wasn't here tonight.

"Now your sister Alice will have to come to Toledo! I just can't wait to meet her. Who knows, maybe I can convince her to move here too. I know that is something that you would like dear," Florence said to a nodding Edward and Sarah.

The club manager was so pleased with the news of Edward and Florence's engagement and stopped over to congratulate them. "That was a great idea, putting the ring in the glass like you did. Maybe you'll encourage others to propose with a ring in the glass. Then they could depart with the glass as a souvenir as I'm sure Florence will do tonight." Florence nodded in agreement.

The glass would be a memento she would treasure forever, for it not only had an "ℒ" on the bottom to signify her new name, it had also contained her engagement ring. "Do you think this will make the news?" the manager joked as Robinson, Edward's business partner in the club and publisher of the newspaper, walked up.

"I think this would make a splendid story for the newspaper, how about it Florence?" Robinson asked her sweetly.

After re-telling the story, for probably the first of many times, Florence and Edward, giddy with excitement, left for a stroll down Madison Avenue to his mother's home.

The next morning Florence surprised me as I was walking into the factory grounds. "Oh Red, what a wonderful morning. I was so happy you and my parents were there last night."

"I can't believe you didn't spot us beforehand or figure out what was going on. Edward has a hard time keeping secrets sometimes! What are you doing here so early?"

"Oh, Red, I couldn't sleep a wink last night. When I got back home I just couldn't believe I was engaged. You know, at some point, years ago I had given up on the notion of getting married and put away the ideas I had scribbled out as a young, hopeful girl into a trunk. The trunk contains fond memories of my childhood. A ticket stub to the first theater I attended with my father, a pretty locket my grandmother had given me, a seashell from my first visit to the Atlantic Ocean," Florence said and then got very quiet.

These things wouldn't have meant much to anyone else, but to her I could see they were warm remembrances of her childhood. I could understand wanting to hold onto precious mementos like that. I still had a worn out note from my mother. I only wish I had something like that from my father.

"Anyway, underneath those trinkets I found an old journal. I held it in my hands almost afraid to open it!" she laughed. "I recalled right away how it contained beliefs about how I would grow up and marry a handsome prince. Oh, I spent many days painting "*great works of art*" that would adorn the walls of my castle."

"Did you have a description of your prince? Did he look like Edward?" Pointing towards the factory I jested, "Did your castle look as grand as this?"

She laughed, "Well, not quite. Oh, I was totally obsessed with stories of princes and princesses and castles and dragons back then. Red, I'm not exactly marrying a prince, but he is like a prince to me. He is certainly handsome, charming and debonair. I don't need rescuing from an evil witch or dragon, which is just as well. Anywhere Edward and I will be will feel like a castle to me."

"I think little Florence would be very pleased with the way things turned out," I said sincerely.

"If only I was more a talented painter. But funny enough, here I am marrying a man who has a small army of talented artists."

I escorted Florence into Edward's office and bid farewell. "Tell Mr. Pomeroy I said hello when you see him later," I said as I left.

Florence knew she had to make a personal stop at Mr. Pomeroy's office to thank him for introducing the two and share their good news.

Florence spent the next few days in pure bliss. She had a wedding to plan! She had no shortage of help on the matter either. She had her mom, her soon to be sister-in-law, and dear friend Hattie. Florence also had many ideas about her wedding day that she had thought about many times as a child.

Mr. Scott was sure everyone had heard about the engagement but he insisted on throwing a party anyway. It seemed everyone in town was invited. Florence had insisted it wasn't necessary but knew once her father set his mind to something there was no changing it. He thought it appropriate to hold the party at the Club where the engagement took place.

On Saturday night all their friends and family gathered in the Red Room. Florence looked beautiful and Edward was charming as always. The band played throughout the night and Florence thought she'd be worn out as she kept trading dances with her soon to be husband and her father.

At one point her father raised a glass and clinked it with a spoon to get everyone's attention. "Thank you all for coming," he began and as everyone quieted down he continued, "I know my finicky daughter had very high standards, and I was starting to think nobody could meet them, but luckily she decided instead to drop her standards," Maurice said as everyone chuckled.

"But seriously, she was waiting until the right man came along and he came along with a glass house and swept her off her feet! I expect and know you will take great care of my darling princess. To the happy new couple, I'd like to present you with a small gift," Maurice said as he waved to get the couple to join him up front. They looked at each other, not knowing exactly what was in store for them.

Maurice handed them an envelope and then said, "This is the deed to land on Scottwood Avenue. You may use it to build your new home."

The couple was elated and didn't know what to say. This was land Florence knew was part of her father's holdings and was near his house. This was a wonderful, generous gift and the couple hugged and thanked him profusely. "I will build you a castle my dear," Edward said joyously as the crowd clapped in approval.

The Woods section in the West End of Toledo was a fitting place for the Libbeys. All the prominent business people lived in the streets ending with Woods – Robinwood, Maplewood,

Collingwood and Greenwood. Tree lined streets with enormous mansions of various European architecture lined the neighborhood. *(These beautiful homes would draw people to the neighborhood for decades.)*

An American Prince Charming and a castle in Toledo? Even Florence as a child didn't really believe all those dreams would ever come true, but they were and I was happy for both of them. Florence and Edward were giddy with excitement that was infectious to anyone around them. The young couple looked full of happiness and hope as they celebrated their engagement and looked on to the future.

"Where will you honeymoon?" one of Florence's friends asked.

"I do think we will go to Europe if Edward can get away for a time. We both adore it over there and it will be fun to see it together again. We got to see a little of it together last year when I ran into him when I was there on vacation with my parents," Florence responded.

"Europe in June, how romantic!" I said chiding my friend.

Edward's elated temperament from the party stayed with him the next day. He refused to be brought down even when he heard of the troubles at the factory. Everyone there soon knew about his engagement, but he tried to put it out of his mind as he listened to the plant manager, James.

The manager told him they were having more problems with the sand. It seems we got a bad load and the glass coming out of the furnace looked a little cloudy. Crystal clear glass was the standard we required of every glass. We had no choice but to scrap all the glass in the lehr. This meant were now way behind schedule for the shipment to Montgomery Ward. The store had ordered 5,000 dozen of the Agata glasses and we needed several thousand more to complete the order. Normally this would have sent Edward into a panic, but not today.

Even knowing he'd soon have a wife to provide for he was determined not to panic. Edward calmly went down to the warehouse and talked with the manager. As he walked up and down the aisles surveying the stockpiles of ware he stopped to consult with some other managers over their concerns of the day. I followed along to see if there was anything I could do to fix the problem. Unfortunately, this was a raw supply problem and not mechanical. But after surveying the scope of the problem, we left the area with a determined plan of action.

Edward saw that they were indeed short of the intended order, but he had an idea. He contacted Mr. Ward and told him that our Agata line was a top seller but he was concerned there was too much Agata product out in the market right now. He told him he may have faster sales with the Ashburton line and if he advertised them for a limited time with a special promotional votive per set he would surely sell them out. Edward hemmed and hawed and then offered to throw the votives in at a reasonable price if Mr. Ward took the Ashburton in place of the missing

Agata. I was impressed how quickly and smoothly Edward convinced Mr. Ward of the new sales arrangement and solved the problem.

Suddenly James came barging into his office, still concerned of the incomplete order, as Edward hung up the phone. "Not to worry James I have convinced Mr. Ward to take the Ashburton line in place of the smaller order of Agata and we will take the pallet of votives to provide as a special promotion."

James looked slightly relieved but then exclaimed, "I'm glad that crisis is averted sir, but I'm afraid I have another one." James went on to describe the next issue and Edward took it all in stride.

There was always going to be one crisis after another he figured, but I think now that he knew he would be coming home to Florence at the end of each day his outlook was a little more relaxed. I knew Edward was looking forward to meeting with Mr. Stine the next morning and apparently he wasn't going to let anything sour his mood.

Edward wanted Mr. Stine to build his new house on the land generously given to him by Maurice. Edward always admired the architecture of Greece and dreamed of a grand palace for his wife. She deserved to live like a queen he told me. I knew it would take some time before he could afford to build the home he wanted but he could at least start drafting the plans.

This was a happy time for me and I was glad to see my friend Edward so blissful. Edward's free time was consumed with his house project which filled him with joy knowing he was designing it for his future wife. Florence happily spent her extra time planning out all the special details of the wedding. Her best friends Hattie and Grace were at her side through it all. I was busy with a special growing project of my own.

Chapter 31

As Spark grew in size, his personality did too. Now you may find this hard to believe, but Spark was turning into quite a character. God must have created him with a seriously large funny bone because the things he did were downright amusing, if not at times aggravating. I told you how he picked up on bringing me things early on, like a golden retriever. Unfortunately, some of the items would be soiled or slobbered on so much that they would be nearly ruined, like the newspaper. Often items ended up with a slight scorch mark on them, as Spark had not yet fully learned how to control his fire breathing breath.

When I worked on a new idea I would get so focused on my work, I would tend to ignore him or forget he was there. So he would remind me by moving something of mine to some strange place. He would find this very amusing. After he did one of his tricks, like taking my pencil and placing it on the doorknob, he would make a silly sound, like someone does when they are snickering and amused with themselves, and then he would go over and lay down on his blanket. I kid you not!

At times I could feel his eyes upon me, wanting me to discover his misdeed and playfully scold him. Watching him squirm a little, as I pretended not to notice, would be my playful revenge. It reminded me of when my son was a toddler and he would do such silly things trying to get my attention.

One of young Robert's favorite games was to take my hat off my head when I was getting ready for work and he would run around the house with it, wailing in laughter, while I chased him. If I teasingly yelled at him, he would squeal in delight and run even faster. He would be so happy when I caught him and spun him around the room.

Those memories of my days as a happy young family were always sneaking up on me lately and making me a little melancholy. Luckily, I had Spark here to perk me up. It's hard to stay in a bad mood with him around.

Spark was also very useful to have around. For one thing, he was a great tea warmer. What do I mean? Well, I think you may have noticed by now that I drink a fair amount of tea. I make a large container of it and bring it down to my office with me when I start my day. The trouble is that it doesn't stay as hot as I like and it is a long walk for me to get back upstairs to get a new hot cup of water. I found, when Spark decided to hide my cup one day, that just by holding the cup in his claws he managed to get the water to an almost boiling temperature again, just the way I like it. I couldn't be upset with him about that. Well, after I found my cup, I wasn't!

One day as I was sitting at my desk, with Spark curled up nearby, I realized I needed to get him outdoors. "You need sunlight and fresh air, boy," I said as he looked at me and made a sigh and a small flicker of a flame escaped in the air.

When he was much smaller I could take him out in my yard at night or when the neighbors were away at work in the daytime. Now with his growing size, it was harder for him to go unnoticed. As I was looking around the room, I noticed a few of the bricks on the south wall jutted out a little in one area that I had not noticed before now.

I walked over to examine the wall, and as I was pushing my hands along the bricks, one came loose in my hand. I noticed it wasn't as thick as bricks normally would be and I was able to pull another one off nearby. Behind it I could see a faint light.

This must have been some sort of opening, maybe a door, at one time. I grabbed my tools off the bench and began chiseling away at some of the looser bricks. Soon I had a large circle opening and a pile of bricks at my feet. But best of all, I had the opening to a tunnel. This must have been one of the original tunnels they built for the gas lines I guessed.

The tunnel appeared to be large enough for me to stand in. I could see a faint light coming from afar. As I started to climb through the opening I stopped short. I retreated back to my desk and grabbed a lantern, just in case. The cool draft in the tunnel was enticing. Even in the sub-basement of the factory, the air could be stifling hot.

I made my way little by little through the tunnel and tried to keep track of my steps to count the distance. The tunnel walls got quite a bit wider as I went along. The ceiling appeared to be maybe ten feet above me, but it was a little hard to judge from the dim light. I crept slowly down a hallway, listening and looking for anything, not knowing what to expect.

I had no trouble getting to the light source which was coming from a large window a few feet above me. Jumping up to look out, I could barely see that this was the backside of the factory which looked over a swampy, marshy field. This is perfect, I thought happily.

The forgotten tunnel and the yard where it led presented me with the perfect solution. The window was quite large, about ten feet by ten feet but it was covered with a thick spider's web which put a little chill down my back. I hated spiders. I went back to my office and snatched my chair and a stick. I dragged both back through the tunnel and placed the chair under the window. I swung at the web and was startled as something landed on my face. I screamed loudly, lost my balance and went crashing onto the floor.

There I sat and listened for a minute. Hearing no sounds, I brushed myself off and climbed back onto the chair. I found I was just barely able to pull myself up onto the window sill and crawl out of the window. I smiled and whispered, "Why didn't I think of this sooner?"

I pushed aside the overgrown vines to get a better view. The back of the property was surrounded by a marshy meadow and a good amount of trees which provided privacy. This would be the perfect place for Spark to get around and explore. I had not been back here since that first day, and from the looks of the grounds nobody else had been here either.

When getting acquainted with the factory a few of us walked the perimeter of the four acres plot that belonged to Edward. We were asked to walk the property line and ensure the fence was completed and in good shape. The men, including myself, found the area a swampy mess and made no plans to return.

Edward was glad to have the extra land though. He had negotiated for it with the purchase to have it available for future expansion. The seller was glad to unload it, as he thought it too marshy to develop and practically threw it in just to sweeten the pot and help seal the deal.

The land was secluded on all sides, three by trees and one with the back of the factory. The building had just a few windows along this back side, but they were set very high, close to the ceiling, and not reachable for easy viewing. This meant nobody would be able to see a dragon romping around the yard. I needed to get back to my office now, but promised myself I would fully scope out the grounds after my shift. Spark deserves a little more freedom and this may be just the answer.

When I got back inside my office I fretted over the mess I had made. I did admittedly break out a good chuck of the wall after all. I looked around for something I could use to cover it so it wouldn't be noticed by anyone coming in the room. I spotted a wide cabinet that held my drawing papers which could work to cover part of the area. I removed the glass samples from the top and set those out of the way so they wouldn't break. Then I carefully pushed and dragged the cabinet across the room. It covered most of the damage but there was still a hole above the cabinet.

I looked around and then grabbed the large piece of cardboard I had been using to doodle new glass shapes on and placed it on top of the cabinet. I lined up the glasses in front of it to hold it in place against the wall. I stood back to examine the wall. The destruction was camouflaged enough for now, but I would have to find something more substantial that I could easily open and close and keep hidden from view.

Just as I promised, I got out to the yard right after work to scout around. Nobody saw me turn the corner and proceed back here so I was able to take my time to access the area. I walked around and took note to understand how visible the area could be from every direction and how accessible it was for anyone to walk back that way. As I confirmed its isolation I became really excited for Spark. I debated about telling Edward first, but I didn't want to bother him.

Edward was so busy these days trying to get an order ready for a major store in New York. The display of products at their store was a big deal because our name would be out there in a premiere shopping venue. Tiffany's was considered the ultimate in shopping places for luxurious items. They carried the most glamorous brands of products. Edward was ecstatic to get the order and his excitement had a way of infecting everyone in the plant. Good news was welcome, especially now, as several men were getting rather homesick and looking a little down.

Toledo had many things to offer and the people were great, but for those who had never lived anywhere but Cambridge, like myself, it was hard to adjust. Several homesick wives kept finding reasons to make trips back to family in Cambridge. The husband's complained the extended lengths of these trips made life harder for them.

The men's loneliness was curtailed by spending time at the local pub. This was a nice way to unwind after work for some. Every now and then, arguments would get out of hand and fists would fly. This was one reason I didn't join in this activity very often. Nowadays my special project gave me another good reason to avoid the pub.

The next afternoon one of the guys asked me to join them for a drink as we were leaving work. Instead of heading to the bar I told the men I needed to complete a project for the boss before morning, which wasn't exactly a lie. My project was to fix up my new office. I watched as the men advanced down the street. When they were far enough way I decided it was a good time for me to search around the scrapyard on the west side of the plant for materials.

I was itching to make a door for the tunnel entrance. I wanted to make it easier for me to open and close, but still keep it hidden from view. I found a broken door that could do the job. I managed to get the door back to my office without raising any suspicion.

A while later I had the bricks attached to one side of the door and had it set across the opening. The new door blended in well enough that it should avoid detection, I surmised. I then placed a small table in front of it, one that could be moved out of the way easily when necessary. I placed a picture above the table and the façade was complete.

Chapter 32

The perimeter check yesterday proved successful so there was nothing stopping me from taking Spark outside, except my fear. I almost hesitated to take him out in the open without telling Edward, but I really didn't want Edward's concerns to delay my plan. If it worked, I would tell him. If it didn't work, which would mean Spark had escaped, or had been discovered, well then, likely many people would tell Edward.

"Here's goes nothing," I said bravely to Spark trying to put out of my mind how this plan could go awry and cause me huge trouble. So, knowing failure was not a choice, I let out a big breath and proceeded. Spark was eager to follow me into the tunnel. He scampered back and forth around me and then took off playfully down the center aisle. There was only one path to take so I let Spark lead the way.

When we reached the window, I leashed him and pushed him up on the window sill while he struggled to help pull himself up. Once we were outside Spark could hardly contain himself. So much new territory to see and explore he realized. I hesitated a little as I glanced back at the factory. I scanned the area again to be sure nobody was in sight. Finding nobody, I gingerly walked Spark around and through the densely forested land. Spark jumped playfully at the bunnies and small frogs that hopped around the woods.

I didn't want to be out too long, so I turned him around and led him back to our cave. "We'll do more exploring tomorrow, I promise you Spark."

On that first visit to the yard I admit my nerves almost stopped me. I courageously forged ahead because I know it was important that Spark have more room to stretch out and exercise. Over the next several days we spent more and more time out there. I could tell Spark enjoyed this part of the day. This was evidenced by how he would pull the leash down from the hook and place it at my feet.

If I tried to pretend I didn't notice the leash, or ignored him too long, he would practically tie me up with it. With the leash in his mouth and me in my chair, Spark would move around me in a circle until the leash was partially around my legs and I was forced to notice him!

At some point I was going to have to trust him off the leash, but not just yet I told myself, maybe next week. I wasn't really concerned that he would fly away, mostly because his wings didn't appear strong enough yet. I was primarily more paranoid about Spark chasing any small creature and causing trouble. I couldn't run as fast as I used to and I didn't want Spark out of my sight. I did notice that Spark seemed to watch the birds very intently as they took flight. I wondered when Spark would realize that he could join them in the air.

After weeks of training with Spark I wanted to reward him. Spark was getting so attached to me that I figured it wouldn't be too risky to let him realize his full capabilities. Who knew, someday he may need to know this, I admitted.

It was time. I had to just let him fly. It was a rather dark evening, and the cloud cover kept any light from shining through. Those conditions made me feel confident that Spark wouldn't be spotted in the air by anyone. Besides it was Saturday night and most people were hanging out with friends or home in bed. "Let's get to it, Spark!"

Spark and I trekked out to the marshy area and when we arrived at the clearing I stopped. I unhooked Spark's leash and folded it in my hand. I looked intently in his eyes and then started running and called for Spark to follow. When Spark gave chase I laughed wildly as I flapped my arms like I was trying to fly. I felt like I was five years old and it felt so wonderful!

Soon Spark was imitating me, but he took it a step further by starting to lift off the ground! He flew a short way and came back to me. I patted him and we repeated the chase and fly motions again and again. After repeating this activity several times Spark took off high into the sky and let out a wild squeal. I was nervous, but excited, as I watched him flying through the air. I soon lost sight of him. Before I could panic, thankfully Spark was back landing down in front of me.

I lay down in the grass and looked up in the sky. I watched him in awe as he flew up, down and around in the air. Every few minutes he came back, almost as if looking at me for approval and praise, and wondering why I didn't follow him. If only I could! I realized then that our bond was secure. I felt better knowing that Spark really wanted to be here with me. He had the chance to fly away and never return. But he had a purpose and wanted to please me, and I felt the same towards him.

When he returned the third or fourth time and bowed down in front of me, a crazy idea popped in my head and I jumped on it. The "it" was Spark's back. Before I knew it, we ascended into the air. I let out a scream of half terror, half delight as we rose above the factory. I was in awe as the building shrunk beneath me. I felt my red hair blowing wildly and reckoned it looked like flickering flames of a fire as we dashed across the sky. My heart pounded so loudly I felt everyone could hear it. I clung tightly to Spark as he gently flapped his wings.

I didn't want the ride to end, but I knew it must. I tugged a little on Spark's neck and pointed down. Spark seemed to understand the command and gently turned around. Slowly he descended, little by little, until we could almost touch the factory. I held on a little tighter as we got closer to the ground. When we landed safely I climbed off Spark's back and hugged him profusely. It was the most magical night of my life!

I don't know if I truly slept that night. In the clear light of day I pulled out a blank paper and jotted down some remarks about Spark's first flight. I refrained from recording my involvement as passenger. That would remain an unspoken and unwritten secret. I didn't expect anyone would read my logs, but I didn't want to take any chances.

Our tests at the factory were also going well. Experiments to project fire into the kilns with the right consistency were leading to some promising results. Spark was getting better at learning to control and release specific levels of fire to add to the fuel going to the furnaces. In time this was going to cut down on a significant amount of cost in the energy bills.

Spark's fuel would come to be a real advantage for us. We were starting to encounter some unexpected service outages. A few months after we started production we began experiencing sudden breaks in the flow of natural gas to our furnaces. We soon learned there were problems throughout the area and all our competitors were affected too. Other businesses in town experienced the same service issue, but the problem is much more damaging to a glass factory than other types of businesses.

In a glass factory, the furnace must run continuously, twenty-four hours a day, seven days a week. The furnace takes several days, when it is initially lit up, to get to the optimal 2,200 – 2,400 degrees Fahrenheit range. It needs continuous fuel streaming in to stay at that high temperature. If the temperature drops, the glass doesn't heat up enough to form properly and the whole batch of molten glass in the process has to be discarded. If this happens it causes idle time for workers and lost production as we have to wait several hours or days for the furnace to be running at the right temperature again to make products.

With Spark's assistance we were now able to ensure the furnaces stayed lit and running properly at all times. Spark is our ultimate trade secret and invaluable to our process. Once Edward had the chance to witness this episode he was even more pleased with his acquisition, and ever more cautious to keep it just between me and him. However, this began to concern me deeply as it brought up the next vexing problem.

Ever since Spark and I were relocated to work in the sub-basement, I had been reluctant to take him off the property. Well, except for a few flying episodes. Due to Spark's growing size, I decided not to risk taking him home at night anymore. I was sure nobody would find him down in the basement at night, but I was too nervous to leave him alone for that amount of time. I started sleeping on a makeshift bed in the office with him. I knew I wouldn't be able to sleep at home, speculating and worrying about Spark being discovered. Besides, I felt the emptiness and loneliness of the house now even when I just went home to clean up and change. I knew it was time to enlist some help.

I knew this day would come sooner or later. Edward did too. We both put it off as long as we could but now was the time to bring someone in on our secret. I lit a cigarette and puffed away as I mulled over in my mind who might be able to handle the job. I thought Edward might want Mike Owens. He would be a logical choice. However, Edward had him focused on many other initiatives. I would have to be ready to persuade Edward otherwise.

My first choice was Connor James, my oldest friend. Connor was 59 years old and a widow like me. Connor didn't have any children, and seemed content to remain single. He seldom went out with our co-workers, and on the rare occasions that he did, he always found a reason to leave early and went home alone, according to the razzing I would hear about from the others the next day. Connor's integrity was impeccable and his lifestyle made him the perfect choice in my book.

When Edward came by the next morning, I was ready. "Before I fill you in on the progress of the project, I need to show you something."

I went over to my makeshift door to the tunnel door and opened it. "What in the h….?" Edward looked a little surprised.

I looked at my friend Edward and pictured him the way he was when I first met him as a little boy. "You'll get a kick out of this," I said amused and then explained my recent adventures in the yard with Spark. Of course, I held back on telling him about the airborne episodes, I didn't want to get fired. Plus I figured that could be discussed later. First, I needed to get to the main reason I wanted to talk with Edward.

As we were chatting Edward noticed Spark retrieving his leash and bringing it to me. Edward was so impressed with Spark. Edward clutched the leash and tied it on Spark and said we should continue the discussion outside as it was clear Spark wanted to show off his yard.

Edward was a bit over-dressed to be climbing out a window and traipsing through the woods, but he didn't seem to care, even when he acquired a small rip in his pant leg, where it caught on a protruding nail. Edward was too distracted watching Spark who ran off to chase a squirrel. I froze as I watched and hoped Spark didn't decide to show off his latest talent now by soaring up to catch the squirrel. Luckily he abruptly lost interest in the squirrel and continued running towards the pond.

Then I blurted out my predicament of sleeping in the factory. Edward, stopped and looked at me, "Why haven't I realized this? Why didn't you come to me sooner?" Edward looked uncomfortable for putting him such a situation. "We must rectify this at once. If that means bringing in another co-conspirator then so be it. I truly wish you would have spoken to me sooner. You know I get busy on other things and I'm sorry I took you for granted knowing that you could run this project. I didn't intend it to take over your life though," Edward said reassuringly.

It was a relief to know Edward agreed with my plan. He fully supported and agreed with the choice of Connor. Edward said, "Well, it's decided, now let's get on with it. I will return within the hour with Connor and we will bring him on board with Project Ignite."

I know it seemed a silly question, but I yelled it out as Edward walked out, "But what if he does refuse?"

Chapter 33

Edward, as promised, returned with Connor about forty minutes later. I tried to keep my composure as Edward briskly shoved Connor in, latched the door and spun around wildly flailing his arms in the air saying, "Connor we have a special assignment for you. You have the option to say no right now, but if you agree, we will expect complete secrecy from you."

Connor looked at me suspiciously wondering what this could be about but I just shrugged my shoulders. "This also requires you to work the night shift for a while. Are you agreeable to those terms?" But before Connor could respond, Edward continued, "Be assured what we are going to show you will blow you away, and I guarantee you will be more than pleased with the assignment. I'm asking you because we both think you are the best qualified to help us."

Not many people ever said no to Edward. Knowing this and with the intriguing way the assignment was proposed, Connor didn't turn it down. In fact, he was so pleased he was singled out for a special assignment that he enthusiastically agreed without knowing anything else.

Edward looked to me, smiled widely and said, "Red, I think the best way to explain this assignment is to just bring it out and let Connor see exactly what you've been working on. Then he will know exactly why you've been tucked away in this secluded area of the plant."

Edward couldn't wait to see Connor's reaction, and neither could I. I hadn't confided this secret to anyone yet. Finally it was my chance to watch someone else react to seeing a dragon.

I proceeded over to the tunnel door and opened it as Connor stared confusingly at me and Edward. I'm sure he would have never guessed what was behind the door if we had asked him to speculate about it. Without any hesitation Spark leaped out of the tunnel. Connor almost fell over as he stammered backward, pointing at the dragon but found no sound coming from his mouth.

Connor's momentarily lost voice was probably a good thing because a scream or a yell wouldn't be a nice greeting to Spark. Spark stopped and stared for a moment and as if sensing our calmness, he then slowly approached Connor to give him a proper greeting. I grabbed my chair and pushed it up behind Connor before he could hit the floor. After a few minutes of catching his breath, Connor just sat staring at Spark with a dumbfounded look of amazement on his face.

Over the next hour, we filled Connor in on our plans and progress to date. Connor asked a few questions, but mostly he listened and tried to absorb everything we told him. I felt so relieved to have another partner in on this project. Edward had his hands full on so many other business matters that I was practically handling everything Spark related alone since he showed up at my door.

"Red, don't you think we need to make Connor a full-fledged member of our secret club?"

"I don't like the way you're looking at me Edward. What exactly do I have to do?" Connor said hesitantly.

"Don't look so worried Connor, it's actually pretty cool, and will only hurt for a minute," I said as I lifted up my sleeve to reveal the tattoo Edward had placed there to commemorate Spark.

Connor walked over to inspect my arm up close. He looked over at Edward who revealed the tattoo on his arm as he pumped his fist in the air shouting, "Spark is in our blood now, so what say *you*?"

"So help me, I'm in, too," Connor said as he removed his shirt.

I pulled out needle and ink and got to work. It was my second attempt and I was still nervous. I tried my best not to shake so I didn't mess up the design. Whatever I did was going to be there forever. It wasn't meant for show to others, but it was a permanent reminder of the bond that the three of us now shared.

Edward could see the shock of it all was taking a toll on Connor so he ordered him to take the rest of the day off. "Well, I'm sure this day wasn't exactly what you expected, eh? Why don't you go home now and take some time to rest. Then pack your bag and come back this evening for your new assignment."

"I'll be here when you get back buddy. It'll be a great night, just the three of us. You two will be great friends in no time," I assured Connor. If all went well as expected, I wouldn't have to be here nights by the end of the week.

Connor headed out the door and assured Edward that he wouldn't tell anyone what he saw. Who would believe him anyway, Connor mumbled almost to himself.

Then he turned back to me shaking his head and pointing his finger at me, "This was it, wasn't it? This is why you acted so strange that night and wouldn't let me in your house! I thought you had a woman in there. Why you little devil!"

I just shrugged my shoulders, "You got me!"

Edward left to talk with Connor's supervisor and advise him that Connor was being pulled out of the department to help on a special project for him. Edward would tell the supervisor it may take a few weeks, and if he needed to find someone to take Connor's place temporarily, he would approve the extra expense. The supervisor had a big crew working for him, so I figured he would take the news in stride and not bother to ask any questions. Who could really argue with the boss anyway?

As Connor left the basement I felt a wave of relief and excitement. I turned to Spark and picked him up in my arms, "Spark you are going to love having Connor around. Thanks to you he is going to enjoy the most interesting assignment ever! Connor was the friend that convinced me not to retire when Edward said the plant was moving to Toledo. You'll like him

Spark, he's a lot like me, but not as good looking," I said with a laugh.

I set Spark down and continued talking as he wagged his tail and hung on my every word. "Connor didn't have any family left in Cambridge and in the end, I convinced him it would be fun to start over in a new town, or maybe he convinced me. Anyway, I've felt bad I haven't spent much time with him since you arrived Spark, but now he can totally understand why. He will surely never regret his decision to move now."

I giggled inwardly and with almost a skip to my step as I moved back to my desk replaying Connor's reaction in my mind. I knew for sure he wasn't going to be able to rest when he got home. His mind must be racing with the vision of seeing our magnificent creature!

"I'll bet when he gets safely inside his house he'll let out the big scream he couldn't find in his throat earlier. It won't be a scream of fright, but one of exuberant joy!" I said chuckling to Spark as I got back down to work.

In no time, Connor returned his new office to find me working on some sketches at my desk. Spark was curled up on the floor next to me. It looked like a normal scene, well, except for the fact that Spark was a dragon and not a dog. I looked up and smiled, "Connor, I didn't expect you for a while yet. Can't stay away, huh? I don't blame you. Spark has a way of doing that to a fellow."

Connor looked relieved to see that I seemed to understand so well. After all, I was in Connor's position not so long ago. Connor walked slowly over to Spark and Spark looked up and moved his tail back and forth before closing his eyes again. I explained that Spark slept restfully most nights, and nothing usually woke him up once he laid down for the night. Connor wondered why we really needed him here then. I assured him that his presence was welcome and necessary.

Life with a dragon is uncharted territory and we didn't want to take any unnecessary chances. I was feeling pleased with my decision as I saw Spark's reaction and acceptance of Connor. Someone to help and confide in was going to make my life much less stressful. As I watched Connor get settled in, I felt I could relax a little, more than I had done in a long time.

Connor's expression had me laughing as he said, "You gave me an impossible task friend! Oh, here's a dragon, yes they are real. Now go home and get some sleep! You dang fool!"

Of course I knew Connor would find that task impossible. Every time he closed his eyes his mind would go back to an image of Spark and then his heart started beating so fast.

"By 9:00 p.m. I totally gave up and got up out of bed. I splashed some water on my face, grabbed my bag and headed back here. The light rain sprinkles didn't even spoil my mood, I don't know how anything could ruin this day," he said looking at Spark.

"Did anyone stop you when you walked through the plant?"

"No. The night shift isn't used to seeing me, but I know most of those guys. I just nodded briefly and walked purposefully towards the stairs. They're all busy with their own work to say much tonight. As I got closer to the door of your office though, I slowed down for a minute and took a quick look around to make sure nobody had followed me. I wasn't exactly nervous as I stood before the door, but as I gripped the handle I felt this strange feeling like this was the start of a new chapter in my life and a very, very special one. Thanks Red."

"Oh, I almost forgot. I hope you're hungry," Connor said to me as he walked over to the large box he had carried in. Connor pulled out a plate that was brimming with chicken, potatoes and gravy and carrots.

"Wow! That looks wonderful Connor. Did you cook that yourself? We are going to get along here just great if this is what I can expect from you!" I said happily as I walked over to the small table where Connor placed the meal.

"Yes, I still love to cook. Although I haven't really had anyone to cook for since my wife passed away. I surely couldn't sleep, as you suggested, so I had to do something." Connor said smiling to see how I much I appreciated the home cooked meal. "I even brought a little extra gravy and the bones in case Spark could have them."

"I don't see why not. Thank you, Connor." I said as I gulped down my first bite.

I didn't care for cooking and since my wife Louise passed away my meals had been less than desirable. My dinners lately consisted of a can of soup or scrambled eggs. That was about as fancy as I got on meal preparation anymore. My wife had been a wonderful cook and often made huge meals that could have fed an army. If any neighbors were walking by or loitering outside our home around dinner time, she would yell out to them to come in and eat. Nobody went hungry with her around!

As I enjoyed the meal I filled Connor in the happenings of the day. Connor had so many questions I didn't know where to start. He listened intently to every word I uttered. I could tell he was trying to commit everything to memory. He was doing his best to prove that I had made the right choice in picking him for this assignment.

"Red, look at my arm. I'm a little bruised up thanks to you. I pinched myself a couple times when I walked home as I still couldn't believe the good fortune I had in landing this amazing opportunity! I bet you're glad I talked you into coming here, eh?"

I smiled at that. I was just so glad to have someone, finally that I could talk to about this secret. I spoke to Edward about it of course, but it was different because Edward was my boss. He gave me the assignment and then kind of left it up to me to manage. The chance to have a colleague here to confide in and share this adventure everyday was just what I needed.

I was determined to keep one experiment to myself at least for now. I wasn't ready to reveal my late night flying sessions to anyone yet. Sometimes a guy has to have a few secrets for just himself.

Chapter 34

"Home at last!" I yelled as I unlocked the door to my house and stepped inside. As I walked home I realized how excited I was just to sleep in my own bed. This was a luxury I had taken for granted, until I started living at the factory the past few months. I was determined to get my normal life back. However, being the keeper of a dragon, *normal* was a relative term. I plopped down on my sofa and stretched out my arms and legs. It felt so good to relax and enjoy the sound of nothing. No machines humming, no banging, no clanging, just silence. Connor was ready to handle Spark for a few hours was my last thought before I drifted to sleep.

I must have really needed that I thought when I awoke to find I must have dozed off for a couple hours. I still felt a little groggy, but I slouched up to a sitting position and studied the room as I rubbed the crust from my eyes. My gaze went right to the kitchen and I realized I was famished. When was the last time I ate here?

From the looks of the fridge it must have been a while ago. The milk was rancid and the vegetables were shriveled and unappealing. I wandered over to check the inventory in the cupboards. I started to ask Spark if he wanted a snack and stopped myself in mid-sentence.

This was the first time in a while that I was alone this long in the house. It was a strange feeling and I didn't like it. My life sure has changed over the past year. I undoubtedly had Edward to thank for most of it. I had a new house, new surroundings in a new town, and a new best friend named Spark because of him.

I was especially thankful to Spark who filled the hole in my life. I couldn't imagine my life without him now. If only I could confide this secret to my son. He'd be on the first train to Toledo if he knew about Spark. No, I knew it was simply too dangerous to tell him, and besides I was sworn to secrecy with Edward and now Connor. "Someday son, you will know about my work with Spark." I said looking at his picture on the wall.

"I dare say if my dad tried to tell me something this outrageous I would have thought he had lost his mind," I said continuing on my conversation to a picture that didn't respond.

I picked up the most recent letter I had from Robert and re-read it. Robert was enjoying school and wrote that his studies were satisfactory. Robert wasn't sure yet if he was going to take a break from school over the summer. He wanted to finish up school as soon as he could and was considering taking a couple classes to get ahead. He was expecting to have time to visit me in my new town, but wasn't making any promises on the timing yet.

Secretly I still hoped Robert would come and join me in Toledo when he finished school, but I kept that wish to myself. I didn't want Robert to come here just because he felt guilty or sorry for me. If I was truly honest with myself I wanted my full dream to come true. That would include Robert at my side at the factory. Father and Son ruling the dragon!

Someday someone was going to have to take over as Spark's caregiver. Connor and I aren't spring chickens anymore, I had to admit. If possible I'd prefer to keep this new tradition in the family. What a splendid family business to hand down, I thought wistfully. All the information I had found about dragons said they lived for hundreds of years, so this wasn't a far-fetched idea. Somebody would have to care for him so why not my future relatives?

I found myself deep in thought about the possibility of a Wynston dynasty as I heated up an old can of soup. I was always a simple man. I worked hard all my life and did the best I could for my family. Although we didn't have vast wealth, we had each other and our faith and happiness. Our small family of three had many great years together enjoying the simple things in life. There wasn't anything more I really wished for in my life, except more time with Louise.

Louise's early passing was a devastating loss, but I had now come to terms with it. I was grateful for the many years we had together and the wonderful son she gave me. I cherished her memory and the love we shared that created our son. Robert was very much like his mother. His looks favored her side of the family. His gentle manner and caring spirit was the embodiment of his mother. I took comfort in that and was fiercely proud of the way he turned out.

My mind wandered back to Spark. What if Edward had found Spark years earlier and brought him back to the Cambridge factory? It would have been more difficult, if not totally, impossible, to keep him hidden there, I figured. I may not have been selected to be the caretaker, especially if my wife and son were still at home. I certainly would not have been able to bring Spark home and treat him like a pet those first few months. I couldn't have taken a chance of endangering my son or wife. I knew now that Spark wasn't dangerous, but I didn't know that when I first met him. Plus our old factory was situated in the big business district with more congestion. The smaller size of that factory would have made it even more challenging to hide Spark. I guess everything worked out for the best in its own way I supposed.

Although I knew Spark was safe with Connor, I found myself missing Spark. I had barely left his side for months. I was anxious to get back to him but I didn't want Connor to think I didn't trust him. Spark can be a handful sometimes but I was sure Connor could manage him. I was actually relieved to have Connor on the team now and I knew that he would be a real asset to our project.

Connor was a pretty crafty guy and was known as "The Fixer" around the factory. He didn't have any fancy degrees or much schooling either, but if any machine was broken, like me, he could be counted on to fix it. When we lived in Cambridge, he would often tell me how he couldn't resist poking around in the garbage cans around town. If he found something that he thought could be fixed he would lug it home. We had this trait in common. He did this to the dismay of his wife. She did not appreciate the "junk" that would be cluttering up the yard. He didn't see it that way. He thought people were too quick to throw things away that with a little tweaking could be put back to a useful life. I could certainly relate to that. He enjoyed tinkering with machines as much as I did and I was confident he could make something that would help Spark with our work.

I awoke the next morning feeling refreshed. As I rolled out of my comfy bed I wondered how Connor faired on his first night. I'd find out soon enough I figured. First I needed to clean myself up and take a few minutes to pick up around the house too. I wasn't here long enough to make too much of a mess but I had been neglecting my chores for several weeks and I could see dust had accumulated everywhere. I grabbed a cloth and cleared away the dust and dismantled the cobwebs from the ceiling corners. That's well enough I thought, I'm ready to get back to the fun work.

As I headed out the door I bumped into my neighbor Herman. "Well, Red, great to see you. Where have you been? I never see you at home or at the plant anymore. I was starting to wonder if you headed back to Cambridge. I know two fellows who left day before yesterday. They couldn't take it here anymore and went home to Cambridge, can you believe it?" Herman said shaking his head.

"That's too bad, but don't worry about me. I really like it here. I don't have any reason to go back, but I have plenty of reasons to stay here."

"Wow, you sound so enthused, what has you so happy about this place?" Herman inquired.

If I could only tell him I thought to myself and then responded, "It's a great place to live, I'm just glad to leave the sadness behind in Cambridge, you know what I mean?"

Herman, sensing what I meant, shook his head sympathetically.

"Well, I'm glad this place is treating you so well. Maybe I'll see you around the plant later. Good day, Red."

"Sounds like a plan, see you later," I replied knowing it was more likely I would *not* be seeing him at the plant if I could help it. Now that I had moved down to the basement level, I remained there most of the day and had minimal contact with the others. If I kept this up, most of them would forget all about me. At this point I wouldn't mind that one bit. It would just make it easier to keep the secret if I didn't have to talk with my old friends and risk letting something slip out about my current assignment.

Chapter 35

Our most important asset, which was our people, was at times a liability. Some of the original Cambridge employees were homesick and left for home. Others were enticed away by competitors. There were many glasshouses operating around the country and skilled workers were in high demand and had several options. Fortunately, there were eager Toledoans happy to take their place and learn the glassmaking business. The new associates' inexperience caused some slowdowns in production now and then. Nevertheless, we were grateful that they worked hard to learn the nuances of the business.

Edward stopped in my office late one day. He informed me he was leaving on another trip and he wanted to check in before he left. "How are you doing Spark?" Edward asked as he walked in and was greeted pleasantly by Spark.

Spark seemed to sense that Edward was an important man and always tried to get his full attention whenever he was around. Spark seemed to enjoy the praise he got when he was able to show off the new commands he had learned. Edward always made such a fuss over Spark and he responded favorably.

"Where are you off to this time?" I asked.

"I'm going back down to Wheeling to see a few artists. Maybe I'll entice a couple to follow me back up here. We are losing a few too many good men. You probably heard that Jones and Richards headed back to Cambridge too? The factories down south have some very talented artists, and Michael gave me a list of people to seek out," Edward said reassuringly.

I could hear the stress in Edward's voice and I didn't like it. Edward looked troubled but tried to cover it up. I assured Edward that I had no intentions of leaving. Then I proceeded to fill him in on the progress I was making on our projects. I didn't want Edward leaving town feeling that he was going to return to find everyone had fled back to Cambridge.

Michael Owens was definitely a lucky catch for our company. He made a big impact on the workforce in such a short time. I appreciated that he was also a tinkerer like me and very adept at fixing machines too. I would have loved to pick his brain on a couple projects I was working on, but I refrained. Michael was a very smart man and I couldn't take the chance that he would catch onto what I was doing, specifically with Spark. No, it was better for me to keep a safe distance from Michael.

Michael had enough on his plate anyway. I could see how Edward admired him and the quick bond of trust the two men forged. I wondered if Edward would confide in him about Project Ignite at some point. It wasn't my concern for now.

Connor and I moved ahead together with the training and testing phase as planned. We were slowly making progress on the amount of energy Spark was able to supply for the small furnace. We continued to test various ways of expanding supply levels. One of the challenges we faced was how to implement the special fuel slowly so as not to arouse suspicion with the furnace engineers. If it was introduced all at once and the engineers noticed no gas was being pulled from the tanks they would start investigating and could discover the truth.

We had to provide the fuel in small amounts for now so we didn't arouse suspicion. One factor that was going in our favor, although it wasn't optimal, was the fact that the more experienced engineers were leaving and being replaced by less experienced workers who would be easier to trick. If the new guys didn't realize how much gas was needed in the first place they wouldn't know the difference. That's what we were counting on anyway.

Chapter 36

We had a few close calls to handle during the early days of Project Ignite. The first time was the night Connor went against my rules and took Spark out for a walk around the yard at midnight alone. It was a night of a full moon and its beam lit up the sky. Connor wasn't planning to go far, but as he started running and chasing Spark he got a little further from the factory than he intended. When he heard an unfamiliar voice, he froze in place. Then he heard another voice. It sounded like two young boys he said.

Connor overheard the taller one say excitedly, "Jimmy did you see it? I told you, I'm not lying, it was right over there by the pond. Don't tell me you didn't see that thing, with the wings? It looked like a dragon!"

The boy Jimmy said, "Tommy, Mom said there's no such thing and you need to stop lying about it."

"C'mon Jimmy, don't get all scared, I'm going to find it and grab it and take it home. Then mom will know I wasn't lying," the boy Tommy said raising his voice as he held one hand high in the air triumphantly.

Connor held tighter to his grip on Spark's leash. He signaled to Spark to stay quiet and tugged him back further behind the tree. The boys must have snuck over here before if they caught a glimpse of Spark. Connor had to think quickly so as not to be discovered. He lifted his head up, opened his mouth and howled at the moon like a wolf. He didn't know he still had that in him he said laughing to me later about it. It was one of the calls he had used with his brothers growing up when they played in the woods and got separated.

The howl seemed to do the trick because he heard the smaller boy Jimmy yell, "Aaaah! Wolf!" and just started running.

The taller boy, trying to look brave, but with his voice a little shaky said, "Fine Jimmy, I'll leave now, but I'm coming back later without you and you better not tell Mom I brought you out here or I'm gonna kill you!"

Connor waited anxiously until it was clear they were gone. Connor and Spark then emerged from behind the tree and quickly proceeded back to the factory. Connor was relieved that the boys didn't come face to face with Spark. That would have been disastrous. He had a few hours to think about how he was going to relay this event to me. He also vowed to do a full perimeter check in the morning. He wanted to find out exactly how those kids got into the yard. As he thought more about them, Jimmy and Tommy, he realized they might be Jim Thorne's boys.

Jim lived a few houses down from us on Ash Street and had two young boys. He had not seen much of Jim since they moved here. Would Jim believe the boys if they came running home with a tall tale about a dragon? Most likely not. Most parents wouldn't take that story too seriously, he hoped.

Still Connor was worried. How much of Spark had the boys really seen? Even if Tommy had just seen a glimpse of a creature with wings what else could he mistake it for, Connor wondered? A duck or goose would be too small if he got a good look at the wing span. There were some big cranes that had a decent wing span. Maybe that explanation would work on Jim. It should be enough, along with the fact that one brother was trying to scare the other.

Connor figured he could persuade Jim with some stories about how his older two brothers were always trying to frighten him when he was younger. He was always trying to keep up with them and they didn't always want their little brother tagging along. They would pretend they didn't hear him running after them and yelling at them to slow down so he could catch up. Sometimes they would run up ahead and jump out him as he turned a corner. Other times they would start telling wild stories about the monsters that lived in the woods trying to scare him into turning back and going home.

Those childish pranks worked for a while, until Connor was old enough not to believe in monsters anymore. He figured those boys tonight were still in the stage where they could convince each other that monsters might possibly exist. And I guess if you consider a dragon a monster, they would be right.

Connor prayed the boys would resist the urge to talk. After all, they had trespassed in an area that was dangerous and off limits to them. Surely they were warned by their parents to stay away. Then he remembered our first official day in town and how Tommy Thorne had been so inquisitive and asking Edward about the yard. He hoped this night cured his curiosity.

Connor wasn't looking forward to telling me about the incident. However, he felt a little more relaxed about it after taking time to think through options of how to react and respond to the little episode. When I stepped in the office that night, he looked at me and immediately started his confession. I didn't know I could have such an effect on him.

"What were you doing out there alone with him, Connor? I told you not to go out that far when I'm not here," I said looking disappointed.

Connor admitted he was a little careless and wouldn't do it again. I sat down and put my hands over my face. I tilted my head down and said, "It's okay, it's okay, we'll figure this out. It's not so bad. Tell me again, how much do you really think the boys saw?"

"The younger boy didn't see anything, I'm pretty sure about that. You should have seen him run for the hills when he heard the wolf noise I made. And if his Mom knew he had snuck out of the house and trespassed near the factory she'd have his head. I don't think we need to worry about him telling anybody what he did. The older boy, Tommy, would likely get quite a lashing I suppose, if his father found out he had coerced his little brother out the home at midnight to go traipsing in the woods. So if we start to hear any rumblings about creatures we can start talking up the crane angle."

Then Connor proceeded to tell me how we could warn others about a large crane on the property if necessary. "I suppose you're right," I said, and then continued, "Let's keep a listen for any stories about a winged creature. Otherwise we'll just keep this between the two of us. There is no sense worrying Edward over what may turn out to be nothing."

Connor looked so relieved I felt this way. I knew he didn't want to do anything to jeopardize how Edward would feel about him. I didn't want to lose my fellow conspirator either.

"I'll make the rounds today before I leave work. I'll see what the current chatter is about and confirm it isn't anything close to the events of last night."

"That'll be fine Connor. I'm not too worried anymore. Make sure you go home and get some rest and put it out of your mind. Everything will be fine. I'll walk with you. I need to pick up a couple parts in the mold shop," I pretended so I could follow him and judge the reactions myself. This episode wasn't as bad as me flying on Spark all those times, I thought, but didn't dare confess that to Connor.

Connor and I went directly to the mold shop. I walked over to the shelves containing spare parts and I heard Jim Thorne yell, "Hey Connor, how's it going? I haven't seen you around in a while. What have you been up to?" Connor smiled and told him he was sorry he hadn't talked with him lately.

Jim then said happily, "Oh my kids are really enjoying Toledo. They are making friends and like their teachers, although they complain they get too much homework!"

"I can't blame them, I never cared much for homework either." Connor said, looking relieved to be talking about school and not monsters in our backyard!

Connor stopped to talk with a few other old friends as we worked our way to the front door that day. To his great relief there was no wild talk, no crazy rumors circulating as far we could tell. I could see that he felt much better and hoped this incident was behind him. There was just one more thing he insisted on doing before he left for the day.

"I'm going to journey out to the backyard before I leave. I want to take a walk about and thoroughly check the entire yard. I'll find out how those boys got in and fix it. No more surprise visitors if I have any say in the matter."

I nodded in agreement and left him. I needed to get back to Spark.

Chapter 37

Edward was depending more and more on Spark every month. Spark was proving to be a great contributor to the running of the factory and keeping our costs down.

Edward confided, "I don't know what would happen to this business if it wasn't for Spark's help."

"From everything I've learned so far, it seems that dragons live for many, many years, so you're in luck," I said supportively.

"But what if Spark doesn't live as long as promised? I've come to depend on all the work you've done with him. I've calculated what it would cost for the extra fuel and I don't like the result. We're just starting to recover from the move to Toledo. Spark's valuable contributions are having a healthy impact to the bottom line."

It would definitely be a tragedy to lose Spark, Edward admitted to me. Edward normally would search for ways to insure big potential and unknown risks to his business. However, he couldn't exactly go and take out an insurance policy on the loss of business due to this key employee's untimely demise! Nor could he insure him for loss due to a kidnapping, or rather a dragon-napping. Spark's importance to the business would have to remain a trade secret. We would have to deal with the loss if and when it happened.

"The best way to mitigate the risk would be to have another dragon. A second dragon would also provide companionship to Spark," I offered hopefully.

"I wish! If only I could get in touch with Mr. Lee. Unfortunately, he's been unreachable ever since our transaction. All my letters have gone unanswered and the last time I was in Europe I tried to stop in to see him, but his shop was all boarded up. None of the neighbors knew what happened to him. I just hope he's safe and that those men haven't not done him any harm," Edward said distractedly.

"What men?" I asked but knew I'd get no answer. Edward had barely told me any details about his acquisition of Spark. He mentioned to me briefly that one night that he was worried someone had followed him from Mr. Lee's store, and that he encountered a couple of strange men on the ship home that had him paranoid and a little fearful about Spark being snatched away from him.

Edward was going to have to give up on looking for Mr. Lee for now. He had other important affairs to focus on now. Ed was going to be married soon. I always believed from the first day we met Florence that he was going to marry her. I knew Edward would be glad to give up the bachelorhood lifestyle he had been living for way too long.

"Have you thought about telling Florence about Spark yet?"

Edward just brushed my words aside. "Are you mad? No sir, what if she changed her mind and didn't want to marry me?

What if she wanted me to expose the secret to the world? No, I told you, I already decided I can't take a chance on losing Florence or Spark. They are both so important to me. Red, I promise I will tell her someday, just not yet."

I couldn't believe the day finally arrived. It was June 25, 1890. I'd known Edward almost his whole life and to see him finally getting married made me beam with pride. The only thing that would have made Edward happier would be to have his parents here. Edward's father would have been so enamored with Florence. But thankfully his sisters were here.

I was honored to stand as Edward's best man. A role I didn't take lightly. I felt like I was a big brother to Edward and now I was gaining a wonderful little sister.

Florence had spent untold hours putting together a lovely wedding with her parents help. I knew that as long as Edward showed up at the event along with the minister she would be happy, even if everything else went wrong. There really was no reason for her to panic. Edward had been looking forward to this day just as much. And I knew Edward's sister, Sarah, was overjoyed with the match and would have dragged him here if she had to.

The couple had originally planned to wed at the Scott family's church, First Congregational Church on Collingwood Avenue, but the lovely park like setting at her father's home on Monroe Street called to her. The house was nestled among acres of trees in Toledo's West End. Some of the most prominent families in town lived in the neighborhood.

I was overwhelmed with all the people there ahead of me and seated around the room. I felt a little out of place at first. I never would have expected to be a part of such a grand event when I was a young lad. The social event of the season, as everyone lovingly called it, certainly lived up to its name. I knew how many people they had invited, but it was still remarkable to see the place practically filled to capacity. Since the Scotts had lived in town so long and Maurice had so many business contacts it seemed as if the whole town was here.

People teased Edward and asked if he was nervous or had second thoughts. I knew he wasn't backing out of this deal. Edward looked distracted as he half-listened while looking around anxious to get a glimpse of Florence. Edward couldn't wait to see Florence. She wouldn't even hint at what her dress looked like except that it was white. He would have to wait a little while longer to view it.

In the meantime, he turned to greet his groomsman, William, who was his brother-in-law. "Don't you look dashing," Edward stated, "I'm sure Alice was happy to see you all decked out for a change."

William replied, "Possibly, but I think she was more excited about being a bridesmaid. She just adores Florence and is glad to see that you are finally settling down, brother."

"I don't know why she was so worried, I'm only 36 years young!" Edward laughed.

"I think this day was part of Sarah's motive for coming to Toledo. She noticed the way you talked about Florence after your first trip here and she was determined to assist in getting you two together."

"Well, I don't think she was the only one. We seemed to have many people on both sides trying to play cupid," Edward quipped.

"That just shows how much they care about you and want to see you happy. You have a tendency to get so bogged down in your work you don't take time for fun," William lectured him, imitating his wife's voice which made Edward smile.

"That's not true, I just enjoy my work so much and I do have a lot of fun when I am meeting people and interacting with my employees," Edward retorted.

I came across Sarah in the hall and she told me the girls were in the back room getting ready. "Florence looks beautiful but Hattie keeps fussing with her hair, even though there isn't a strand out of place. I pulled it up in a bun and weaved baby's breath and mini red roses around it that-"

Sarah left me and went running over to Edward as he was approaching the room that held his bride. She quickly stepped in front of the door while chastising him that he couldn't see Florence yet. "Calm down, be patient, no peeking!"

Edward put his hands over his eyes and said to Sarah, "I'm not here to peek, I just want to give this to Florence."

"I'll take it to her, just move back!" Sarah said as she stepped inside with the little box in her hand. Edward stood near the door in anticipation as he heard the girls giggle as she opened the box. Florence squealed with delight discovering a pretty pair of earrings that were shaped like champagne flutes, and made of glass.

Edward smiled as he heard her read the card which said, "Here's your something new. They sparkle in the light just like you."

Sarah came out of the room and reported to her brother that he made his bride cry. "She's in there messing up her make-up! She teared right up as she held the earrings in her hand and recalled the champagne flute that held her engagement ring."

"How clever and thoughtful you are big brother," Sarah said reporting that all the ladies admired the one of a kind gift.

"I'm just glad she liked them. This is just the beginning of many surprises for my new wife," Edward said and looked at me with a sly smile.

"Gentlemen, we are about ready to start, please take your places. No getting out of this now," the minister advised, half joking as he patted Edward on the shoulder.

Edward and I looked toward the back of the yard in great anticipation when the music started and we saw Florence and her father appear. As the bride stepped closer, we all saw how extraordinary she looked and how he beamed with pride. I just knew he had made the right decision. I hope he knows he is the luckiest man on the Earth, I thought.

The ceremony left everyone with misty eyes of joy. After the newlyweds kissed, I watched as they were greeted by a line of well-wishers that seemed to go on forever. Everyone wanted to acknowledge the Libbey's and compliment Florence on her exquisite dress. It sparkled so brilliantly in the sunlight. Edward agreed heartily that he had never seen a more beautiful bride. She truly was a vision. Her look would surely be imprinted on his heart forever. If only the new *Glass Queen* had a dress made of glass I thought and then laughed at that absurd idea.

Edward pulled me aside later that evening and said as he looked at Florence coming down the aisle holding her bouquet of red roses he was struck with an idea. "I'm going to create a line of glasses with a rose etched on the side and call them Florence Rose. Don't say anything. I want to keep this a surprise and show her when it is done."

"You know I can keep a secret," I said nodding.

"I try not to mix business with pleasure normally, but in this case I don't think she will mind. Can you keep Florence busy for a few minutes? I need to grab some paper and sketch out this design while it is fresh in my mind," Edward said as he sauntered away.

I smiled as I looked around at all the happy people enjoying the day. The weather really cooperated for them. It was a sunny, pleasant, 70 degree day. My mind wandered to Spark. Too bad he couldn't be here to enjoy this day. Someday I hope to share him with more people I thought wistfully. My daydream was interrupted by the photographer calling the wedding party to gather together for a picture. I'd love to have a photograph of Spark I thought as I smiled for the camera.

The festivities went well into the night with everyone laughing and dancing and having a grand time. Around midnight Edward and Florence said their farewells. I would see them in the morning before they left for their honeymoon.

The honeymooners were going on a short trip to Edward's hometown of Boston with a stop in New York City along the way. They were hoping to take a longer trip to Europe later in the year. Edward wanted to show his new bride off in Europe. He was also anxious to track down Mr. Lee. I knew he was hoping to make a second purchase from him soon.

I helped escort the new couple to the train station bright and early the next morning. After a wonderful night, they were both very much looking forward to more time alone. Florence only hoped that Edward would refrain from trying to conduct business on their honeymoon.

"I feel a little guilty leaving my business for so many days but I know it is in good hands with you and Michael," Edward said.

"Yes, we'll keep it running smooth. Don't worry about a thing. And when you return your architect should be ready with new drawings of your house plans."

"Florence doesn't care too much about the exterior design phase, she's leaving that part up to me. She is really looking forward to the interior decorating part. Luckily we have similar tastes so I don't expect many disagreements on style. She just hopes the house won't overflow with too many pieces of glass. But can you really have too many exquisite glass pieces?"

"I know I'll have to fight for his attention when we get back in town, but I at least want his full attention for our honeymoon."

"Don't fret my dear, I have every intention of keeping this a pleasure vacation," he said convincingly and then turned to me. "Actually I heard some rumors that Mr. Lee may be in New York now. If I'm able to find my old acquaintance, I would love to see if he has any other rare souvenirs to buy."

"I can't blame you there," I said knowing that except for this one slip up, he would be true in his promise to be one hundred percent devoted to Florence on the honeymoon.

Chapter 38

"Edward, did you see the news about the labor strike at Corning?" I said rushing into Edward's office one morning.

I was sure if Edward hadn't seen the news, he would want to know this right away. The article said that a strike at Corning was causing problems for Thomas Edison. It was 1891 and orders for his light bulbs were growing by the day but production was ground to a halt by the slowdown in New York. Edison must have been worried about upsetting his customers until he came upon a solution.

As Edward and I were discussing the matter, I could see his mind churning with ideas. He didn't have to remind me that our company had made some of the early light bulb prototypes and even sold the bulbs for a while. However, Edward was more interested in making tabletop glass products and didn't want to spend precious time producing light bulbs, and eventually halted production.

Times being what they were for Edison, he must have reviewed all his options and figured it was worth a shot to approach Edward. The next thing we heard was the phone ring and Edward's secretary waving frantically towards us.

"Oh, Mr. Edison, yes, I think Mr. Libbey may remember you," she said trying to contain her composure, "Please hold one moment sir."

It must be nice to get that kind of reaction, and I'm sure Tom never tired of it, I thought to myself. I could see the pleasure Edward felt to hear that Mr. Edison had called him. He waited a moment before answering the call, not wanting to appear too anxious or not so busy that he could just rush to the phone.

A few moments later Edward picked up the line, "Tom, I'm sorry to keep you waiting. I was down the hall. How have you been?" He said while smiling at us and waving to his secretary and motioning for a pen and paper.

"Yes, I'm sorry to hear of the current labor strikes going on in New York. I'm sure this must be cutting into your orders." I watched as Edward shook his head and scribbled something down on the paper. Finally he said, "Business is going very well for us. However, we may have some room in our production schedule to produce some bulbs for you. Let's get together and see what we can do."

Edward, never one to turn away the prospect of new business, looked ecstatic about the new opportunity. He put down the phone and told us excitedly that Mr. Edison was coming to town on the next train. This unexpected turn of events brightened Edward's mood.

I think Edward always regretted his decision to stop making light bulbs. Lights were an undeniable "must have" in every home now. Edison had created a huge industry so the strike at the plant was devastating to his business. If he lost out on critical business deals it could cripple the company's sales for several years I imagined.

"This is great news Red. Westinghouse has been pulling out every maneuver to take market share from Edison, so this partnership with me is critical."

Edward and I went out to the production floor and pulled the plant foreman aside. After a quick discussion, we learned it wasn't looking good to add in another product to the schedule. We were already behind on our own orders to a big retailer.

As we walked back to Edward's office and thought over what to do to secure the Edison business, I reluctantly threw another problem his way. "Mike is starting to get suspicious," I confided as I closed the office door.

"What exactly do you think he knows about?" Edward asked.

"Well, for the past couple years he's been focused on the workforce, increasing production and developing his inventions, but now he's restless and starting to inquire about what exactly we are doing down in the basement. He caught me off guard one day as I was heading to my office and tried to follow me in asking to see my lab. I wasn't sure if Spark was out, so I couldn't let him enter and I made up some excuse about being late for a meeting with you and he backed off. But now that he is curious, I have a feeling he'll be back soon," I said with a look of deep concern on my face.

"Yes, I understand your distress. Thanks for letting me know. I wondered if Mike was getting suspicious of something because he's been asking me for a lot of information about energy costs. Luckily he wasn't here before Spark so the numbers he has seen so far all include Spark's helpful contributions. Confidentially, I've been working on some ideas which would get Mike out of this location, but I'm not quite ready to move forward with those plans just yet. Truly, this request from Edison couldn't have come at a better time. I could assign this project to Mike. Let's go have a talk with him. I've got a plan."

As we walked to Mike's area Edward told me about his back-up plan. He had already been discussing with Mike the possibility of expanding out to another site. To my surprise, he advised me that just a few months back the two of them had scoped out a closed facility in Findlay, Ohio. Several glasshouses that set up shop in the town were closing down. Findlay was one of the towns that offered free gas a couple years ago to entice new business, but now as the gas wells went empty, the companies found they weren't profitable enough to stay in business.

We found Mike Owens in his office and filled him in on the conversation with Edison. After telling him our foreman didn't think we had room in their schedule for added production Edward brought up his next idea, "What about that old factory in Findlay? I think we could set up a small operation down there. What do you think?"

Mike nodded agreeably that it was a possibility and then replied, "I'd like to look it over again. Maybe we can get down there this afternoon? I know some of the men would jump at the chance for some overtime."

Edward asked Mike his thoughts about running the operation, to which Mike quickly exclaimed, "I'd be honored to run the production crew in Findlay."

Edward looked relieved as he glanced at me. I had no doubt Mike would agree to it. He would have to get the line up and running quickly to keep Edison happy Edward warned him. Further he would have to manage a team from Toledo along with the New York workers that were coming in from Corning to help. Mike was always up for a new challenge and this fit the bill.

(These were busy and exciting times for Mike. Mike and Edward were negotiating the final details of their new venture. Mike invented, and perfected after several trials, an automatic bottle making machine. The machine made it possible to make thousands of glasses a day more than anyone could now. I knew the advent of the bottle in the market place would provide a huge convenience for food storage. Edward decided he wanted the bottle production set up as a separate business. Mike would be running it day to day. In fact, Edward insisted that it be named the Owens Bottle Company. (This would later become Owens-Illinois). Mike had come a long way and worked hard and must have certainly been glad he had pressed Edward to hire him. It was a partnership that benefited both men. Their new business marked another milestone in solidifying Toledo as the Glass City).

"Mike, I appreciate your enthusiasm of taking on the light bulb operation. You know I'm still working out the financing details of the new venture you proposed. I will continue working on that matter while you are away. When the strike in New York is over and we get back to normal operations, we'll talk more about it."

"How quickly can you get the plant running?" I asked Mike.

"Well, Red, it depends how good of shape the furnace is in and how fast we can get raw materials down there. I'll look into the logistics before we leave and see if we have enough in our inventory that we can use until our next shipment," Mike responded.

"I'll set up the travel arrangements and let you know what time we can leave," Edward said.

The issue that caused Tom to call Edward was advantageous on two fronts. First, more business was always welcome and secondly, it would get Mike away from Toledo at least for a short time, I hoped. This new opportunity would cause Mike to drop the subject of the basement project. Who knew Tom's problem could solve my problem too?

The facility checked out to Edward's liking. Edward worked out the details with Mike to get the new operation up and running. When Mike informed the Toledo staff of the opportunity to work in Findlay we were all pleased with the response. Luckily enough of the men jumped at the chance. We expected to be completely operational within no time. Corning was sending some of their staff down to help as well. Tom was relieved to have a supplier for his bulbs. Who knew how long the strike would last? Labor negotiations were always very unpredictable. I was just glad to have Mike out of my business for a while.

Now that the light bulb project was underway Edward soon turned his attentions to his next dream.

Chapter 39

"Chicago won! We're going to put on a show for the world Red!" Edward exclaimed as he walked into my office that morning. Edward practically skipped over to Spark and patted him on the head.

As he turned to me I said, "Sir, what has gotten in to you today? What are you so happy about? What does this have to do with Chicago?"

"Red, it has just been announced that the World's Fair is going to be in Chicago. I've just decided that we are going to be there too."

"What do you mean, as visitors?" I asked confused.

"No, no, we are going to be there showing our products on the world stage. Just think, people from all around the country, no all over the world, are going to be there. This is going to be the biggest gathering the world has ever seen! The organizers are going to go all out to show off how far America has progressed and prospered in just 400 years since Columbus discovered it. I imagine there will be crowds of thousands, maybe millions of people. Chicago is only a few hundred miles from here and we will be there, Red."

"That sounds wonderful, but how? I know you've been struggling to get this place running at full capacity and the costs have gone way over budget. How will you get the board to agree?" I asked.

"You leave that to me Red, but somehow we will be there, I guarantee it. You know I always keep my promises Red," Edward said seriously.

"Yes that is true sir, I would never doubt you," I said as staring at Edward's serious face. I laughed to myself as Edward went down the hall, practically bouncing with joy.

When Edward later suggested that he wanted to take Spark to Chicago though, I nearly flipped out. Have you lost your mind, I wanted to scream. Instead I said calmly, "But how will we get ever get him there unseen and unheard?"

The thought of taking Spark on a trip had me fretting all day. Ever since Edward dropped the news that he wanted to take Spark to Chicago I was a nervous wreck. Was Edward serious about this outlandish idea? I was seriously questioning his judgement. The three of us had been keeping Spark hidden in the basement, except for his jaunts out in the yard (and a few escapades I wouldn't mention out loud), to ensure his safety and secrecy.

Putting Spark on a train and whisking him away to Chicago was crazy enough. But then to think he could be kept hidden among all those people was simply ludicrous. This idea was too foolish. Too many things could go wrong. Spark wasn't the size of a sparrow anymore, he was practically a full size…well I supposed he was reaching full size anyway, and he would be impossible to hide.

When Connor showed up that night I filled him in on the conversation with Edward. "Chicago, really? That sounds wonderful. I've always wanted to go see the glorious city they rebuilt after that horrendous fire a few years back. And to have a chance to tour the World's Fair, that would be terrific!" Connor said enthusiastically.

I couldn't believe his reaction, he simply was thinking about the fun he'd have in Chicago and wasn't listening to any of my concerns about Spark. "Did you hear what I said? Edward wants us to take Spark. He wants us to take a dragon on a train across Ohio, Indiana and up to Chicago, Illinois. Then if that's not impossible enough he wants us to set him up in the booth so he can save on expenses, bloody nuts I tell you," I yelled.

As I spoke those words out loud the thought of it formed pictures in my mind and I couldn't help but laugh in fright. As a laughing attack hit me, I couldn't stop myself. I kept giggling louder and louder and tried to get my words out. I walked over to Spark and started pretending I was a passenger on the train seeing him for the first time. "Oh pardon me sir, is that a, a, a, dragon seated next to you?"

"Oh he seems like a friendly fellow, what's his name? Kids, come meet the dragon riding the train with us to Chicago!"

The two of us were soon howling in laughter. Spark looked up at us curiously but didn't seem to think it was so funny. When the laughter finally subsided Connor said, "Look, he's the boss, and the boss man always get what he wants right? So I say let's go with this. Just think about what a grand adventure this will be? Think about how great it will be to pull the wool over the eyes of millions of people at the fair. Someday they'll write stories about us, we'll be famous. We'll be heroes Red! We are the legendary secret keepers of the magical glass factory! We can do this! Don't worry about a thing!"

Connor said this with such conviction I almost believed him. Well, it would be amazing to pull this off I reckoned. If only someday I could tell this story to my son.

So we jumped full steam ahead and started working extra hours to prepare for the Chicago trip. We figured it was only a matter of time before Edward found the financing and we wanted to be ready. We had to devise a plan to get Spark out of the factory, to the train station, hidden on the train, off the train in Chicago and into the booth without being seen or heard at any point along the way.

It sure seemed we had enough on our minds to work through without adding additional stress. However, another mistake by Connor almost ended the project one night. We had been working long days, trying to do our normal work, taking care of Spark, and planning for the trip. The stress was starting to get to Connor. I could see that Connor needed a rest, so I encouraged him to take the night off. "Connor there isn't much critical going on tonight. I'd like to keep working on my experiments, so why don't you take the night off. I'll stay here with Spark while I wait on my test results." I said encouragingly.

Connor normally would protest and rarely took time off these days, but he surprised me and said, "Thanks Red, I really could use a little fresh air. I think I'll walk home and read a book," Connor said as he grabbed his coat and headed towards the door. "See you later Spark," he whispered as he walked by him.

Connor was looking better already. He really just needed a breather, a chance to get away and relax. I believed he had every intention of sitting at home on the sofa quietly with a cold beer. Apparently that plan was all forgotten as he got closer to the bar. The neighborhood pub was just up the street from the factory and just a block before his house. Normally he walked right by without giving it much of a thought, but tonight it seemed to be calling to him. Well the bar wasn't exactly calling to him but some of the patrons inside of it were.

"Connor, hey Connor, come inside, have a drink with us!" Connor heard someone yelling out the window of the bar as he approached. Connor looked over and recognized Jim Thorne. Jim and Connor worked closely together back in Cambridge. They even lived in the same neighborhood back then. It wasn't surprising that they both found themselves working at the glass factory. It was one of the largest employers in Cambridge when they were younger and many of the kids from their school ended up working there at one time or another. Some even managed to hang in there as long as they did.

"Hey Jim, how are you doing?" Connor asked.

"I'm great, why don't you come inside, I'll buy you a drink and we can catch up. I haven't seen you lately in the breakroom," Jim said as he smiled happily at Connor. Connor was planning to have a beer so why not stop inside and have one there instead of drinking at home alone, he thought to himself.

"Sure, I got time for one drink," Connor said and walked into the bar. Connor hadn't been in the bar since he started working nights. He walked in to find the bar fairly full of people he recognized from work. Some nodded friendly towards him and returned to their conversations. Jim raised his hand to get the attention of the bartender. The bartender came over and took Connor's order.

Jim started off by saying how much he had been working lately. He didn't complain so much, but was just filling Connor in about how busy it was in the packaging department lately. "We've been working a lot of extra hours the past few weeks. Did you know we got a special order for LaSalle's department store? Their order got mixed up with another customer's order and we spent the week packing the Pomona glassware in the wrong boxes. Boy those guys were fuming when we found out! We had to pull back a few pallets full of glassware from the warehouse, pull the glasses out of the boxes and repack them in the right ones. It was so frustrating, but it would have been worse if they were shipped out wrong. The customer would have been furious! Thankfully we got it all fixed up before for the train departed. If we didn't I would probably still be there. I'm still not sure how the mix up occurred, but I'm just glad it's behind us now. After all that, I just needed to have a drink and clear my head," Jim said tapping his beer bottle.

Then Jim started asking Connor questions about what he had been doing lately and how he was adjusting to Toledo. He really wanted to know if Connor was going to leave like some of the other guys had done.

Connor let Jim know that he was very fond of Toledo and had no intentions of leaving. He liked the area and his new house. Jim then confided that he liked the place more than he expected and didn't plan to leave. Jim admitted his wife still wasn't so keen on the place but his boys really liked it.

"I told my wife she has to give it time but she is complaining every day that she wants to go back home. I know she misses her sister and nephews, but she realizes too that we need to stay here for the job. Money doesn't grow on trees I tell her when she starts in about leaving. In time she'll come to like it here as much as I do," Jim said.

Connor agreed that time has a way of helping things. Connor and Jim had a few laughs about the good old days when they were kids and Connor was really glad he stopped at the bar. Just hanging out with Jim reminded him of how much they had been through in their life and the unlikely circumstances that kept them friends after all these years.

At this point Jim was the only one left of the old gang that Connor even knew where to find. Funny how when you're young you figure you'll always be friends and see each other every day. Then you all grow up and suddenly life has a way of spreading everyone apart. People drift so far away that you lose touch and almost forget about how close you were once. Oh no, Connor thought, this beer is starting to make me melancholy.

"I need to shake this off, I don't have time to be sad right now," Connor whispered quietly to himself. Connor looked around the room and heard a few guys arguing about who was telling the biggest whopper. There was a small group around them and they were all having fun laughing and carrying on.

Jim noticed Connor watching them and said, "Hey, that's some of the people from my department. Follow me and I'll introduce you. Connor picked up his beer stein, his favorite one made at our factory. It was dimpled around the outside and had thick sidewalls and a heavy handle.

As they approached the group Connor heard one of them saying something about the Lochness monster.

Connor listened as this guy told about his childhood back in Ireland. He bragged about a day when he and his friends were out playing in the countryside and saw a leprechaun. Of course his story was all nonsense but he told it with such conviction that you almost felt it was real. I guess the drinks everyone had in them probably helped that as well. The evening went on that way with each man trying to out shine the other with their outlandish tales.

Eventually someone spoke up and said, "Hey Connor you haven't told us your story yet."

"Oh that guy couldn't tell a story to save his life," said another and everyone in the place was soon looking and laughing at him.

Well Connor took that as a challenge. He had just enough beer in him to make him feel cocky and boy oh boy did he have a story that would knock their socks off. He would get the last laugh on this group. So with everyone staring at him Connor stood up and began his tale. He told the group how he once came face to face with a monster. It was a legendary monster that nobody believed existed, but he now knew it to be true he said convincingly.

The more the group laughed and hung on his every word, the more animated Connor got. He had them eating out of the palm of his hands. He was really enjoying all the attention his story was getting from the group. As they cajoled him into describing this monster he had encountered, he envisioned Spark and described him, except that he made him bigger and meaner.

"How did you get away?" "Did you kill it?" "What kind of monster was it?" The crowd shouted out.

As the crowd got quieter, leaning in to clearly hear every word Connor uttered, Connor stopped himself. Just as Connor was about to reveal the secret he looked up and noticed the water tower of the factory across the way. The tower had the Libbey name painted on it. Connor stared at that tower and name and thought it was like a warning from Edward. Connor realized he had almost revealed to everyone that dragons were real and there was one living across the street. The men were just staring at him, and he panicked as he remembered his close call with Spark and Jim's boys. He stared at Jim for any inkling that he knew anything about Spark. He felt somewhat relieved that Jim didn't seem to know anything about his kid's adventure. Connor then told the crowd the monster turned out to be a crocodile.

The men all booed as they realized they had been snookered into almost believing another big tale. "Connor that was intense, you really had us going there. Boy, the way were describing the monster I thought you were going to say you saw a dragon!"

More laughter filled the air. Connor looked around and could tell nobody would have believed that ending. But if Jim's boys were here he wondered what they would have had to say. He so much wanted to tell everyone the truth that it really was a dragon, but he was sworn to secrecy. The fact that he almost blew it again, weighed on him and sobered him up instantly. The fact that the fellows were all laughing about the absurdity of a dragon at least made him feel relieved that none of them had any suspicions about Spark.

As the next storyteller began, Connor quietly slipped out of the bar. He cursed at himself all the way home. His close call was enough excitement for him for the night. By the time he reached his house he wanted no part of any more stories so he skipped out on the reading he had planned to do and headed straight for bed.

The only time I came close to spilling the beans about Spark had been when my son came to town for a visit. Robert had originally planned to go to Florida with a group of friends over school break but at the last minute he had a better idea. Robert decided he would take the train to Toledo and surprise me. I was certainly surprised but mostly I was elated. I missed my son so much now that he lived too far away to come home on the weekends. I buried myself in work, especially grateful that I had Project Ignite to help distract me from the loneliness of missing my son.

I had brought some of my work home that afternoon and had it spread out on the kitchen table. I was surprised when I heard a knock at the door. I didn't get many visitors these days. I figured it was one of the neighbor kids as I walked toward the door. I opened the door to find Robert.

"Oh my God, what a sight, do my eyes deceive me? My boy is actually here?" I said excitedly as I grabbed Robert in my arms.

"What are you doing here? Why didn't you tell me you were coming? I would have picked you up at the train station, you know? How long can you stay?" I peppered him with questions and gave Robert no chance of responding.

I grabbed Robert's bag from the porch and as I brought it in, I suddenly panicked. I realized I had papers out on the table about Spark along with a couple of drawings. I noticed Robert walking towards the kitchen, just curiously looking around at the house he had only heard about in letters but had never seen. Robert didn't understand my reaction as I practically pushed him aside and entered the kitchen first. I began furiously scooping up the papers and putting them in a folder.

I realized I was acting rudely and then tried to recover by saying, "Sorry son, these are some papers from work and I just didn't want anything to get spilled on them. Help yourself to a drink. Are you hungry? How about we go out and get something to eat?"

"Dad I'm fine right now. I'd really just like to sit down and catch up," Robert said as he walked back towards the parlor. Robert took notice of how sparse the house looked. It didn't look like his Dad even lived there he complained. He wondered what was going on, and he wondered if I was really doing as well as I had claimed. He was really glad that he had come to check in on me. He would have a few days to assess the situation and learn the truth he muttered as he strolled through the house.

I stayed in the kitchen another moment, looking for a good place to hide the papers and trying to recall if I had anything else incriminating lying around. When I couldn't think of anything I rejoined my son in the parlor and tried to act normal.

I sat down, half listening as Robert filled me in on his classwork and school happenings. I just found myself swelling with pride at my son and remembering all the good times we used to have together. He looks so much like Louise, I thought nostalgically. Robert had happily reported that he was planning to stay for a few days if that was okay. It was more than okay with me. I would take anytime I could get with my son.

"I'm looking forward to checking out the town. I'd also love to see your new office and the plant if I can," Robert said.

I hoped he didn't detect the glimmer of dread on my face. "Oh," I said slowly as I tried to think. I certainly couldn't show Robert my office or my current project.

"Well you've seen all that before, I don't want to bore you when you're here on vacation."

"Not at all Dad, as I get closer to finishing school, the business world is getting more interesting to me. It won't be long before I'm out here in the real world in search of a job," Robert said.

"What's going on with Rosemary, are you still seeing her?" I asked, slyly changing the subject. If only Robert could be working with me that would be perfect. I was thinking that over as Robert was telling me that he wasn't seeing Rosemary anymore. I feigned disappointment, but secretly I was glad because if he wasn't involved with anyone he may feel more inclined to give Toledo a chance.

I was going to work hard over the next couple days to make Toledo seem irresistible. I knew how to do that in ten seconds flat, but I wouldn't do it that way, it wouldn't be quite fair.

I was determined to play tour guide to my son but I would have to find a way to avoid the office. I was glad I had Connor to help out. If my son had shown up when I was living at the factory he would have probably barged in Edward's office to demand to know why he was working people so hard!

The next couple days were wonderful for me. I had my son, I had my work, and my life was almost perfect. I still missed Louise, but I knew I couldn't replace her. Robert tried to broach the subject of me dating a couple times, attempting to let me know he'd be okay with it. Robert knew I didn't need his permission, but he didn't want me to feel I had to hide anything from him if a special lady entered my life.

"This is the best news ever!" I yelled out loud to nobody but myself. I was reading the latest letter from my son Robert and I couldn't contain my joy. Robert had decided to move to Toledo. He wasn't sure where he would live or work, but he thought it was important to be near his family.

"I really enjoyed the city when I visited and I could picture myself being very successful there," I read out loud the beautiful words from Robert's letter. Of course I would welcome Robert to stay with me, at least in the beginning or for as long as he wanted. I scanned the letter to see when he was coming.

"It looks like I have a lot to do before my roommate shows up in three days," I spoke merrily and I jumped in the air. Now if I could bring Robert in on Project Ignite I would feel secure knowing Spark would be cared for, for a long time.

I broached this very topic with Edward a few times. Edward trusted me implicitly and said he couldn't see any reason not to bring him on board. I still had some time before my shift started so I figured I better get moving and prepare the extra bedroom. I had been using the room for storage and boxes were all over the bed. As I worked, I thought about the best way to introduce Robert to my friend Spark and the lifetime job offer.

Let's not put the cart before the horse, I reminded myself. I should wait until Robert got here and find out if he had any other job prospects or aspirations before deciding if it was the right time to make the proposal. I didn't want to rush Robert into working with me. I wanted to give him a chance to see if he had any other plans for his life before springing my idea on him.

I picked up Louise's picture that was on the dresser and said, "Thank you honey, I know you must have had something to do with this. You always wanted to keep your boys together. I can't wait to see Robert's reaction when he finds out what his old man has been up to since moving to Toledo."

Robert arrived by train on a sunny Saturday. The pleasant weather only added to my good mood. Since I knew of his planned arrival time, I was at the train station plenty early and ready to meet him. I felt like a kid on Christmas morning anxiously awaiting to open my presents. My son coming to Toledo was the best present I could have received. I had nothing else I wanted from Santa anymore.

I sat eagerly on the bench inside the station. I closed my eyes and thought back on my conversations with Edward and Connor over the past few weeks. All three of us were in agreement that bringing Robert on board would ease our burden and more importantly, secure a long, safe future for Spark.

Getting Spark integrated into the energy production of the furnace was an amazing feat. Now whenever we saw the product going through the lehr to be cooled, or being packed in a box, we smiled knowing that a part of Spark was there too.

Connor and I had mulled over how to bring Robert in on our special project. Connor thought our secret society should have a special ceremony to initiate in the newcomer. Connor wanted to name it "*HIC SUNT DRACONES*" and make it unforgettable. I reminded Connor that the introduction of Spark would be unforgettable on its own and it wasn't necessary to make a big fuss about it.

Connor wouldn't let his idea go. He knew it wasn't everyday people find out dragons are real, let alone get to meet one and be asked to take care of it. Connor was always fond of Robert. He remembered him as a shy but polite little boy. If he had a son, he'd want him to be like Robert he told me many times. Connor soon wore me down on the idea.

I finally realized that we only had each other and having a small ceremony would be the proper thing to do. We were a celebration business after all. Our products were made to celebrate life's moments, big or small. I would have to say this probably fit in the big category!

Connor didn't share too many of the details with me and said he had it all under control. I was now glad to have a special introduction scheduled for Robert. Who knows, maybe this is a tradition he will pass on to his kids, or grandkids someday. I liked the thought of that. Although the reality of Robert having a wife and kids would complicate the project, if he accepted it, I wouldn't mind having a grandkid, or two, to spoil.

I was lost in thought until the whistle of the train blared. I looked up to see the approaching train. "Robert your adventure awaits!" I said under my breath proudly as I stood up to walk to the platform.

I stood to the side of the door and smiled as I saw other passengers reunite with loved ones. Every time someone stepped off the train I thought it would be Robert, but it wasn't. Be patient I told myself, but the anticipation was overwhelming me. I started to get really concerned when the conductor got off and it appeared everyone had vacated the train.

"Dad, Dad don't leave without me. I fell asleep and woke to find an empty train. I would have been upset if I would have missed my stop and ended up in Chicago!"

I laughed in relief, "You're just like your mother! She could fall asleep anywhere, anytime, no matter how much noise was blaring around her!" We hugged and then I stood back to look at Robert. "You look so much taller son, but I know you're not growing anymore, it must mean I'm starting to shrink!"

We walked happily side by side to the awaiting carriage. I kept telling the driver to slow down as we made our way through the downtown so I could point out the new sites to Robert. I hoped Robert could see how happy I was and that he would be content that he had made the right decision.

"What's gotten into you tonight pops? You've had this mischievous look on your face since I got off the train?"

"Oh, do I?" I said innocently as I pictured the introduction of Spark to Robert.

Chapter 40

Robert's initiation ceremony was ready to go on Thursday night. If all went according to plan the new member would accept his destiny and be brought into the fold. Connor was excited. He had lived with this secret and wasn't able to share it with anyone except the two that had brought him into it. It was going to be rewarding to see Robert's reaction and be able to have someone else to confide in, he confessed.

Connor prepared the speech that he expected Edward would deliver as the Master of Ceremonies. Edward was briefed little on the event but thought it would be amusing. He left the details to Connor and said he would be there.

Before the initiation meeting could take place I had to make certain it would be something Robert would want. Once we told him, if he refused, I knew he wouldn't tell anyone about it, but it would put a strain on our relationship thereafter. I had given Robert some time to settle in at my house and gently probed him with general questions about his future aspirations to see if his plans could fit with what I had in store for him.

Robert was young and still a little unfocused on a specific career. He had studied business in college and that could open many avenues for him. He wasn't set on a specific industry, at least none that he told his old man about. Luckily for me the couple of interviews that Robert had since he got to town had not interested him.

Robert wanted a job, but not just any job. He wanted something that would "spark a fire within him" he told me more than once. Well, little did he know how much I could help him in that! He figured since he had a place to stay with me, he had some time to be a little selective about where he would work. He knew that once he landed a job it likely would be a place he would spend many years, if not all of his career. He wanted to make the right choice. All these factors were playing right into my hands.

I told Connor that evening about my discussions about Robert's future. Connor was ecstatic, "Oh, Red, this is great! I know once Robert hears the job description, or rather sees it, he wouldn't turn it down in a million years!"

By Thursday afternoon Robert was starting to get nervous. He told me he was looking forward to his interview with Mr. Libbey but he didn't want to say or do something stupid that would embarrass me. "I know Mr. Libbey had a very high opinion of you back in Cambridge and from the way you talk it seems your bond has strengthened even more since you moved to Toledo."

"We do have a great respect for each other. Mr. Libbey, eh, Edward, allows me a great deal of freedom to do my work. He has put me in charge of a very special project since we moved from Cambridge." I bit my lip to stop myself from revealing the project too soon.

Robert straightened his shirt collar and tie again and I noticed his hands were shaking. Well, I guess it's good to be nervous I thought, that must mean he really wants to work here. Maybe he did miss being around me.

Robert was as ready as he could be. He picked up his hat, placed it on his head, and we walked down the street. The brisk air felt cool on my face but I noticed beads of sweat dripping from Robert's forehead. I didn't perspire at all when I went to the Libbey factory for a job many years ago. I guess I was too young and desperate back then to be nervous. We didn't say another word until we arrived at the guard shack a few minutes later.

"You have an appointment, son? He doesn't see anyone without an appointment." The guard asked as he looked at the young man.

"Oh yes sir, I do, my name is Robert Wynston. I have a meeting with Mr. Libbey at 6:00 p.m. I'm a little early I know, but better to be early than late," Robert rambled on nervously as the man looked him over.

The guard opened his appointment book and found Robert's name. "Oh yes, there you are, I guess Red here can escort you in." The guard said as he motioned to me.

I led Robert up the walkway in front of the factory. We passed by what Robert could easily see was the warehouse and shipping area. There were several barrels of glass stacked up near the large open doors. To the right of the main building was a smaller building. Robert saw the sign on the door which read "*Glass Display Building*".

"Maybe you'll get a tour of that building later. Many samples of our products are displayed on several shelves around the room. It is an impressive line-up, especially when the room is lit up and the glass is all sparkling," I said.

"I hope I get a chance to see it later. I don't recall anything like that at your old factory."

I held the door to the factory open and motioned Robert inside. I told him to turn left and we ascended up the stairs. At the top of the stairs there were offices to the left and right and a hallway that looked like it led directly into the manufacturing area straight ahead. Robert followed my instruction to go in the door to the right.

Robert looked spellbound as he gazed around the room. On the wall hung a painting of Edward Libbey, whom he recognized, and another gentleman, which Robert could see from the sign was Edward's father William. The men both looked stoic and stately. They looked like men of power, but the artist also subtly conveyed a side of warmth to them. Robert was captivated as he pointed out the cut glassware designs featured around the room.

In front of Edward's office was a large ornate desk that belonged to his stenographer. A hand carved glass paperweight on the desk was etched with the name Lillian. "That must be Ms. Halpin, I'd forgotten about her. I remember meeting her back in Cambridge when I visited the factory. She was always so kind, she reminded me of my grandmother." Robert said as I turned to hide a little tear forming in my eye.

Robert was admiring the facets of the design when Edward stepped out of his office. "Robert, welcome! Come on back. It's great to see you. You are looking more like your father these days," Edward said as he led us into his office.

Robert looked awestruck with the beauty of the office. The antique furniture and artwork on the wall always made me feel I was going back in time. "My father told me about your love of European art and antiques. Your office is exquisite. Did you find all these on your travels Mr. Libbey?" Robert asked.

Edward took great pride in the treasures he collected and proceeded to tell Robert about where each piece was acquired. "I'm afraid I have an obsession with collecting fine art and antiquities. My house will soon be overflowing. I'll need to open a museum to house everything soon!" Edward laughed heartily.

As the men were ready to get down to the usual questions of a job interview, I started to excuse myself. I hoped Edward would find Robert to be a passionate, intelligent young man. Robert didn't know that he was interviewing for more of a unique, secret life-long position at the company.

Robert would be happy if he could get a clerk job, or anything really, as he was just starting out his career. Most of his friends were jealous that he was interviewing with the head of a major manufacturing company. If only they had that opportunity, many of them remarked to him.

"Excuse me, Mr. Libbey. I'm afraid you need to take this call, it's Mr. Edison." Ms. Halpin said excitedly.

"Robert, I'm terribly sorry but I need to address this call. Red, could you take Robert around the factory and show him around? I'll catch up with you as soon as I can."

"Certainly, come along Robert."

The two of us left the administration area of the building and headed down the hallway which led to the manufacturing area. Suddenly the noises from thc machines became louder and there were people moving about everywhere. Robert was always intrigued by the glass-making process and took tours at the old factory whenever he could.

When we approached a large furnace Robert stopped. It was a couple hundred feet high. Robert looked up as I gestured and pointed with my hand so he could see the window. I encouraged Robert to climb the ladder propped against it and peek inside. The furnace was brimming with flames, which was mesmerizing. Robert smiled as he descended the ladder and caught up with me as I walked on towards the other side where there was a crew of eight men near one of the furnace openings.

One of the men was blowing into a blowpipe. Another guy was gathering molten glass onto a rod. I knew the process well. The molten gob would be rolled and worked into a round ball and then given to the glassblower. The blower would work the ball into a shape either by rolling it out by twirling the pipe in his hands or he would have an assistant help him shape it into a pattern by using a mold. Making a glass into the right shape took a lot of skill. You also had to watch your time. As the glass started to cool it would start to harden and you had to work fast to shape it properly. If you didn't shape it properly in time, one of the crew members would have to take the gob of glass and reheat it in the furnace until it was smooth and malleable again.

When the blown shape was formed as intended the glassblower would put the glass on a rod and then he would further refine and shape the glass using metal or wood tools. If the glass piece called for a handle one of the assistants would bring small pieces of molten glass that the glass artist would shape and press onto the glass. That was the process Robert was watching today. I'd seen it many times before but I was always captivated by it. And the men worked in such harmony. They each conducted their job with such precision and seemed to anticipate just what the other needed without uttering a word. Robert continued watching the team until another man took the finished product and put into the lehr.

I explained to Robert that the lehr is an annealing furnace where the glass is cooled ever so slowly to prevent the glass from exploding. The glass would remain in the lehr for eight to ten hours until fully cooled. If the glass isn't given time to cool slowly in the lehr it would most likely break in the cutting or finishing stage. I didn't reveal that I found that lesson out the hard way when I started out my first job at the factory as a taker-in for the annealing area.

As I directed Robert around the work area, Robert could see some men taking glasses out of the lehr that had been in there overnight and fully cooled. They put them on a cart and then took them to the finishing area. There was a group of master cutters in the next department who were taking the cooled glasses and cutting into them ever so gently. One guy in particular that caught Robert's attention was using a cutting blade and cutting what appeared to be a starburst pattern onto the glass. Robert remarked that it must have taken years for the man to learn to do that so well. It was truly extraordinary. I cheerfully greeted the men throughout the department as Robert stopped to study what each man was doing.

Soon Edward caught up with us and tapped Robert on the shoulder. He motioned at us to follow him down the hall. We walked by the engraving area where a row of workers were carefully etching designs on glassware. Robert nodded and smiled at one of the men when he looked up. The workers were used to having visitors. Edward often brought in customers to let them see how the products were made. When they saw the quality craftsmanship for themselves they were more likely to buy. Edward encouraged them to tell their customers about the manufacturing process when they were in their stores. Edward thought the more people that saw the process the more people there were to talk about his products.

Edward walked Robert quickly through the packaging area, but it was notable as well. The men carefully inspected each glass individually by holding it up to the light. There were posters on the walls with information about what the glass should look like and what imperfections to look out for that would prevent the glass from being sold. The imperfections listed were blisters, bubbles, misshaped rims, and other unwanted blemishes. Edward explained that each glass was carefully checked and if it didn't meet his quality standards it was discarded. The discarded glass would be smashed down into cullet and later re-melted and formed again. It was a relief to see that the undesirable pieces could be recycled in that manner.

When Robert asked to see the warehouse area, I escaped back to my office. I wanted to make sure Connor had everything set up. Edward would keep Robert busy for a while with questions and the rest of the factory tour. If this proposal was going to work the way Edward wanted, he needed to make sure Robert loved the glassmaking business as much he did. If everything went as I suspected, Edward would see that Robert was the right man for the job. Then he would lead him to the basement.

I could imagine Robert would find it a little strange to be taken down to the basement. It wasn't part of a typical tour. Most people would want to see the glassblowing process as it was like watching a show, but who would expect to go down to the gritty basement with the pipes and fixtures? Oh well, he was quite a curious lad and would follow Edward anywhere. Before they reached us they would walk past a large tank that contained oil and he would see several pipes that carried the gas to the furnaces.

Goosebumps went down my arm as Connor peaked out the office door and let me know that they were coming. I pressed a glass to the door and put my ear against it. I liked that our glasses had multiple uses!

I closed my eyes and concentrated and could hear Edward say to Robert, "This is your father's office. He is working on a top secret project for me. This is extremely confidential. If you accept a position here, you will be working here with your father. He needs an assistant and from everything I can gather you are the perfect candidate. Do you have any reservations about taking a position at this company? For if you do, please tell me now, and we can turn back."

I couldn't believe what I was hearing. Did Edward honestly think there was any chance that Robert would say no I'm not interested?!

"Sir, I would be honored to work for you. I know I'm just out of school and have little experience, but trust me, I'm a very hard worker and anything you want me to do, I will work hard to learn as quick as I can," Robert said in a very serious tone.

"That is just what I was hoping to hear! Your father will be so excited when I tell him," Edward said and rapped on the door. I pulled down the glass so quickly I nearly dropped it as I stumbled briskly away from the door.

No need to tell me, I heard it loud and clear. A moment later Edward opened the door. I looked smugly at Edward. Edward winked at me and said, "Red, I have a new apprentice for you. I think you already know him."

Robert looked and probably saw the twinkle in my eye as I tried to remain serious and businesslike. "Robert, I'm glad you could join us. Please come in and have a seat. I think you remember Connor. Connor also works with me on Project Ignite."

Robert said hello and shook Connor's hand. Robert sat in utter stillness as I pressed upon him the confidentiality and secrecy of this project. I paced back and forth in front of him as I told Robert that I had been working on a most amazing project almost the whole time I had been in Toledo. The three men in front of him were the only ones in the company that knew about Project Ignite, I divulged.

"If you commit to the project you will have to work in secrecy alongside us. This will require many long hours and anything you see or learn here would stay here just between us. This is top secret and nobody else can know."

Once we were convinced that Robert was ready to join us, the ceremony began. Connor stood up and walked over to a table in the back of the room. He lit one of the candles and said, "Ubi concordia, ibi victoria."

I glanced at Robert, who sat with a look of wonderment on his face, and took a handsomely carved pendant from the box Connor gave him. The pendant had the new Libbey trademark engraved on it. It said LIBBEY CUT GLASS around in a circle about the top. The bottom of the circle said TOLEDO, OH. Inside the circle was an eagle with his wings spread. I told him that there were only four of these pendants and by taking this pendant he was joining the secret club as its newest lifetime member. Robert stood up tall and expressed an enormous sense of pride as I pinned it on his shirt. He couldn't know it, but the best was still yet to come.

I then turned to Connor and said, "Bring it on!"

Connor had built a small stage in the area near the tunnel. Earlier he had positioned several glass candlesticks around the edges of the platform. I wasn't quite sure what his plan was but I expected it to grab Robert's attention.

Connor guided Robert to stand in front of the stage. Robert looked perplexed but he followed along. Connor directed me to turn off the lights. That was also my signal to blow my trumpet. I played it slowly and then picked up the beat with a thump, thump, thump. The others all stood breathless and quietly waited for further instructions. Without the lights on we were in total darkness. I turned my eyes forward as I heard Connor unlatch the tunnel door.

Connor cleared his throat and spoke this eloquent verse:

"No longer will you be in the dark,
For today you'll learn the mystery of our spark.
A greater secret you'll never know,
May our Spark shine within you, wherever you go."

I knew what was coming, but still those words gave me goosebumps. The next thing I heard was a familiar whoosh as Spark's flash of fire illuminated the candles in one quick breath. As the candles flickered and light returned to the room, Spark stood on the stage spreading his wings and looking truly majestic.

I stepped around so that I could have a clear view of Robert's face as he laid eyes upon Spark. Robert's eyes were so wide they looked like they may burst out of his head! He was utterly speechless as he stared at Spark and stared back at me. The look on my face told him it was real and not to be scared of it, but Robert kept shaking his head back and forth and saying "No, this can't be, this can't be."

Edward went over to Spark and led him off the stage and over to Robert. Edward told Robert that this was Project Ignite and he would be working with this lovely creature. Spark sniffed him out and looked at him curiously. Spark hadn't been around many people so he was just as curious to see Robert. Once the initial shock subsided the four of us sat down, with Spark near my side, and filled Robert in on the details of our work.

"Dad, you sly devil! How could you have kept this from me all this time?" Robert said as we talked about the progress we had made and what other plans we had.

"Red, aren't you forgetting something?" Connor asked as he pulled up his sleeve to reveal the tattoo I had placed there some time ago.

"Bloody hell, did you do that father? I feel like I don't know you at all!" Robert said looking at me in astonishment.

I smiled at that and retorted, "Another reason to work here with me. Get to know your old man again, Robbie."

"I'd be honored, but don't call me Robbie! So who's going to ink that wonderful design on my arm?" Robert said anxiously glancing at each of us.

"Connor, grab my supplies, would ya?" I said as I walked over to wash my hands. "Now, remember you can't reveal the true meaning of this tattoo to anyone, you understand boy?"

Robert smiled and nodded. I couldn't help but wonder what Louise must be thinking if she was looking down at us at this moment. Not only was I allowing my son to get a tattoo, I was the one inking it on his body for all eternity. But the tattoo had become an important symbol of our mission and our bond. He was one of us now and I couldn't be happier, I thought when I stood back to admire my work.

We were all relieved that Robert was so excited to work with us and with Spark. I could tell that Robert was over the moon. He never, ever could have imagined doing with his life, but it was something he would have never turned down for anything else.

When Robert got home that night, he was too restless to sleep. He knew that he had a long day ahead of him tomorrow but he couldn't turn his mind off. Beginning early the next morning he would be starting his new career as a dragon master. He sat down on the edge of my bed talking over details of his day, as if I hadn't been there!

I smiled as he unpinned the pendant and held it up, admiring it in the light. It shined brightly. The carving detail was exquisite. Then he grabbed his magnifying glass and studied it a little closer.

"How amazingly clever," he mumbled quietly to himself. "I just realized something I didn't notice before, something you probably didn't notice either, Dad."

He studied it a few minutes longer as I stood wondering what he was thinking. Then he looked at me and smiled, "Dad, the eagle in the middle of the design isn't an eagle after all. Sure, looking quickly at it, it resembles an eagle, and with the word American above it, it tricks your mind. But looking very closely at it, especially under the magnifying glass, you can see that it is really a dragon! A dragon cleverly disguised to pass for an eagle by the unknowing eye! The hidden secret of the company Edward has stealthily made a part of his new logo. His most valued secret hiding in plain site!"

Robert was truly astonished and proud to be working for such a clever, ingenious man. I knew he had so much he could learn from Edward. He would be wise to take every opportunity to learn everything Edward was willing to teach him, I told him.

Robert went into the kitchen for a glass of water. As he stood over the sink admiring the glass he turned back to me and said, "I saw a glass like this being made today. I know you've seen it a thousand times, but it's really remarkable. I can't believe my luck. A few days ago, I was leaving school and fretting about the future and where I would go and what I would do and now, today, everything has magically fallen in place."

I joined him in the kitchen and started laughing wildly. Robert looked at me and I grabbed his hands and swung them in the air as I did a little jig. When I caught my breath I yelled out, "So son! How did you enjoy your first day at work?!"

Robert hugged me and said, "Thank you Dad! You have made me so proud and so very happy. I'm honored to be your apprentice!"

I just hugged my son very hard and tried to hold back the tears. I hadn't felt this happy in a long time. My son was here with me and I was on cloud nine. Tomorrow I would begin training Robert to work with Spark. Tonight we would enjoy the start of a new special bond.

Robert didn't get much sleep that night. However, waking up in the morning was not a problem. Robert suddenly had so much energy he felt he'd never need to sleep again. He was energized by all the possibilities and discoveries that would fill his day with joy. Since he was up, he decided to treat me to breakfast. I taught Robert how to make nest eggs when he was a young boy. It was about the only meal that Robert took an interest in learning to make. My wife and I enjoyed cooking together and Robert was happy to let us keep that chore. Today was different. He wanted to make me a nice meal that we could enjoy before going into work together.

"Robert, you're actually cooking? This is a strange new day! Thanks son." I said grabbing a tea bag. This was a welcome change. I was in the habit of reading the *Toledo Blade* before work. I always started with the business section to see what was going on with other local businesses. As I began to read Robert picked up another section. I said, "The news in that section is light and a perfectly enjoyable way to start the day. But keep an eye on my eggs, I don't like them burnt."

Robert put the paper down and picked up another slice of bread and generously spread butter on both sides. He found a small juice glass and pressed the top into the bread and cut out a nice round circle from the center. He placed both parts of the bread into the skillet and broke an egg into the center of the bread where the piece had been removed. As that was cooking, he did the same to a few more pieces of bread and gave the sausages a turn. It wasn't too glamourous of a meal but it was the thought that counted, I figured.

I glanced at the clock and noticed it was nearly 7:00 a.m. "Oh, shoot, we need to get going now. Son, need I remind you, you are to keep Project Ignite confidential? Not a word to anyone ever."

"You can count on me Dad. Now is there anything else you've been hiding from me?"

Chapter 41

Robert threw himself into his new job. He was eager to learn everything he could about Spark and the glass industry. He was anxious to prove we had put our trust in the right man. He didn't want us to regret the hire, which he worried could have a negative impact on me too. Robert's only regret was that he couldn't tell his friends about his nifty new job and what he was up to.

We agreed he would tell anyone that asked that he worked in accounting. That was partially true, so it wasn't a total lie. Robert would be in charge of addressing the expenses of the project, and projecting cash flows and budgeting.

"I know if someone told me they were an accountant, I would consider the topic so dreary I wouldn't stick around to ask further questions."

I wondered if any of those other accountants I had met over the years had to hide a big asset like Robert was going to do. It just goes to show, I thought, you should never make a rash assumption. Robert had not planned to look for an accounting position anywhere, but the fringe benefits with this job were irresistible.

Once Robert was settled into our shared office I stepped out for a meeting with the New Product Development Manager and his group. Edward had some new ideas and we were going to discuss the viability of them. Edward was always traveling the country, visiting with customers and listening to their needs, I explained to Robert. If something was proposed by the customer, no matter how impossible it seemed, Edward would take it upon himself to see if it could be done.

Edward believed everything should be made of glass. He had such high regard for quality though, that nothing would be produced without undergoing rigorous quality tests first. Quality wasn't the only obstacle. The complexity of the design would also be scrutinized by the artists, mold makers and engineers. *How difficult would it be to design? Could it be easily replicated over and over by the majority of glass artists? How much raw material would be required for each item? What is the cost for product and personnel time to create it? What would the market pay for it?* All these questions and more were discussed and deliberated with several departments before a new product would be cleared for approval.

Edward and his team would then go whole hog at creating the market demand. Simultaneously the master scheduler would be trying to find a way to get the product into production without jeopardizing any other orders already on the schedule. Robert found all of this very interesting and I promised I would explain it to him in more detail later.

I felt rather proud as I could see that Robert had gained a new respect for me and all his new co-workers. While growing up he knew that my company employed hundreds of workers, but I don't reckon he ever really stopped to consider and understand what all of them actually did. He learned just a small fraction from meeting with Edward yesterday. Robert realized now he had so much to learn.

Robert was encouraged to keep a list of everything he needed to do to learn about the company and his new role. I noticed Robert wrote down that he would personally get to know what each man did to help the company. Everyone had a crucial function and it was exciting to see that he wanted to know how each person's role made the operation work. I knew it would take quite some time to accomplish that task, but he had been given a lifetime commitment, so I was optimistic he could fit it in!

"Keep Spark in the cage until I return." That was the only real instruction I gave him before I left for my meeting. I expected Robert to get started by reading the files on the project and getting up to speed on all the work that had been done to date. I should have known my one directive would have been too hard to keep.

I realized I left my notes on my desk so I turned back to get them. I slowly opened the door and was about to yell out to Robert, but stopped myself as I saw what a rip-roaring good time he was having with Spark. I should have known that Robert would mosey right over to Spark's cage within a minute of me leaving the room. Well, it was impossible for anyone to ignore Spark I figured, especially as Spark would be looking at him so curiously. This is the dream of all kids I imagined, to see a real live dragon.

I held my tongue as I heard Robert introduce himself to Spark and proceeded to tell him about himself. Spark didn't know what he was saying, but he looked intently back at Robert and seemed to enjoy every word.

Robert asked Spark questions but didn't expect to get answers from Spark or from anyone anytime soon. "*How in the world did you end up in a glass factory in Toledo? Are there other dragons out there somewhere? And where was somewhere? Where did you come from?*"

Some of the answers would come in time, but the three of us told him last night as much as we could for now and told him to be patient and more would be revealed in stages. Robert was relieved that Spark didn't seem to be a man-eating dragon. "My friends would think I was plum crazy if I told them about you Spark," Robert said staring into his cage.

"Damn it, I know what my father said, but I can't resist. You look a little peaked and I think you'd feel better if you could get out and move about the office."

Robert found the key to the lock in my desk drawer and used it on the lock. At first Spark just sat still and looked at Robert. Robert opened the door wider and stepped in. Spark just sat there. Robert then made a rookie mistake that would reveal his naivety.

Robert set the key down on the ground and reached out to pet Spark. Spark kicked the key across the room, leaped out and pulled the door closed so quickly that Robert was knocked to the ground. Robert was stunned and couldn't do much but laugh. He was now the caged animal and Spark was on the other side.

"You clever little rascal!" Robert said.

Well, this day just got a whole lot more interesting, I chuckled. He sure wouldn't want his old man to come in and find him this way so I watched quietly as my son spent the next several minutes trying to get Spark to kick the key back his way. Spark seemed to know what he did and appeared pleased with himself. He kept running around the room and to make matters worse he managed to knock the papers Robert was supposed to read all over the room with one swipe of his tail. Robert better make a mental note to add another item to his list. Always listen to Dad's instructions, oh and, don't turn your back on Spark!

As Connor walked up behind me, I motioned for him to be quiet. I pointed into the room and Connor looked over my shoulder and surveyed the situation.

I nudged Connor in front of me and motioned for him to knock at the door. I smiled and managed to suppress my laughter. Connor appeared and looked at Robert in the cage and Spark laying nearby. It looked as if Spark was guarding his prisoner.

"Oh, Connor I'm glad it's you. Could you please let me out of here before my father returns?" Robert said hopefully.

Connor ignored his pleads and asked Spark what his dumb prisoner had done to get locked up. After some unflattering jokes at Robert's expense, Connor decided it was time to let him off the hook. I almost felt a little sorry for Robert. It's not easy being the new guy.

"I'm guessing you will listen to our instructions going forward, Robert? Spark is a mighty intelligent and clever lad. You see how he got the best of you today? Don't forget that. Spark is turning into quite a jokester and likes to play tricks. All three of us have been tricked by him. Now I guess we can call this your formal initiation from Spark. Welcome to the club!" Connor said as he unlocked the cage and let Robert out.

Connor helped Robert pick up the papers and they had them in fairly good order before I decided to make my entrance. Robert looked thankful that I didn't find him before Connor. He didn't suspect I would be quite as amused, especially with it being his first day on the job. I decided not to pile onto his agony.

I could tell Robert felt guilty that he hadn't studied the project information he was assigned to review while I was out. However he did learn a very lesson instead. Never turn your back on a dragon. Never!

For the rest of the morning Robert was at my side. Robert watched his every move with Spark. He longed to develop an unbreakable bond with Spark the way I had. I told him it took some time, and he had to be patient.

Robert revealed he was thinking of his mom. "Mom, sure would be pleased with how things turned out. She was always encouraging me to ask for your help with everything. It would drive me crazy sometimes because I wanted to show off to you how smart I was by doing things on my own. I sure am glad you asked me to help with Project Ignite because I would have never known about it to ask!"

The afternoon was fairly routine for the three of us. Routine in Robert's new world meant that he was not duped by the dragon. Robert let Connor and I deal with Spark the rest of that day and he kept his distance. One screw up in a day was rather enough for Robert.

We spent most of the day all quietly absorbed in our work. It was fairly quiet in the sub-basement office and that was the way I liked it. The isolation and quietness of the location was something that would take time for Robert to get used to though. He had spent the last few years on a crowded campus, constantly moving from one building to another for classes and back to a large dormitory each evening. He didn't have much time alone the past few years.

Being an only child, I reckon I wasn't too surprised that Robert confided that he liked sharing a space with three roommates. The other guys would complain at times, none of them ever had much privacy as they each grew up in a large family with several brothers and sisters, but Robert really enjoyed all the noise and commotion. He enjoyed growing up with his parents, but it was a quiet household, with nobody for him to argue and fight with and tease.

"Man alive, I never realized the fun I could have had if I had some siblings to grow up with," he said then stopped for a moment realizing this was a sensitive subject we rarely discussed, but then continued, "Don't get me wrong, I had a great childhood with you and mom, I just always felt like mom wanted more kids, although she never said that to me directly."

"We would have loved to fill the house with ten children, but life didn't work out that way. Louise, your mother, realized early on that we had a perfect son on the first try and needed no others," I said truthfully.

"I have a surprise for you Robert!" Connor said one morning when he entered the office.

I hesitated and wondered what kind of surprise was in store for him. I wasn't sure Robert wanted to know, especially with the way Connor said it.

Connor held up two tickets to what looked a baseball game and waved them in the air. Robert sighed in relief and yelled, "Wow, thanks!"

"I have two tickets for the Toledo Pirates game tonight but I can't go. I thought you and your dad would enjoy going to the game. You like baseball don't you?" Connor asked.

"I sure do! You know I played in high school and really enjoyed the game. I wasn't good enough to make the college team but that gave me more time for my studies I suppose," Robert informed him.

I realized Robert had been working nearly night and day this past week and it would be nice to take a break and watch a game. "What do you say, dad?"

"The Black Pirates, eh matey, Aaaarrgh?" Robert said in his best pirate inspired voice. *(The Black Pirates name would be changed a few years later to the better name we know them as today, the Mud Hens.)*

"Yes, they are a pretty good team. They are in the International League. They play over in Speranza Park. It's just a short trolley ride from here, over on Cherry Street and Franklin Avenue," Connor advised.

"Oh, I remember seeing that place. Speranza is the name of it you say? Where did that name come from?" Robert asked.

"I'm not sure. I think I heard someone say it was the name of the owner's yacht! The Ketcham family owns the ball club. The Ketchams are a very important family here. You may also have noticed that baseball is a popular thing around here. Every time there is a game during the week, the Ketchams hang big signs across the streets downtown that say "Baseball today". The businessmen probably don't like it because everyone tries to get out of work to get to the ball game!" Connor said laughing.

Connor was usually among the baseball fans. He loved watching the games and being part of the crowd. Today he sacrificed that to let me and my son enjoy it.

"Take me out to the ball park!" Robert sang to his Dad while waving the tickets in the air.

"I guess we do need a night out." I turned to Connor and thanked him for the gesture.

"Red, you've been working this guy too hard. A young man needs time to get out and have fun. I'll handle things here. You guys go and enjoy some peanuts on me," Connor said and handed Robert a few coins.

"Did you know that Robert was a good outfielder back in school?" I asked eagerly and full of pride.

"I might have heard that once or twice or maybe a hundred times," Connor said jokingly. "Robert, your Dad has told me every move you've made every step of your life. I was surprised he let you get away for school where he couldn't document your every step," Connor informed Robert.

I looked down a little embarrassed. Hearing that out loud made me feel a little over-protective but I couldn't help it, he was my only son.

We put away our tools and headed home to change for the game. Robert laughed when I stepped into the living room with a Pirate shirt and eye patch. "You must have been to some games already I presume? Are you giving up on your Red Sox?"

"No, I'd never be unfaithful to my Sox. Toledo is in a different league so they don't compete."

Robert claimed he was staying true to his Sox, his favorite team, and it showed on his choice of shirt. "Luckily Toledo now has many Sox fans so you'll fit in well," I told him as we left the house.

"Look at the crowd! Everyone from Toledo must be here," Robert said, truly impressed with the number of people in the stands. "Is it always this crowded?"

"Every time I've come here so far, it has been," I responded and then continued in a whisper, "Maybe they just heard the dragon master was making an appearance."

Robert couldn't help but smile at that. He enjoyed the fact that he shared such a tremendous secret with his father.

We Wynstons enjoyed the game immensely. The atmosphere all evening was joyous, even if the Pirates were losing, the crowd just had a great time enjoying the game together. The Pirate mascot didn't have to try hard to get the crowd cheering. Seeing the pirate dance around got everyone yelling. Robert was impressed with all the families there with young kids. The kids were watching the game and enjoying the antics of the pirate. Robert could see why they had such a large crowd if this much fun was going on at each game.

As Robert was looking around at the spectators, we heard someone yell "duck" and turned to see a ball coming towards us. Robert stood up and caught it in his right hand. The people around us went crazy cheering. "You should take this as a good omen of good things to come for you in Toledo," I told him sincerely.

Robert turned around and noticed a young blond boy behind him. "Sorry lad, if I didn't stand and get in your way you would have caught this ball. Why don't you take it?"

The boy got a big smile on his face and turned to his father who nodded his head, letting his son know it was okay. The boy took the ball and held it high in the air as the folks cheered even louder.

"Catching a fly ball is exciting, but nothing could beat the excitement in the office with Spark." Robert whispered to me.

Thinking of Spark, I pictured him now and thought of the chaos he would create if he was here flying around trying to catch all the balls!

Chapter 42

People from around the country would soon be descending on Chicago for the nation's biggest celebration. Edward was a showman, a people person, a master marketer. He knew that if he could get his products in front of people he could get them hooked for life. How to do this wasn't the issue, the issue was having the money to do it. Edward was determined to find a way, come hell or high water, to be at the fair.

Edward had to convince the board that the show was vital to the company's long term success. This proved to be an impossible task. No matter Edward's reasoning, pleadings and demands, the board didn't share in his vision. "They just don't get it Red. They just cut me off and say it's simply too much money to spend on such a temporary venture."

I knew Edward was frustrated but that only made him more driven to find a way to fund this scheme. After all, Edward repeatedly said, "How can I miss out on what is being billed as the greatest show the world has ever seen?"

I never underestimated Edward and the board shouldn't have either. Edward was not one to give up. He sure wouldn't be running the company today if he backed down easily. He always soldiered on. "What is going on in that head of yours, Edward?"

"If the company won't back my dream, then I will have to find some private lenders."

While waiting on news of the financing, Edward plowed ahead on what he called the fun parts, the design and marketing plans.

"Where do you even start to plan such a project?" I asked naively.

"I've already reached out to David Stine. David thought I was joking when I first approached him. However, realizing I don't joke about such things, he said there was no way he was going to turn down this sensational project. I didn't have to say much for him to grasp that this would put his work on the world map. Millions would see his creation I told him!"

David was the architect Edward hired to build his house. It seemed like no time before David was coming to Edward with sketches of his ideas for the fair. The design of the building was fitting of the Greece and Roman classical designs, the theme of the other pavilions. The name Libbey was front and center over the large doors of the building in bold capital letters. The words "AMERICAN" and "CUT GLASS" were engraved on either side of LIBBEY name.

Several American flags waved proudly in the wind around the outer edges of the roof of the building. The building was made of white plaster like most of the other buildings at the fair. This gave a clean, crisp, bright new city feel to the site. Electricity, which was still a luxury, was used at night to light up the grounds. That in itself was going to be a delight to the fairgoers I sensed.

Edward was able to raise the necessary funds and spent around $250,000 for the mini factory. Since he was spending such an enormous amount of money, he insisted upon certain conditions. Most importantly he was able to guarantee the exclusive rights to be the only one at the fair permitted to make and sell glassware. This was a genius move on my boss's part and I was quite impressed.

The working furnace which was constructed under the dome of the building was expected to be a huge attraction. The visitors would be able to watch several glassblowers working at stations set up around the furnace. The visitors would also have the chance to purchase the wares being made in front of them or other trinkets designed as souvenirs that were made at the Toledo factory in preparation for the fair.

One of the more unique items we produced was a small glass hatchet. First President George Washington's face was etched on one side of the blade and Libbey's name was etched on the handle. This was made to go along with the replica of George Washington's home that was designed and displayed by the state of Vermont. Other souvenirs included small pins, tumblers and shot glasses.

The fair organizers told Edward they wanted a spectacular setting that would attract millions, and they certainly achieved that and more. (Later it was reported to be the most well attended fair in the nation's history and drew in over 27 million people, which I think was almost half the population of the country!)

"Make Libbey a household name." That sentiment was Edward's dream to achieve by being at the fair. The fair was set to run for six months. Attendance at the event was expected to be over twenty million. If only a fraction of those attending visited our exposition that was millions of potential new customers. This fair, so far, was exceeding all our expectations and it hadn't even begun yet. As long as I can keep our secret in the dark nothing could ruin this event, I thought.

We were at the fairground weeks before the opening overseeing the construction. There was no shortage of things to do. "Red, we need to get those few hundred free glasses to Pabst so that they can display them and allow patrons to sample the beer, as it should be tasted, in a tall beer mug!" Edward had met Pabst brewery owner Fred Pabst several years ago in Germany. Their partnership was another potential boon for the company.

As we carried a few boxes towards the Pabst display we came upon Mrs. Roxbury and her clever invention. I could almost see Edward's wheels turning in his head as he found another way to display his products. He complimented Mrs. Roxbury on the dishwasher development, as we approached her display.

"I know your invention will be an instant success with anyone who is tired of washing dishes every day. If you like, I will have my assistant deliver a few cases of dishes that you can use for your demonstration," Edward said as he winked over at me.

"That is most generous, Mr. Libbey, if you do that I will be sure to point out their origin to our visitors." Another win for Edward. His ingenuity ensured his product would be scattered all over the fair for added exposure. The man was the ultimate promoter and always found unique ways to market his ware.

I had been at the factory site since dawn. It wasn't necessary to be there so early, as the fair didn't open for a few more weeks, but I wanted to make sure everything was just right. I took great pride in my work. My work was important to me, and I always worked hard and was meticulous about every detail.

These days though, ever since I was entrusted with the secret, my work took on an even more serious tone. The weight of the secret was a burden, but just knowing that Edward had chosen to confide in me and put me in charge of this made me feel very flattered. Nobody had ever entrusted me with this level of authority before, and I wouldn't let Edward down.

When the possibility of having an exhibition at the World's Fair first came up I thought it was going to be a low key event. Our company had displayed booths at fairs before, mainly for industry folk, and I assumed this would be a similar venture. Yet as Edward thought more about it and all the publicity that it could bring, his plans grew exponentially. This is not going to be a one-horse show, he muttered to me several times. Nonetheless, I don't think Edward seriously envisioned bringing our secret along.

When I overheard Edward saying to another manager, "Why Herman, you are my best artist, wouldn't it just be grand to put you in front of an audience at the fair?" I wondered to myself the possibility of Spark going too, but quickly dismissed it as absurd.

Edward had said it maybe half in jest at first, knowing that Herman is quite introverted and would never dream of "performing" his work in front of an audience. However, as the words were flowing out of Edward's mouth, I could see the wheels churning in his head, and the idea actually becoming a possibility. Herman was working on a special new project and it actually would be a showstopper that would wow the crowds I surmised.

As that day progressed, Edward spent time scribbling madly in his workbook. Edward was an idea man, and because you never knew when an idea would strike, he carried around a workbook. This book was always with him and shared with no one. *(It was actually burned years later by Edward before his death, as he didn't want to take the chance of anyone else seeing it).*

I went home that night and thought and thought about the secret. If Mr. Libbey was going to have a live show of glass blowing, would he, could he, really ever consider bringing the secret along? To most it would never even be considered a remote possibility, however, Mr. Libbey wasn't most people.

I chuckled to myself and remembered that just a few years ago, with the company on the brink of financial ruin, he convinced us all to move our glass factory 700 miles west to a swampy land! That was no small feat and just shows the lengths Edward can go when he makes up his mind.

That night was a restless one for me. I heated up a kettle of water for tea and spent most of the night at the kitchen table thinking. I just knew Edward would approach me soon. Sometimes I thought Edward was as crazy as a loon. This far-fetched idea was too much and I must be ready with all the reasons why it wouldn't work. I was not always this pessimistic, but I was realistic and this task would be utterly impossible, not to mention downright dangerous.

The very danger of the idea would only intrigue Edward more I fretted. He did love a challenge and any kind of adventure. If it wasn't for his adventurous spirit we'd never have this secret to deal with in the first place. About 3:00 a.m. after several cups of tea I was wired up and almost convinced of the fact that I would surely be dragged into this ridiculous plot. So I resigned myself to that inevitable fact and thought of all the ways we could put the plan into place and keep the secret at the same time.

The investors, and especially the bankers, will be pleased if they are able to get their money back quickly. There was concern on their parts to get the financing for this fair project, but Edward was able to convince them it was a minimal risk. Libbey was well on its way to becoming a household name. Edward assured me that the advent of the automatic dishwasher would diminish the reluctance of setting a formal service of tableware in the American home, prompting more sales.

In spite of my initial misgivings I actually started to warm up to Edward's idea. Life was sure more exciting with Edward around. Pulling this off would just be another affirmation of his ingenuity. Imagine, Connor, Robert, Edward and I engaging in such tomfoolery!

Chapter 43

"Time for an adventure Spark!" I yelled as I entered the office. It took me all night but I set up the last details to get Spark on the train. I still wasn't totally convinced this was the smartest plan Edward ever had, but we were too far down the path to retreat now.

I easily coaxed Spark into the large crate by tossing his favorite snack into the box. The crate was marked "DANGER – FLAMMABLE LIQUIDS INSIDE", which wasn't entirely false. By the time Spark was securely contained inside the box Connor arrived.

"This is going to be fun, eh?" Connor remarked.

"I won't stop shaking until we get this box safely delivered without the content spilling," I said in response with a huff to show my continued unease about this venture.

Connor didn't outwardly show any anxiety about this assignment and that frustrated me. He never seemed too concerned about the possibility of Spark's discovery the way I did. I guess he figured I did enough worrying for the both of us. Connor pushed one end of the crate, which moved fairly easily with the help of the cart beneath it. He helped me escort the crate to the train station where we would stay with it for the entire trip.

Normally passengers wouldn't stay inside the cargo area of the train, but I told the conductor I had to watch it to be sure nothing spilled out on the trip or everyone would be in danger. My look of authority and foreboding did the trick and the conductor quickly agreed. It wouldn't be the most comfortable seat on the train for me, not really much of a seat at all, but Spark wouldn't be out of my sight once we got underway.

Robert arrived at the station as the crate was being loaded. "Oh Dad, that looks mighty cramped. Why don't you sit in the passenger car and I'll watch the cargo." Robert shoved his ticket into my hand and coaxed me along to the passenger car. He assured me that he had everything under control.

Connor and I rode in the passenger car closest to the one containing our precious cargo. If Spark made any noise we would be the first to hear it, along with a car load of people. Hopefully we would be able to distract them from the truth somehow. Spark was fairly complacent so I didn't expect any issues, but I tried to be prepared for the worst. After all, I'd never ridden a train with a dragon before, or maybe I did and didn't know it!

I wondered now suspiciously if there had been dragons in my company before that I never knew about? That thought kept playing in my head as I tried to relax and enjoy the ride. I gazed out the window and tried to concentrate on the adventure ahead. The click-clack of the tracks provided a relaxing rhythm that made my eyes feel heavy and I started to doze off with the thought that I hoped someday I'd be able to share my tale with someone. Tale, tail? Were my eyes deceiving me or did I just see a reflection of Spark's tail out the window behind me?

No, it was definitely his tail, I realized as I saw it again. I rubbed my eyes in disbelief. What the devil was going on back there I wondered? Before anyone else could gander back there I stood up and moved to the other side of the aisle and asked loudly, "Has anyone been to Chicago before?" Everyone looked my direction which was just what I wanted. I kept talking and kept their eyes focused at me until I could no longer see Spark's tail. Connor looked at me bewildered because he didn't see what I saw.

I couldn't believe what just happened. I wondered if Robert let Spark out of the crate to stretch out. "That damn fool!" I cursed to myself as I sat back down. He must have been thrashing about and trying to fly when I noticed Spark's tail flapping out the window. We were passing mainly farm field areas so I tried not to be too concerned. Nevertheless, I sat there worrying someone from one of the train cars would see it and scream and alert the others even if they didn't know what it was exactly.

Nobody was happier than I was when we finally arrived at the station in Chicago. Edward arranged to have a carriage waiting for us to get Spark to the fair. I set off to the freight car and approached Robert who was standing just outside of it and asked, "So did you have an uneventful trip?"

He looked at me and said, "You could say that, but not quite. Spark was a little frisky when we started out."

I responded, "Yes, around about the Indiana border I caught a glimpse of him waving out the window. I almost had a heart attack!"

"Oh you saw that? Do you think anyone else did?" Robert asked regretfully.

"I told you I should have been back there with you son," I scolded. "I hope nobody saw anything, I kept everyone distracted in my car, so I know none of them did. I can't say for sure about any of the others but probably not. I'm sure it's fine." I said trying to reassure myself before we heard a young boy walking by with his family.

"But Mommy, I did too see it. It was a big scaly tail and it was in the train with us. I know it was a dragon tail."

"You need to stop with this crazy story son, you're starting to worry your sister and you know there are no such things," the father said and rolled his eyes and tried to smile as he looked at me, Connor, and Robert as they walked by. The three of us just looked at each other. I didn't need to tell Robert again, he got the message, and we all knew we were going to have to be more careful.

We only had to keep Spark hidden at the fair for six months. Sure, no problem at all, I bravely thought to myself. It had been fairly easy to keep Spark out of sight at the large factory on Ash Street but at this smaller replica it was going to be a challenge. This place also included a basement level and in it contained a hidden room. That would be our home for the next several months. We would be spending a lot of time down there with Spark. And to make matters more interesting, Mr. and Mrs. Libbey would be living in the top story of the building.

What a strange time this was I thought! Connor just thought of it as another part of the adventure. All of us were looking forward to spending time in Chicago too. The town had been rebuilt after the great fire and I wanted to see everything. Up until now I'd only been as far west as Toledo. We had heard stories about a great fire, but everything we saw so far looked very elegant, although some of the buildings looked very new.

I was getting impatient, but then Robert pointed out our carriage arriving with two men. The men jumped down and walked up to me. I saw them exchange a small glance of concern between themselves when they saw the warning on the crate. "It's not as dangerous as it appears. It's just some parts for the furnace that are very delicate. We can all help you load it on the wagon and ride in the back to assure it doesn't tip."

Connor shook his head bravely at the men too. He made it appear that he would reluctantly do the same. The five of us carefully picked up the box. Connor yelled, "Oh no, it leaked look." He laughed heartily as the two moving men looked down and appeared a little rattled.

I almost looked myself because Connor sounded so convincing. Instead I gave Connor a stern look and said to the men, "No, sorry, we're okay, let's just keep moving and get this box loaded."

After a short ride through town we arrived at the fairground. It was still under construction here and there, but it was still impressive. I really had no idea it would be so big and grand. It looked like a small city being built before our eyes. The buildings had a white façade that made everything look so shiny and new. I had never seen anything quite like it.

I couldn't wait to go explore it. First, we had to get Spark securely in place. Just to the right I saw the Libbey name prominently on what was shaping up to be a grand mini-factory. "Wow, Mr. Libbey has outdone himself, eh Connor?"

"It's simply marvelous! This is going to attract many visitors," Connor replied.

"I'm not surprised that Edward managed to get this great location in the Midway!" I said admiring the location.

The carriage stopped at the entrance and I hopped off the back. I briskly went over and opened the door to the factory. "Edward we're here," I yelled out but got no reply.

I looked back at the others and shrugged. "Looks like nobody is here right now, let's go ahead and move this down to the basement."

The two moving men seemed surprised there would be a basement in a temporary building but what did they know about glass factories? I could see they just wanted to get this flammable package safely off their cart and get on their way. I suspected they wouldn't be helping us when it was time to go back to Ohio.

Edward was in the back of the building and appeared when we entered with the crate. He greeted us and followed the delivery men to the basement as they carried down the precious cargo. "Be careful, very gentle with that box please. Remember, it contains very flammable liquid and we don't want an explosion."

My team shared a knowing glance as the movers glanced nervously to each other. "I'll be glad when this job is done. I'm just used to moving furniture for people," one of them said under his breath so I could barely hear him.

Edward gave them a very handsome tip and that seemed to lift their spirits as they departed. Connor was about to open the crate but I cautioned him to wait, "I'm going to go look about first. I want to make sure nobody is around in case Spark gets a little noisy when we first get him out."

Edward turned to me and asked, "How did the train ride go, Red? No issues I hope?"

I spoke out before Connor lost his nerve and blurted out the mishap which would have caused Edward undue alarm. "Oh, it was fairly uneventful. Spark kept quiet the whole ride," I lied. Well, this wasn't exactly a lie, I just omitted the one eventful part.

Connor smartly kept his mouth shut.

"Let's get him out and let him stretch. It's been a long journey for him. Connor, go and lock the door. We don't want any unexpected visitors."

Edward and I carefully opened the crate. Spark looked around curiously before walking out of the box. We were petting Spark and laughing about something when Connor returned. He didn't know what we were laughing about but I gave him a signal to let him know it wasn't about the little excitement on the train.

As Spark moved about checking out his new home, we unpacked the rest of the supplies. "We are going to impress the world with our dragon-heated glass!" Edward laughed as he patted Spark on the head.

Most of the glasses we made were clear. However if you knew to look closely, as we did, in some you could see the faint cloudy swirl of dragon's breath in the glass. Those are the really valuable ones.

"It looks like you have everything under control here. I'm going upstairs now and attend to some other matters. Let me know if you need anything," Edward said as he left us alone in the basement with Spark.

"We're fine for now," I replied, locking the door.

When Edward was gone Connor burst out, "I thought for sure you were going to spill the beans to Edward. I know from playing poker with you that you can't tell a lie. Your face always gives it away. Not this time though. I guess I better be careful if I ever play cards with you again." Connor laughed.

"Edward has enough to worry about without me adding to it. Besides if the only one who saw anything was that boy, I think we're in good shape." I said hopefully.

I looked around and noted that a few things were missing. "I'm going upstairs to look for our other box of supplies. Keep him quiet."

Spark just looked up and rested his head down on the table. He looked so innocently at me I couldn't help but smile.

"Sparky this is our new home for a while. I hope you like it," Connor said scratching his head. "Let's find you something to eat," Connor muttered as he began looking for the box of food.

As I started up the stairs I overheard Robert say, "Enough of that now Spark. Sorry, but your wings are grounded until we get back home. We can't take a chance of anyone else seeing you. There will just be too many people here to risk a midnight flight."

I stood by the stairs for a moment and thought of confronting Robert. He didn't know that I knew of his antics. Robert had taken to walking Spark late at night, well if you could call it walking. In the darkness of the night he and Spark would soar in the sky. It was an amazing sight that I came upon one night. I had taught Spark to fly and now he was taking my son on midnight rides.

I didn't let on to Robert that I saw him and wondered if he would confess to me he had broken my rules. Never mind that I had been doing the same thing. I guess that is why I didn't bust him on it. Robert and I both would have to forgo any sky rides for a time. I prayed Robert could refrain from that activity.

When Spark was fed and content, Robert asked if he could go have a look around the grounds. "Let's go check it out together, Connor can watch Spark for now."

"The enormity of this place is so extraordinary," Robert remarked as we walked.

Each display we passed was in some state of construction. Robert really liked the way the log cabin looked. It reminded him of the cabin we had stayed at in his youth. It was one of the few times Robert and I went anywhere on our own back then and we thoroughly enjoyed it. We loved his mom but she wasn't the type who enjoyed hiking through the woods or fishing or living off the land.

I wondered if it would be possible to own a cabin someday. Maybe out in the Oak Openings area, where it wasn't too far from town but close enough that I could take Spark there, or rather Spark could take me there, I thought optimistically. All in due time I gathered. If everything goes well here at the fair and we get him back home unnoticed I would look into that idea. My real dream would be to allow Spark to fly free as a bird whenever he wanted.

Robert was intrigued when he came upon the partially built Ferris Wheel. We had never seen anything like it. "Imagine how excited people will be to be so far up in the air!" Robert exclaimed.

We secretly already knew that feeling thanks to Spark. I will have to pretend like it's my first time in the air when we ride the wheel. Robert didn't know of my flying stunts with Spark. I was fairly certain Connor didn't know either, but if he did, he didn't let on to anyone.

"We'll have plenty of time to explore the grounds over the coming months, we better get back now," I said as I turned around.

Chapter 44

We returned to see our team all busy on their special contributions. Connor had already started working on the furnace to get the "fuel" set up. Herman Hammesjahr was finalizing his genius plan. Herman had perfected the art of spinning very fine slivers of glass. The thread like quality gave him a wild idea and he was working frantically on it. Edward busied himself by checking on every detail of the construction. He would make a list of anything awry and discuss it with Mr. Stine straight away.

The fair would be opening to the public soon and he wanted everything perfect. "Many people in the country know my name but some still may not. Red, the display here will change all that and nothing can go wrong!" Edward stated.

I knew Edward's pride was also at stake. Those board members, of Edward's own company, didn't share his vision of this project and he wanted to prove them wrong most of all.

"We have everything under control," I assured him while my team nodded in agreement, including Spark.

"Is everything squared away with the living quarters?" I asked changing the subject.

Edward's wife would be staying with him at the fairgrounds most of the time. Edward wanted to make sure she would be comfortable when she was here. They would be spending their third anniversary here after all. He still couldn't believe how lucky he was that she had married him he told me several times.

Edward instructed that the second floor be sound proof. The architect assumed it was so they'd have privacy from the public but Edward had another bigger reason for it. And that big reason would also be residing here.

Edward didn't want his wife or anyone else hearing Spark from below. Spark was fairly well trained now and didn't often roar loudly, but Edward sure didn't want to take any extra chances. We would test out the sounds tonight. The fair wasn't open yet and only a few people would even be staying here like the Libbey's planned to do. Luckily, most were staying in hotels in the nearby downtown area.

Edward knew bringing Spark would save on his expenses and therefore he had to stay close by and watch over his investment. Imagine if anyone knew there was a dragon here? It sure would cause a chaotic scene! The four secret keepers would pull this off. We just had no other choice.

Edward made another inspection of the building. The furnace looked to be in good shape. We would be ready to fire it up in a couple days. Edward was pleased it would be running for opening day. Next he walked over to the Crystal Art Room. Our most grand glass piece took center stage here. It was an exquisite punch bowl engraved with scenes of the fair. We expected it would draw a lot of attention. (We were elated later when it won a gold medal and international press.) The inside of the factory was shaping up to look like a real glass museum. Something unexpected and delightful to the fairgoers was on the horizon.

As night fell on the fairground all the workers went home. They would all return early the next morning. The rest of the evening the four of us were alone in the park. When Edward was certain that everyone was gone he joined us back down to the basement.

He was pleased with the progress we made so quickly. Just about everything was set up in the area thanks to his three co-conspirators. "Men, this looks great, let me know when you are ready to do a sound check with Spark. We'll wait a few more minutes to make sure everyone is far away from the park. You know, I had this room built with the best sound proofing materials," Edward said puffing up his chest. "We need to make sure the sound of Spark doesn't reach the display area and my apartment on the second story. Red, you stay here with him and in minute let him roar. Robert you go to the display area. Connor to the outside and I'll be upstairs."

"Let's do it." Connor said and led the way with the others close behind. I waited the allotted time and then told Spark to speak. On command Spark let out a loud roar. It was a majestic sound that I never tired of hearing. I wasn't sure if the men were in place, so I had Spark do it again, just in case.

A few minutes later the men appeared, "Well did he speak?" Edward asked.

"He belted out two giant roars. So nobody heard him?" I inquired.

"Not a thing," Robert responded and the other two shook their heads in agreement.

"Fantastic, I'm glad I got my money's worth on that investment." Edward said relieved.

I wasn't sure exactly how much Edward had spent on this mini-factory but it had to be a small fortune I reckoned. I heard rumors of it to be around $250,000. This amount of money was unfathomable to me. No wonder the board balked at the request.

Florence arrived by train in time for the grand opening. Edward and I went to the train station to greet her when she disembarked. Edward was anxious to take Florence on his arm and show her off around the fair.

"Oh Edward, this is amazing! Look at all the people, the laughter and joy in the air. I can't wait to take it all in. I hope you haven't been working Red and the other guys too hard already!" Florence said glancing to me for confirmation as we made our way to the entrance of the fair.

The handsome couple made heads turn as they proceeded down the midway. Florence looked like royalty wearing a large blue bonnet, with exquisite flowers and ribbon entwined around it. Her beautiful flowing dress, made of fine silk, glistened in the sun. She elegantly carried a parasol to ward off the sun's rays. Edward, looking dashing as always, was dressed in his ditto suit, a crisp white shirt, Astor tie and black top hat. He had one arm holding onto Florence and his other hand twirling his mustache.

Florence couldn't help but notice the huge Ferris Wheel under construction that was already towering over the sky on the right. "Oh Edward, we must ride on that wheel. Just imagine what this city looks like from way up there!"

"But, Florence, I don't know, that goes awfully high, are you sure you could handle it without fainting in fright?!" Edward loved teasing his bride and she enjoyed their playful banter.

"You should know me better than that, when I have ever shown fear?!"

"Florence, why don't you stroll the sights and make a list of what we must see and do, I must go with Red to check in on my team at the factory, I promise I won't be long."

"Oh no Edward, you mustn't leave me just yet. You've been here for a month preparing everything just so, certainly you can take the time to stroll with me while I gaze upon this wondrous place for the first time."

"I know just what you'd enjoy first, come this way." Edward said as he motioned that we follow him to the right. They strolled, arm in arm, laughing and smiling to each other, as I trailed further behind to give them some privacy. I did enjoy seeing Florence's eyes sparkle as she drank in the atmosphere, and listened to all the foreign tongues. It seemed people from all over the world were here for the grand opening.

"This is so elegant, it's like a whole new city, a wonderful, clean, white city. I feel like I'm in Europe again!"

Soon Edward was pointing out that they had arrived at the The Great Wharf, a moving sidewalk. He found a seat and took Florence's hand as she sat upon the bench. The "travelator" looped around the lakefront pier. As they sat and gazed around, Edward couldn't help but smile. The splendor and magic of this place was a delight to see.

I knew now that Edward had made the right decision to be a part of this historical moment. This was a shining example of all the good that could be accomplished in America and how far this great country had come in the past 400 years. America was always looking to Europe as the star to emulate. Well, today the world was looking at America, and seeing what it could do. This was a day that made all Americans stand a little taller, including me. I was so excited to be a part of it.

After the couple completed the loop around the lakefront pier on the moving walkway, Florence began to feel anxious for keeping Edward away from his exhibit. "Let's get you two over to the factory, Edward. I know I've kept you both away too long. Although, you've told me all about it, I want to come upon it along with a crowd of visitors and soak in their astonishment and compliments. You two go ahead and I will be along shortly."

That's all Edward had to hear, his beloved understood him so well. She had put up with him being away from home this past month as he and our team put the factory together and set everything up just right to delight and amaze the visitors. Edward knew in his heart this was his chance to shine and make his name known throughout the land for quality glassware. The opportunity to watch live demonstrations of the glass blowing technique would astonish most people. Glass blowing was around for thousands of years but it still was a magical sight to witness the process in person.

I admired Edward, he was as smart as a steel trap. He was determined to make the most of this opportunity, and he wasn't going to blow it. He knew if he could get the people coming to the exhibit they would be leaving as life-long fans of Libbey Glass.

Edward's showmanship and personality was one that immediately drew people in. You just felt comfortable that he was telling you the truth and was genuinely glad just to talk with you. Edward's generosity and humor was a part of every product that bore his name.

The only thing the visitors wouldn't be able to see was our secret accomplice. That must remain a secret from the world I thought wistfully. I was entrusted to keep this secret well-hidden and well fed. Can you imagine what would happen if this secret was uncovered at this populated event? The utter terror and confusion it would unleash would be plum ugly. I shuddered at the thought and quickly stepped up my pace to get to the factory site.

"Ring a ling". "Ring a ling".

"That's music to my ears!" bellowed an animated Edward to a couple of ladies several paces in front of us. The ladies turned around and smiled widely when they realized it was Mr. Libbey. They probably recognized him from the large picture that was hanging in factory they had just left.

"Oh Mr. Libbey, I must say your factory was wonderful and this bell you made will be a cherished souvenir of our visit here," said the older of the pair.

Before Edward could respond the younger lady exclaimed, "I do suspect my mother will get great joy ringing us for dinner with her new bell."

Edward chuckled and thanked the ladies for their purchase. "I do hope to see you at the factory again. We have several artists making different products throughout the day. Have a glassy day, ladies!" I was as pleased as Edward to hear that the bell, etched with the words "World Exposition 1893" was already a hit with fairgoers.

I wondered what kind of reaction we would have produced if we let them tour the basement?

Chapter 45

Libbey had no shortage of fine works to display at the fair. Amberina glass, invented and patented by our best designer, Joseph, a few years earlier (with Edward's secret inspiration) proved to be a real crowd pleaser. The two toned glassware was red at the top and various shades of red, orange and amber down to the bottom. It was one of the highlights of Joseph's demonstrations.

When the glass piece was reheated, it was twirled and spun and worked on carefully to get the various tints of color along the full length of the glass. The hot glass looked like the flickering flames of a fire. The colors slowly changed and danced before your eyes. A small amount of gold was added to the amber glass as the top of the glassware cooled.

Joseph showed off his artistic abilities by making vases, pitchers, tumblers and compotes and other popular wares in front of many adoring fans. Most were seeing glassware being made for the very first time, but even those who had seen it before stood in awe of his talent. Watching artists create something so masterfully in front of your eyes was an inspiring feature of the fair, precisely as Edward knew it would be.

"Careful how you sit in this dress!" I wanted to yell out to the lady bravely considering this dress. I held my tongue. I didn't dare to question an artist! Georgia Cayvan, a famous actress of the stage, somehow got it in her head that wearing a dress made of glass would be so fashionable but I think she found out how brittle little strands of glass could poke you.

Of course, you know my boss by now, he sure wouldn't miss any opportunity to show off what he and his master artists could do with glass. Ms. Cayvan was ecstatic that she would be able to model the glass dress to the world at the Exposition. *(And would you believe, it was such a huge hit that Princess Eulalie of Spain insisted that one be designed for her too?)*

I was not a woman, so I didn't claim to be any kind of expert of fashion, but really what were these ladies thinking? I can't imagine thousands of slivers of glass pressed against my fair skin! I must admit though, that as Ms. Cayvan walked across the stage, the glittering dress was a sight to behold. All the ladies swooned over the glamourous dress. Most men were like me, and just shook their heads bewildered!

The fair proved to be a roaring success! Edward's board members would be eating crow! The number of people that toured the factory was astounding. The early days of the fair was admittedly a little slow and could have spelled disaster, but Edward was quick with a plan.

Edward realized as he tried to coax people inside to look at the factory and his wares that they were a little reluctant. They didn't want to take the time to come inside, opting for other fascinations along the midway. Edward was not deterred, he was determined. He had all his money, and his family member's money riding on this venture.

While in a state of frustration one day, he said, "Well, if I charged for entry, they would think there was something magnificent to see!"

As he said that I looked at him, and we nodded in unison. "Of course, that's brilliant! Make them realize you have something valuable in here that they won't see anywhere else and they'll line up in droves."

That was all it took. An admission fee was set at twenty-five cents and it was like magic. People stood in line, happy to pay to see what was inside. Of course, they could have seen it all for free, earlier that day, but they didn't seem to remember that.

Once the people got inside they bowled over. Some days several hundred at a time entered. They stood just behind a railing and watched the glass masters carve the glass, while sitting at their cutting wheels, and shaping their masterpieces. It was certainly something I never tired of viewing. The ladies fawned over the care and precision it took to make the beautiful glassware. They all wanted a lovely piece to take home. So the plan worked. Many walked away with a lovely piece of glass and the memory of how it was crafted.

Charging admission seemed to be the tipping point to profitability. Once people saw the admission charge, they couldn't line up fast enough. The factory was bursting with customers for the remainder of the fair.

Edward was in his glory. The bigger the crowd, the more animated he became. Showing off his wares, and charming the ladies just came naturally to him. He stood like a preacher on Sunday and enlightened everyone on the beauty and mystical powers of glass. The glass glittered in response. The glass objects flew off the shelves and into the hands of admiring guests.

In the end Edward would make enough to pay back his investors and pocket a tidy profit of over $100,000. Plus over two million people from around the world came through the factory and would undoubtedly remember his name. Edward's biggest satisfaction would come when the board would have to admit they were mistaken about the venture.

The crowds that continued to fill the fair in those final days were great on the one hand, but not on the other hand. My concern was all the extra people that would be on the train on the way back east. We barely made it here undetected. Could we be so lucky again?

The more I thought about it, the more concerned I became. Days on a train or a quick flight in the air? The solution was clear as glass to me. Would I be able to convince Edward? Could I get Spark home without revealing my method? I had to try.

I decided I would tell Edward that I urgently needed to get Spark back to the factory. Connor and Robert could stay behind and help with the final days and shut down of the furnace. I would have to convince him this was the best way to protect his investments.

Fireworks would make the perfect cover. The closing ceremony was planned for October 30th and everyone would be distracted with that. "While everyone is looking to the sky for fireworks, we can fly in the other direction," I told Spark as the escape plan unfolded in my brain.

If anyone caught a glimpse of Spark's fire they would assume it was a stray flicker from the fireworks. Now that it was set in my mind, I was relieved and excited. This would be a great ending to the world's greatest fair! But I wouldn't feel at ease until we were back in Toledo under the cover of darkness.

"I see your point, Red," Edward said as he listened to me and walked through the sales area checking on the remaining pieces of glass for sale. "Taking the train ahead of the crowd, makes the most sense. Are you sure you should go alone though?"

"Oh yes, it will be fine. Besides you need the rest of the crew here to dismantle the furnace," I said. Letting Edward believe we were returning by train was necessary. I didn't feel it was good for him to know about the flying part just yet.

"We have enough fuel from Spark stored in the basement now that will get you through the final days." In case Edward wasn't totally convinced of my early departure I threw in, "However, I'm a little concerned about how much special fuel we may have left at the factory at home, and I'd feel better getting Spark back there as soon as possible."

"Oh, yes, that could be a problem. We'll take care of things here, you get packed to go."

I told Edward I had a ticket to leave the next evening. I felt a little guilty lying to him, but it was better he not know about the exact mode of transportation. I spent the rest of the day packing up my things and putting away as much as I could.

The next day I was nervously excited about heading for home. I had only lived in Toledo for a few years, but it was now my home. Connor and Robert were excited for the fireworks that evening. They were not as anxious to get home as I was it seemed. Connor had found a lovely woman that worked at another building and he wasn't looking forward to saying goodbye to her. The lady was from California, so there wasn't much chance they would see each other after the fair.

As evening fell, the fairgoers and my co-workers made their way to the lakeside. They wanted to scope out a good place to sit and watch the fireworks. When darkness descended, I rousted Spark awake and led him up the stairs. Just as I opened the door to the first floor, I heard a noise.

Florence turned towards the door, "Red, is that you? You startled me. I thought you were out watching the fireworks?"

"Oh, sorry dear. I was working on something and lost track of the time. I'm going out there soon. What are you doing back?"

"I wasn't feeling so well, so I decided to come back and rest. What are you doing? Are you smoking again?"

"What?" I said bewildered. Then I saw it. Spark had let a puff of smoke escape his nose and it wafted past my head. "Oh, shoot. You caught me. Nasty thing, these cigarettes. I keep trying to quit, you know, but everyone now and then I have to have a few puffs." I lied, hoping it sounded believable. I sure couldn't let her find Spark after all this time keeping him hidden.

"Red, I understand, but I hope you quit again. Those things aren't good for you."

I nodded sheepishly and looked back, signaling to Spark to stay put and out of sight. Florence must have felt she had admonished me enough, so she quietly slipped upstairs. When I was sure the coast was clear, I quietly got Spark out of there.

The fireworks were already going off on the other side the fairgrounds. There was not a soul in sight. We were able to sneak behind the building undetected and waited for our cue. When the next firework blasted into the sky I latched onto Spark's back and we departed. Not that it mattered, but I held my breath until we were way above the clouds.

Spark was so joyous to be flying that he did a flip and nearly lost me. The notch in the belt I had strapped around him came loose and I was in trouble. I grabbed onto his scales and prayed. He seemed to sense my distress and straightened out. When we were flying in a steady line I was able to tighten the strap and breathe. I let out a loud scream of relief.

The wind was a bit chilly tonight but I didn't mind. I was alive and flying in the sky. It was an exhilarating feeling but soon I was ready to get back on the ground. On second thought, since we weren't expected back to Toledo for another day I decided to take a detour. I signaled to Spark to head north.

I figured we could take some time to look for his family. I couldn't believe Spark was the only one of his kind. I was still committed to re-uniting him with other dragons. I didn't know how Edward would react to that but I had to try.

After some time, we landed on a remote mountaintop. If I was a dragon, this is where I would choose to live I supposed. The mountains are remote enough to provide protection and would also provide food, water and shelter.

We trekked through forests and over valleys for hours but to no avail. I knew if there were any dragons around Spark could have sniffed them out. We left deflated, but I was still hopeful. "Someday, Spark, we'll find them!"

Spark seemed content as I climbed on his back and I signaled him to go home. The flight was never long enough for me. Spark had us home in Toledo in what seemed like no time at all. When Spark noticed the familiar water tower he began the descent. We landed gently in the underbrush of our woods. I stumbled off his back and laid on the ground with my hands spread out and kissed the ground. "We're home, thanks Spark."

It was late and at this time of night, I didn't expect too much trouble getting back into the factory. I tied Spark to the tree and told him to keep quiet. I wanted to make a quick trip around to our tunnel entry and make sure nothing was amiss. We'd been gone for a few months and who knows if someone could have disturbed our area.

Once I confirmed there were no signs of trouble or people I returned for Spark. He looked as anxious as I did to get inside.

He followed alongside me as we made our way to the window. Once we got down into our old familiar tunnel I felt much relief.

"Let's get some rest and re-charge for tomorrow." I said and Spark seemed to agree. Edward was expected back here tomorrow.

Rest was easier said than done for me. I thought we made it out of Chicago undetected but a lump formed in my mouth as I looked at the newspaper laying near my door. An article about the fair commented that a few witnesses reported seeing a strange winged creature in the sky the night of the fireworks. The comments were followed by continued concerns of people disappearing or missing since going to the fair.

I held my breath and hoped that police wouldn't try to link the events. Being back in Toledo, far from Chicago, gave me some comfort. I vowed to keep Spark grounded and out of sight for a while. I just hoped that the person looking for Spark overlooked the story.

I was up all night going over all my steps and trying to recall if I saw anyone strange or anything amiss while we were in Chicago. Eventually, totally exhausted, I fell asleep in my chair. I awoke in a sweat screaming, "No you can't have Spark – he's mine!"

Chapter 46

"I'm ready to shout it out from the rooftop!" Edward exclaimed as he ran up to me when I arrived at work.

"What has you in such a chipper mood?" I asked curiously. Edward was pretty enthusiastic about many things, so I just wondered what this latest news could be. You could have knocked me over with a feather when he told me that he was expecting a baby, or rather, his wife was expecting one. After all, she was the one that would have to deliver the baby.

Edward divulged to me he was overcome with tears when Florence announced she was pregnant. They had been trying for five years and I was really beginning to wonder if it would ever happen. Both families were secretly waiting for this news from the couple.

"That's splendid Edward! This is such a joyous occasion!"

"I want to scream out to everyone around. Florence however, is more cautious. You know she's prayed for this for so long and doesn't want to jinx it."

I could understand her hesitation and sadly could relate to it. She was afraid to tell everyone in case she suffered a miscarriage. Many women her age had endured that fate, including my wife, and while she was so happy, she likely had her doubts as well. Edward would hear nothing of her worries and convinced her to embrace only good thoughts.

The couple invited everyone they knew, it seemed, to dinner on Friday night at the Club. It seemed all their good news was shared there and this certainly more than qualified. In fact this was the best news ever. Edward had Florence's favorite room, the Garden Room, reserved for Friday's big announcement.

For the next few days, I was entrusted to keep the couple's secret. But when I bumped into Florence the following day when she stopped into the factory she couldn't seem to talk about anything else. Florence knew that Edward had told me and she seemed okay with that.

"Oh Red, I'm so eager to share the news with everyone, but I also want to surprise everyone with the announcement at the party." Florence whispered quietly while pacing back and forth in front of the office before continuing, "I know Edward wants a son more than anything. He is looking forward to having a son to work alongside him someday as he did with his father. I want that too, don't get me wrong, but a little girl would be so welcome too."

I waited with Florence until Edward arrived. She apologized that she kept talking about babies. I listened as she went from one concern to another about the changes a baby would bring to her world. The couple was still living in their small apartment and it would be cramped with the addition of a baby. Luckily the house that they were building on Scottwood would be finished soon.

"I had not exactly planned out a nursery for the new home, since I wasn't pregnant when the project started a couple years ago," Florence muttered.

"This is perfect timing if you ask me. You were worried that the house was too big and grand, for just you and Edward, and now comes along another one to fill the house with joy," I said patting her on the shoulder.

It sure was a grand house they were building, and fitting of Edward's style. He always went above and beyond on everything he did and the house was no exception. It would have every modern amenity available too. They expected to move into the home in January 1895, which I just realized would be shortly after the birth of their first child, if the calculations on the due date were accurate. What a special home welcoming that would be!

Friday night finally arrived. Florence and Edward were at the Club earlier than necessary to make sure everything was set up perfectly. After all, Edward told Florence, it wasn't every day you got to tell your family the greatest news in the world!

Red wondered if anyone else caught on to the theme of the evening as they were served mini foods of every sort. Edward made sure the drinks and appetizers were served in mini glasses and the main course featured mini shrimp, baby carrots and mini potatoes. As dinner was served, Edward stood to propose a toast.

"Florence and I would like to thank our families and friends for joining us here tonight. We've enjoyed many special occasions here at the Club since it opened and could find no better place to share this joyous news. Florence is with child!" Edward said as the audience sat stunned into utter silence. Then as if the trance was broken they cheered and yelled all at once.

Florence's sister-in-law screamed the loudest and jumped out of her chair. She went running over to Florence, crying and laughing as she hugged her. "This is the best day ever! I'm going to be the best aunt!"

Florence stood up and hugged her mom, and then her father and then walked around the table as everyone stood to give their blessing. Sarah shared a quiet nod of happiness with her big brother. She was so happy to see that all his dreams were coming true.

"I can't wait to meet my niece or nephew! Have you picked out names yet? When did you find out?" Sarah said peppering the happy couple with the questions everyone else was thinking too.

Florence's life had changed so much over the past couple years since I first met her. She was happily married, pregnant and building her dream house. She knew she was such a lucky lady.

A few days later Florence received a letter in the mail from her Aunt Martha and she was worried about what it didn't reveal. She knew her aunt had been ill the prior year and wasn't totally cured yet. She told me how fond of her aunt she was and how much time she had spent with her when she was younger. I recalled how she was so sad when her aunt left Toledo to move to California. It was so far away and she wasn't able to see her as often as she did when she lived just down the street.

Florence worried that when her child was born she wouldn't be able to travel much. She would be stuck in Toledo for quite some time. Not that she would mind, she would have her baby, but she wondered how much longer her aunt had to live. I knew her aunt wasn't likely to travel to Toledo anytime soon.

"Edward is getting ready to leave in two days for another business trip and you will be left alone. Why don't you talk to him about traveling to California with your mother to visit your aunt while he's away?"

"Oh Red, that is exactly what I was thinking. I know Edward will worry about me traveling and being pregnant and all, but I'll be back in plenty of time before the birth. Maybe you can assure him that I'm not a fragile flower and I can travel in my condition," Florence said hopefully.

"Leave it to me Florence. I'll put a bug in Edward's ear. Besides, there isn't anything he would deny you anyway."

"Red, I'm so excited at the thought of seeing my aunt again. I won't be able to sleep a wink tonight. It's been so long since I've been to California. I just love it out there. I secretly hope to coax Edward to move out there someday, maybe when we retire."

"With the great weather in California, I'm sure you won't have any trouble convincing him." I said a little reluctantly thinking it might be impossible for Edward to leave Spark behind.

The phone rang as I was walking by Edward's office one morning. Ms. Halpin, yelled out to me, "Red, where is Edward? This is urgent, it's about Florence."

"Hang on, I'll run out to the factory and find him," I responded as I took off down the hall and into the factory. I nearly knocked someone over, but I didn't stop, if Florence was calling, I worried it was about the baby. I knew Edward didn't want her leaving town in her fragile state, but he couldn't say no to her about anything. If he missed the birth of the baby he would be so disappointed.

"Edward, there you are, come right away. Florence is on the line," I yelled as I turned and raced back to where I had come with Edward running right behind me.

"Hello, hello? What is it darling?" Edward yelled into the phone panting and nearly out of breath.

"Oh, oh, of course, the line is dead." Edward said as he turned to Ms. Halpin. "What did she say? What is going on? I can't get through…"

Before I could ask what the news was, Edward sat down and covered his hands over his face. He looked up at me rather sad and distraught. "It's really happening…and I'm not going to be there. Florence is having the baby isn't she?"

"Oh Edward, isn't it wonderful!" Exclaimed Ms. Halpin.

The news was exciting and upsetting at the same time. I could feel the sadness fill the air. Edward was trying to put on a brave face, but I knew where he longed to be right now. He would crawl over broken glass to be there. But even the fastest train couldn't get him there in time. There was only one way he could make it.

I puzzled it over in my mind, but before I fully thought it through I heard myself saying, "Ed, come with me, I have to show you something."

He looked bewildered as if nothing could be so urgent in the factory at this moment. However, the insistent look in my eyes and my steps encouraged him to follow. I quickened my steps down to the basement as my mind raced. I kept trying to convince myself it would be okay to tell Ed of my experiments.

We reached the lab and I whispered in Robert's ear, "I need your help. Go find Connor and tell him that I'm conducting work with Spark today and that he can take the day off. You are excused as well."

Robert looked at me, but he knew better than to question or argue this abrupt directive. He grabbed his things and quickly left us alone.

I caught my breath and turned to Edward. "I know of a way to get you to California. You can be there to see your child being born. That is what you want, right?"

"More than anything, you know that, but it is impossible. The baby is likely arriving today."

"Mr. Libbey, if I learned anything from you it's that nothing is impossible!"

Before Edward could say another word, I turned around with a saddle and handed it to him. I grabbed the handle to Spark's cage as Edward stepped back. "You're not serious? What's going on with you?"

I ushered them both towards the tunnel and said, "I've never been more serious. I've been all around the world with Spark and he is an excellent flyer. He will get us there in no time." Spark and I raced down the tunnel before Edward could object.

As Edward stood there trying to decide to follow me or scold me, I yelled to him as I started climbing out the window. I had not taken Spark out in the daytime for quite some time but I couldn't stop now. I knew nobody was in the immediate area so I waited patiently as Edward hesitantly climbed out the window. He followed as I led Spark through the wooded area. When we got to the clearing I jumped on Spark and waved for Edward to mount on behind me.

Edward was likely worried about following me to his death and never meeting his child. My only concern was being spotted as we ascended. Once we were high above the clouds I let my shoulders relax. It was then I felt the death grip Edward had on my coat strap. Spark handled the flying like the pro he was. This was my first tandem ride and it was exhilarating.

"Are you frightened?" I yelled back to Edward.

"You know I fear nothing," Edward muttered bravely, but I could feel his body trembling against mine and I smiled with giddy satisfaction.

I tried to explain to Edward why I had not told him of this secret, but I don't think it mattered anymore. I knew if, no when, I got him safely to California all would be forgiven.

Spark seemed to have an internal sense of direction and flew with purpose. We landed near a patch of woods in the town of Ojai. The gloomy skies didn't match our moods. Edward had the biggest grin on his face as we dismounted and jumped to the ground.

"How in the world could you keep that from me?" Edward admonished me.

"Well," I stammered, but Edward just let out the biggest holler and I couldn't help but laugh.

We laughed louder as Edward went over and thanked Spark profusely for another great deed. Edward said he was indebted to Spark and would never be able to repay him. Spark had helped save his factory and now was able to help reunite him with Florence.

"Florence, yes, I must get to her now. What am I going to say?" Edward said looking to me and Spark for an answer that he could plausibly provide for his sudden appearance in California.

"Ed, you just tell her that you couldn't stand to be without her and you jumped on the train days ago to get out here. You don't know anything about the baby coming yet. It is just a happy coincidence." I said proudly thinking that would be a good plausible story since she wasn't able to speak to him directly on the phone when she called the factory. I didn't like the idea of lying to Florence but we couldn't exactly tell her the truth could we? No, Edward didn't want her to know about Spark, especially with a baby about to be born.

"That might just work Red. Now I want you and Spark to get back to the factory as soon as you can. We can't take any chances of anyone spotting Spark. You know I'm still concerned about that man that Mr. Lee warned me about when I got Spark. He feared a very bad man wanted to harm Spark. That is why he wanted me to take him far away and keep him safe. Spark being out in the world like this is a real concern to me."

I gulped. If Edward only knew of the several trips we had already taken. But I knew the dangers and was always extra cautious. We never aroused any suspicion or encountered anyone. Spark was like one of my children and I would never put him in harm's way.

"I think it would be best if we hide out here until dark. You go and be with Florence. Go now."

I watched as Edward made his way up to the side of the house. We figured Florence, and her aunt, would be in such a tizzy about the baby, they wouldn't think too much about Edward showing up unexpectedly. We thought his story was plausible enough. After all, it was his first child and he did regret that she talked him into to a trip across the country at such a fragile time in her pregnancy.

"Well, lookey there Spark. It looks like you got us here in the nick of time!" I slapped Spark gently on his back as I saw what I was sure was the local doctor arriving at the house.

After waiting for what seemed like forever, but actually was only a few hours, Edward came running out to the barn to tell me that his little baby boy had arrived into this world. Mother was exhausted, as was the baby, but they were both healthy and happy. I jumped up and down and gave Ed a hug after hearing that wonderful news!

"The healthy scream of the newborn was music to my ears. Florence is so happy and can't take her eyes off the new baby. He has dark brown eyes and just a whisper of hair on his head!" Edward exclaimed.

"So what do we call this new bundle of joy?" I asked. I couldn't wait to hold the baby boy in my arms.

"His name is William Langdon," Ed said joyfully.

"Of course, I should have known. Your father would be mighty proud that you gave him his name."

"Well, I better get back up there. I owe you both for getting me here in time. I'll see you back home in a week or two. I'll have to see when Florence and William are ready to travel."

I watched as Edward sprinted back to the house. I found myself pacing back and forth, waiting for darkness so we could leave, and wondering what that baby boy looked like. Finally, my curiosity got the best of me. I decided I would sneak up to the house and peer through the window. As I approached the house I could see Edward in the kitchen holding a bundle in his arms. It looked like he was alone so I quietly inched closer to get a better view.

I was so enthralled, trying to get a glimpse of the baby, that I failed to notice my companion had followed me. It wasn't until I felt a hot stream of air rush by my cheek that I regretted my mistake. "Get back, Spark." I hissed at him. But it was too late.

Spark's tail had banged into a pail that was on a table and it went clanging against the house.

Edward turned quickly and caught a glimpse of Spark and me. His eyes looked startled as he glanced at me and then to Florence's aunt who was walking into the kitchen. I ducked as quickly as I could and pulled at Spark. I could faintly hear the lady questioning Edward about a strange figure she saw through the window. I could see her approaching the window and I prayed Spark stayed quiet. All I needed was for him to breathe and let out a flame. We would be busted and Edward would kill us.

"Spark, I think it's time to fly." I was ready to get some distance between us and this house. I didn't stick around to hear everything Edward said, but I knew I'd get an earful later.

Chapter 47

Finally, I saw the train in the distance. I stood frozen on the platform as it made its final descent to the station. Everyone here knew by now that Edward was returning with his newborn son. That's because I couldn't hide my enthusiasm and told everyone that showed up.

The others waited in anticipation along with me, just curious to see the glass king's little prince too. They were not disappointed. Edward's face was all joy when he stepped off the train with Florence and little William. The onlookers cheered and clapped when they saw the little family for the first time. Several men walked up and shook his hand and congratulated him as they waited for their own families to disembark the train.

I wanted to hear every word of William's first couple weeks of life but I knew Edward was tired and anxious to get his family home. He had everything set and waiting that a little baby could need. I had the carriage ready and got Florence and the baby settled in the back. Edward sat up front with me and quietly asked about Spark and the factory. I assured him everything was fine.

"I had a bit of trouble convincing Mary there was nothing outside her window that night. As the week went on, she kept looking and trying to convince everyone that she saw some kind of large winged creature. I told everyone I had seen her drinking quite a bit and that she was making up stories. I felt a little bad about that, but I couldn't let anyone believe her story."

The next couple months were by far the most wonderful in Edward's life. William was a happy, content little baby and barely ever cried. He was lucky to have two doting parents who fussed over him day and night. Florence didn't mind that William had to stay in a little crib in their room. But Edward was ready to move from the cramped apartment. Edward's only complaint was that the construction of their new house was taking longer than expected to end.

Florence's mother and stepmother-in-law both doted on the baby as well. They were both ecstatic to have a new grandson in the family. Edward remarked that they were both over almost daily to check on William. They both tried to take William off Florence's hands to give her some time alone, but that rarely happened. Florence never wanted to spend even a few hours without William by her side.

That Christmas was a very happy one for both families. I had my son with me and Edward had his baby's first Christmas which made it an extra special year. I noticed that Santa didn't miss hearing that William was born. Under the tree were several presents for little William.

"We both agreed not to get the new baby too much, as he is too young to appreciate it anyway, but as you can see we just couldn't help ourselves." Edward said.

"I just wanted to drop off this gift from the guys." I said as I handed the package to Florence.

The men at the factory, engraved a special glass vase with William's name and birthdate on it. It was a really special gift that the parents admired as Florence lifted it out of the box.

"Oh, this is so stunning and thoughtful," Florence said as she looked at it. "Tell the men, how very much I will treasure this always."

Edward agreed and added, "Yes, they certainly outdid themselves. I didn't know anything about it." Edward said thoughtfully and was truly pleased to have such a good group of men working for him.

Edward led me into the kitchen to get a drink. I took a seat at the table and he turned to me and said, "You know, I feel like I have two children. My first born is quite scaly, but lovable. How is Spark doing today?"

I filled Edward in on some of the new tricks Spark was mastering. I wanted to tell him of our strange encounter the other night when we went looking for his dragon family, but I stopped myself. It was Christmas after all, and I didn't want to dampen Edward's spirits.

There wasn't much to tell really. We had a close call upon landing in Ireland, nearly landing by a pack of wolves, but we managed to escape with barely a scrape. I felt sure we were getting closer to finding more dragons, but it turned out to be another dead end.

"Come see what I got for William," Edward said as he led me into the other room where the table contained a toy train set. Even though it would be years before he could play with it, Edward couldn't wait to get it. I sat with Edward that afternoon and we put the train set together.

William was close by listening as Edward explained every step of the instructions. I could see William just loved listening to his father, although it was doubtful he understood a word. Edward spoke with such intensity and expression that William couldn't help but laugh and coo along. This only encouraged Edward more. Florence found it hysterical when she came upon us.

"I think you will have that train track wore out before William ever gets old enough to play with his toy!" Florence teased. She seemed to get a kick out of seeing Edward playing so intently with the toy and his son.

Edward looked up and smiled and informed her, "I have to make sure every part works just right. William will be playing with this before you know it. I think this makes a great addition to his nursery."

As New Year's Eve approached I insisted the Libbey's go out and celebrate at the Club. "Uncle Red can handle the little one for one night," I assured Florence.

It was the first night Edward was able to get Florence away from little William. She felt guilty leaving him, although he was in good hands with me. Don't worry, I won't let him play with the dragon, I wanted to yell out, but I refrained. I only hoped they would both Spark someday.

By February the young Libbey family was on the move. Their new home was finally ready. I arrived early that morning to help with the move and found Florence looking around nostalgically at the apartment. "Why does it suddenly seem so small, Red? I have so many happy memories here, but since William moved in the apartment is a bit too cramped for comfort."

"You won't have that problem in the new house," I remarked.

The new house on Scottwood was a masterpiece. It was two years in the making and it was exquisite. The house boasted over 10,000 square feet. Their apartment could easily fit in just one room of the house. The new place was more extravagant than Florence ever expected. Edward may have gotten a little carried away but he wanted his queen and little prince to live in a magnificent palace he told me many times.

The house was built in the Colonial Revival pattern that Edward always raved about after his trips to Italy. Florence loved the wrap-around verandah. I knew she would spend a lot of time out there once the weather got warmer. For now she would enjoy the interior. The two-story bay window in the living room looked like an inviting place to sit and read I remarked as I helped Edward with the furniture. Reading was one of Florence's favorite pastimes and it was important to have a cozy well-lit corner to curl up and read a book he told me.

"I can't wait to try out this window seat in the early morning light," Florence said as she plopped down on the chair. "Mornings are my favorite time of day. If I can enjoy a cup of tea and read before Edward and William wake up, I feel so invigorated."

It was a snowy February day but we didn't notice the cold for long. Edward soon had all five fireplaces throughout the house lit up. William was mesmerized by all the flickering fires as his mom walked him from room to room. She couldn't wait to hear the pitter patter of his little feet on the hardwood floors in the next couple months she commented.

I busied myself moving boxes from room to room and eventually came upon Florence rocking William in his nursery. She sang quietly to him and he just stared up at her. I couldn't help but stand quietly near the doorway and listen happily as Florence sweetly sang to her son and told him about his future in their new home. *"I said Ohio is the place you ought to be, so he came to make Toledo the Glass City…"* Florence suddenly stopped and looked a little embarrassed when she noticed me there.

"You know you weren't supposed to hear that. William can't tell how bad I sing but I'm afraid you can," Florence said quietly.

"Nonsense, you have a beautiful voice and anyone would love hearing you sing. Was that a song you made up about Edward, has he heard it?"

"I hope not. I was just goofing around and telling William a little about his father."

Once William was resting quietly Florence put him down in the crib and we left his room. We descended the stairs and found Edward arranging an array of books in his new study. He smiled broadly as he saw us approach the doorway. "I have a feeling you will be spending a lot of time in this room," Florence said smiling as we entered.

The oak paneling lining the walls reminded me of the Red Room he had designed for the Club. The rich wood trim of the room was adorned with paintings he had picked up in Europe a few years ago. It was looking more like a home than just a house.

"It took a long time to get this house built, but well worth the wait," Edward remarked as he got up and gave his wife a big hug. "At last we are at home. I know we will enjoy many happy years here together," he said lovingly to his wife.

Edward had so many reasons to be happy with his life. He had his wife, son, a new house and family members close by. His business had been going well the last couple years too. He knew he was a lucky man.

The movers had set up some of the furniture over the past week but there was still plenty to do. I thought the rest of the unpacking could wait until tomorrow. I could see Florence was ready to enjoy one restful evening with her two best men in their new home. Besides, I made my farewells and departed. I had to check on my *two* sons.

Chapter 48

The next few months of 1895 went by quickly. Florence was engrossed with the joys of motherhood and Edward enjoyed his new fatherhood status and the joy of a bustling business. He had always worked long hours at the factory, but now he found himself getting home by early evening. He wanted to get home to hear all the details of his son's day.

Florence never tired of retelling almost every moment of their day. It seemed that each day William was doing something new that made his parents so proud. Florence's days were often filled with family or friends that visited to spend time with little William. Those first months with William were the happiest of Florence and Edward's life.

Unfortunately, the happiest year would end as the most tragic and heart wrenching they would ever encounter.

It came on, out of the blue one night, when William was just ten months old. Edward said the whooping sound of William in the other room woke Florence in utter panic. She raced down the hall to William's room with Edward close behind her. Florence picked William up in her arms and tried to comfort him. His breath was so irregular and he was gasping so hard.

Edward took him from Florence and held him tightly in his arms. He rocked him gently until the coughing subsided. They stayed there with William for a long time until he was finally asleep again. Edward returned him to his crib and gently coaxed Florence out of the room. She was reluctant to leave William but was exhausted and he didn't want to risk waking William again that night.

The couple returned to their bedroom and got back in to bed. Edward assured Florence that he would be okay and that she should get some sleep. As Edward turned and tried to fall asleep he heard his wife's quiet tears. He wrapped his arms around her and tried to calm her down.

"I could tell she was thinking the worst, but I tried to assure her it was just a little cold and that all children get a cold sooner or later. The trouble was the sound of his cough. Florence knows people that had children die from whooping cough and she is frightened to death that William could have it."

"I'm sure you did your best trying not to worry yourself and trying to keep Florence calm," I remarked.

To their horror, William didn't get any better. The coughing continued to get worse throughout the next day. Florence got so worried she contacted Edward and he came racing home from work. It was the only time she ever asked him to come home early. She was beyond frightened as William got worse and worse. He had trouble breathing, he was running a fever and he was miserable. They contacted the doctor, but there wasn't much they could do about it.

A couple weeks later, on September 9th, little William passed away in the loving arms of his mother.

Florence's mother was in the next room when it happened. She was bringing some food to her daughter who had barely left William's side the last couple weeks. She was devastated and didn't know what to do for her daughter or what to say. Their beloved William was gone. It was a tragedy that many women endured in these times, but you never expect it will happen to your family.

Florence was inconsolable. A darkness filled the new house. The echoes of silence covered the house and its occupants. What should have been the happiest time of their lives turned tragically into the worst. Edward tried to put on a brave front for Florence but he was suffering just as much.

How could this happen? They had both waited so long for a child and were so happy when they found out Florence was pregnant. Those months of anxious anticipation were exciting and fun, but nothing could have prepared them for the joy little William brought to their lives. It wasn't uncommon for babies to die in their first year of life in these times. Like all couples, they knew the odds but brushed those thoughts aside and hoped for the best.

They lived every moment rejoicing in William and the love he brought into their home. They had not thought of life without him. He was just ten months old and was so happy and healthy up until those last couple weeks. It started with that little cough and quickly turned into a wheeze as he got sicker and sicker and could barely breathe. William just slipped away from us too soon.

It wasn't fair. He didn't have a chance at life. He would never experience the freedom of walking, talking, going to school or doing any of the normal everyday things that people take for granted.

I was just as devastated as Florence and Edward. I knew how much Florence had wanted children. I was there at William's birth and saw those special moments they shared when mother and son laid eyes upon each other for the first time. I was only blessed with one child and couldn't imagine the heartbreak I would have encountered if Robert had died in my arms as an infant, or even now. It just wasn't right that a parent should lose a child.

Regrettably, I knew nothing I could say would make Florence feel better. With Edward at her side Florence would eventually pull through this tragedy. Florence was still young and possibly could have another child someday. I knew that would be the last thing on their minds in the near term, but maybe in time it could be a reality, I hoped silently.

The funeral was a quiet, small affair. It was a place nobody wanted to be, but we had to be there for the parents. Florence was in such a grief-stricken state, it was difficult for the minister to get through the blessing.

After the service we left the church and made our way to Woodlawn Cemetery. It was one of the oldest cemeteries in the town. Many of the well-known families were buried there. The cemetery had a beautiful, serene, park-like setting. A pond was on the east side. Along the western side was the river and a bridge stretched across it. Flowers were planted all around the pond. The pond was a favorite spot with the geese. It would be a place Florence and Edward would get to know very well as they would often visit William's grave over the years to come.

It was early September and the groves of trees around the cemetery were just beginning to transform to their autumn hues. The colors reflected beautifully in the pond and made a pretty scene, if not for the headstones and monuments. William's headstone listed the year of his birth, 1894 and his death, 1895. The stone also listed his parent's names below his own. *(They both would join William again, here one day, but it would not be until many years later.)*

I knew Edward reluctantly returned to work the day after the funeral but I felt he had to for his sanity. I knew he needed to immerse himself in work to help numb the pain he was feeling, just as I did when my wife passed away. That was a pain so deep I didn't expect it would ever leave me. I've carried that sorrow every day, but feeling the pain of loss of your child must have been a thousand times worse.

Florence insisted Edward return to work too. She wanted to be alone, but her mother insisted upon staying by her side. Florence was a strong person and needed time to pull herself up with that strength.

Mrs. Scott was also there to run interference for anyone wishing to stop by to see Florence. She would take their condolences and well wishes and assure them that Florence would contact them when she was up to it. The vast number of people that stopped by was a testament to how well Florence was thought of by so many people in town.

Chapter 49

When will the rough times end, I wondered? The next few weeks were tough for me. It was hard to see Edward and Florence endure such deep grief over William's death. Edward wanted to be home to comfort Florence but he became a big reminder of the loss. He told me that every time Florence looked at him, she teared up and he felt helpless. At least he could get away to the factory and escape for some time.

"How good to see you Edward. How is Florence doing?" I asked as Edward entered the room.

"Not so great Red, it's going to take more time. Florence needs something to keep her busy that would be just as rewarding and distracting as my work. She had such a love for art perhaps she could do something with that, I don't know but I need your help," Edward said as he walked closer to his desk.

"Of course, anything. Whatever thing, big or small, I could do to help Florence just tell me," I said most sincerely.

"Thanks Red, you're a great friend."

Edward knew that I meant every word. Edward was there as a friend when I lost my wife several years back, and that had just cemented our friendship. He knew I understood somewhat the heartache Florence was experiencing. Unquestionably losing a child must have been so much worse, but a loss is still a loss.

"She's barely out of the house these days. It's not healthy for her and I'm worried," Edward confided to me.

"I'm glad Sarah is visiting her today. Sarah is a fun spirited girl and always has a way of brightening everyone's day. I'm sure she'll find a way to help Florence," I said reassuringly.

Edward went over to Spark. "Any luck with the latest tests?"

I could see Spark was able to put Edward in a better mood. You couldn't help but smile with a dragon around. As I thought about that, I had a sudden pang of guilt. How could we feel a moment of happiness when Florence only felt sorrow and remorse?

That's when the revelation finally hit me. Florence needed to be brought in on Project Ignite. I knew Edward had always planned to do it, but something always got in the way. Understandably when they had their baby, Edward decided it wasn't a good time to tell a new mother there was a dragon in the neighborhood. Her protective motherly instinct wouldn't let her be so open-minded that he would pose no danger to her baby.

We seemed to have the revelation at the same time. Edward turned to me and said what I was thinking, "You know, I've been meaning to do this for years, and maybe now is the perfect time. It certainly would give her something else to think about, if even for a few minutes."

With the words not even uttered out loud I knew what he meant. We realized we couldn't think of another thing that would make her feel better. We could set up the introduction for tomorrow.

"There's no more time to waste, Red. No. Otherwise, I'll find another excuse and it may never happen. I don't want to withhold this joy from Florence, or anyone for that matter. Yet, sharing it with more than the few we already had could pose a danger to Spark and I won't allow that to happen."

As we sat in Spark's headquarters in the lower basement we thought of a plan to coax Florence to the office. She had been refused to leave the house since the tragedy, but Edward hoped that the day with Sarah would put her in a more congenial mood. Edward would tell her he needed her to come to the plant to review some important papers that he didn't want to take out of the factory.

Edward explained further, while convincing himself, why it was time to bring Florence into the fold on our special project. "I never intended to keep this secret from her, but you know all the trouble we had from the beginning. I just didn't want her to worry, especially with the danger that Mr. Lee had alluded to when he told me about his troubles with Spark and how he wanted him safely out of the country. Now, I think knowing about this and what we're doing here will actually help her, at least in some small way. If nothing else, it will certainly get her mind off her troubles for a spell," Edward stated.

"That's putting it mildly!" I responded. "I'll tell Connor when he shows up. You know he'll want to perform the initiation ceremony."

Edward smiled at that and said, "Yes, I fully expect that. I think it's a good idea too. It helps to realize the significance of the secret."

Plus it was fun to watch their reaction I exclaimed with a hearty laugh. I thought back on that happy day when we brought my son onboard the project.

"I will get Florence in here first thing tomorrow morning. Ask the others to be ready, I'll check back with you later." Edward said as he left me alone with Spark.

Now that the plan was in place Edward must have felt like he was doing something positive to help his wife and surely felt a small bit of relief. The rest of my day went better. I even caught myself smiling a few times throughout the day as I imagined Florence's reaction to meeting Spark tomorrow. It was going to be grand!

Towards the end of the afternoon I made my way to Edward's office. He had hung up the phone and looked more relaxed than I had seen him in weeks. "Florence is having a good day, I could hear the sounds of the piano when I phoned home. Sarah made a breakthrough with her today that I couldn't do these past few weeks. While the melody was a little melancholy, I was just pleased that at least she was playing again."

Florence had taken lessons for years in her childhood and her parents surprised her with the piano when they moved into their house I recalled. It sure wouldn't have fit in the tiny apartment they first lived in or her parents would have given it to her sooner.

"I told her I had something very important to discuss with her and she would have to come with me to the office tomorrow."

"Did she question why you couldn't just tell her on the phone?"

Edward looked at me and said, "No, I convinced her it was something she must see and it would be too difficult to bring it home."

"Don't worry boss, I'll have everything ready to go in the morning," I replied and then added reassuringly, "You won't regret it so don't look so concerned. It is all going to be fine."

Edward confessed that having his secret revealed to Florence tomorrow would be a relief. He knew it was a long way from the joy they had known with William, but he was taking it one day at a time now.

I stepped out of the room before Edward could back out of it or pester me for more information.

I was at the front entrance as the couple arrived at the plant the next morning. Edward greeted several people as we walked through the hall and Florence gave a cheerful smile and nod to the curious onlookers. Florence looked a little bewildered as we passed by Edward's office, wondering why they didn't stop, but she knew better than to question it.

As we walked into the noisy manufacturing area, I yelled loudly, "Follow me. Watch your step, these stairs are starting to get a little slick from the grease already." Florence was glad she was wearing sensible shoes and looked down at the steps as she descended.

As we reached a level below the basement, I could see a curious look on her face. It seemed that she didn't know this area existed. What the heck could be so important it was down here she probably wondered.

Edward unlocked the door which read, "AUTHORIZED PERSONNEL ONLY" and opened it to reveal a long hallway. There were different hallways that led to the large holding tanks. You could also view underneath some of the machines from here. It was also dark and gloom and not a place many wanted to walk around.

A large pile of broken glass was kept down the north hallway. The floor above it was grated and discarded pieces of glass landed here throughout the day. The broken glass, known as cullet, was re-melted and reused in the manufacturing process.

"I never thought about where you kept all this cullet during the waiting period. It is a little dark and creepy down here, but also fascinating," Florence yelled just barely loud enough for me to hear. She marveled that she never thought the underbelly of the factory would be so remarkable. *(Little did she know the most remarkable thing to see was still to come.)*

We arrived at my office door and Edward gave a quick knock as he opened it with his key. Florence saw a couple familiar gentlemen inside, Connor and Robert. Both of them rushed over to shake Florence's hand and welcomed her to our office.

"This is your office?" she said trying to be polite as she looked around. It was a nice enough, large size laboratory I always thought. However, as I watched her look around I could tell she wondered how we worked in such a place each day. I guess it did look a little drab with no windows and no natural sunlight. "I don't know if I could work down here alone, it would be rather creepy to me. What if something happened, who knows when someone would ever find you."

Edward directed Florence to a table in the corner and she sat down. Edward sat next to her as we hung back not sure how Edward wanted to start this conversation. At that moment Edward spoke, "Florence these gentlemen here have been helping me on a most incredible project. It is highly confidential. Only the people in this room are privy to it. I would like to bring you in on this project. I don't like to keep things from you and though you are not involved in my business, you are my wife. If something would happen to me, this would all be yours."

Florence cleared her throat, and I could see she didn't want to think such unpleasant thoughts. Edward saw her flinch and realized he shouldn't have said those words to her, especially now.

Edward started again, "I think this will go a far way into you understanding all the extra time I spent here, especially in those first couple years of our marriage."

I shared a glance at Florence and thought back on some of the strange times in their early marriage Edward had gone running out into the night claiming there was some sort of emergency at the plant. Edward always told me that she didn't press him for more details. She knew if he wanted to tell her more he would and if he didn't she would try and be there when he was ready. Apparently he was finally ready.

"Is this something you just started working on in Toledo or does this go back even further?" Florence asked now that he had more than piqued her interest.

She noticed the other men just standing behind Edward, staring at her intently. She slowly looked each one in the eye. They looked like they were validating whether it was a good idea to bring her into the fold on their project. She likely couldn't tell if they were concerned about telling her because technically she was an outsider, or was it because she was a woman? She may not have an engineering background like we did, but we knew she was plenty bright.

She decided to try and ease our minds. "Gentlemen, won't you please take a seat. Let me assure you that I have the utmost respect for your work and the expertise you provide to the company. I am here solely at Edward's request and I have no intention of getting involved in my husband's business unless he truly finds it necessary."

Of course it was none of our business how Edward decided to run his affairs. We were his employees after all. We knew she technically owned the company too, but we all appreciated her words just the same.

Once everyone seemed content that the preliminary caveats were out of the way, Edward was ready to continue.

"Florence this is a new concept, a revolution that came about after I was already here in Toledo."

He stopped and we shared a glance. I bit my tongue to prevent myself from blurting out the fact that she was actually with him upon the date of discovery. I watched and waited. He wasn't ready to divulge that point yet, as I suspected. I guess he didn't feel it was totally relevant, so he decided to omit that intriguing detail.

"These men here have helped me enormously and I couldn't have done any of this without them. Nobody else in the factory knows now, or will ever know about this project. This goes without saying, but for the benefit of my team here, we must have your word that you will never breathe a word of this to anyone."

Florence wasn't concerned about keeping a secret for her husband so she looked at all of us and said, "You have my word, all of you."

Connor clapped his hands together and smiled when he yelled, "Marvelous!" He was enthusiastic to get on with the initiation and then warned, "Before we do the big reveal, we have a formal ceremony to initiate you to our club."

Florence laughed at that part. I had not heard her laugh in weeks and it made me smile. "You all sure like to drag things out. I can see you've all been around Edward, the showman, too long! Well, let's get on with it. What do I need to do? Is there a secret handshake or secret language I need to learn?" She said it in jest, but could see by the way we looked around at each other, we were considering this now.

The stage was set with the candles placed around it. Connor looked and pointed at me to turn off the lights. I played my trumpet gently as I heard Connor step towards the tunnel door and said,

"No longer will you be in the dark,
For today you'll learn the mystery of our spark.
A greater secret you'll never know,
May our Spark shine within you, wherever you go."

Spark lit the candles on the stage in one quick hail of fire as he moved onto the platform. As Spark stood there spreading his wings in the circle of flickering light, Edward grabbed Florence's hand and looked excitedly into her eyes.

Spark was greeted with Florence's scream. It was a blood-curdling scream, one of which I had not heard before. Boy I was glad this area was sound-proof! Spark felt her terror and sprang behind Robert. Florence stepped back and tried to speak but no words escaped.

Edward squeezed her hand and told her Spark was real and he was harmless. When Spark heard Edward say his name, he poked his head out from behind Robert and looked at Florence. He looked out with his big brown eyes and had the sweetest look on his face, at least I thought so. Florence watched us as we coaxed and calmed Spark down. It was the strangest sight. Four grown men fussing over a dragon like he was a small child.

By that point Florence had regained her composure and with everyone's encouragement, she ambled slowly towards Spark. "A dragon? But how can this be? They aren't real. You didn't perform some crazy experiment down here to create this, did you?" Florence asked as she looked around the room at all the lab equipment trying to make sense of this all.

This made Edward chuckle loudly. He wasn't sure how she was going to respond to meeting a dragon but we never expected she would think they had created him in their lab! Edward's laugh prompted the rest of us to laugh too. When Florence heard us all laughing she realized how preposterous that sounded. But it was a day for preposterous things to happen she retorted.

Of all the things she could have learned that day, this is the last thing she would have ever guessed. Dragons are real and my husband, no we, own a dragon, she uttered several times! Spark was ready to win her over and walked over to her slowly. She hesitantly grabbed his claw and shook it.

"Sorry I screamed, I just never saw anything like you before. You are magnificent!"

I'm sure if Spark could talk he would have said the same thing. He's never met a girl before, let alone such a beautiful one.

"His name is Spark," Robert offered.

"Nice to meet you Spark," she said as he nudged his head up under her arm. Spark knew how to win her over and it definitely worked. She was taken with him from that moment on. Florence delighted in all the tricks he could do. He really put on a show to make a great impression.

I sat back and smiled as the rest of Edward's team went on and on explaining everything they'd been doing with Spark and bragging about all the money we had saved the company. Florence couldn't have been more thrilled to listen to everything and marvel at the wondrous project. She was so impressed with Edward that she wasn't even upset he had kept it from her for so long. When Robert told her about the mishap on the train to Chicago she couldn't stop laughing at the picture of it in her head but then realized she had been living with Spark at the fair.

"You mean, all that time I was staying that apartment in the factory, Spark was right there? How could I not have known that?"

Edward just smiled sheepishly and nodded his head. I could tell he was relieved to see Florence back to her old self. Even if her mood only lasted for the morning, it was a good start.

"Wait a minute that tattoo on your arm, was that really something from your childhood or was that because of Spark?" Florence asked suspiciously at Edward.

Connor chimed in excitedly, "Oh that's Spark alright, look we all got them!" Connor said proudly as he lifted his sleeve to reveal the same marking.

"Well, if I'm to be a true member of this club, I insist on one too," Florence said loudly pointing her finger at Edward.

It would have been scandalous if discovered on such a lady. Ladies didn't spoil their bodies with tattoos, at least none I knew. But Florence liked to buck the system and start her own fashion trends at times. That type of thinking may have been what intrigued Florence about it. It didn't take her a moment before exclaiming, "I'm in. If I'm to be a full-fledged member of this secret club I insist on wearing the mark. Red, pull out the ink."

Florence took a chair and pulled it to the center of the room. She sat down and pointed her index finger at me and motioned me to come towards her. Edward shrugged his shoulders and threw his hands up in defeat. Florence smiled in triumph at Edward as she rolled up her right sleeve.

In less than an hour she stood proudly admiring the symbol on her arm. "Thank you all," she said as she turned around towards us, "you really have no idea how much this means to me. We five are bound together to keep the secret of the flame!"

She hated to leave but said by now she had taken up too much of our morning. She thanked us all profusely, especially Spark, and said she would be back. We all said she was welcome to visit anytime. She definitely would be back she told us and thanked us again.

When the Libbey's reached the hallway Florence hugged Edward. He looked back at her in surprise and delight as she said this was the best morning she had in a long time. I could tell Edward was just content to see her smile and laugh; it had been way too long.

"Gentlemen we did it!" I said as I gave Robert and Connor a vigorous handshake. "Spark, you little sparkling heart throb! You really lifted her spirits more than anything has in a long time," I said patting his back.

Florence got home that day with a renewed vow she told me later. She was determined she would also find a project that would be stimulating for her. Although it would be tough to beat Project Ignite, she had an idea. Her biggest passion was to the arts.

She felt art was so essential to a well-rounded education. She always felt guilty that many of the children in the community didn't have access to the cultural arts that were such an important part of her life. She decided it was time to find a way to change that.

Florence's first order of business was to organize the artwork that she had acquired over the years. She was fortunate and traveled with her parents extensively while growing up. Her parents indulged her hobby and even provided her with teachers and private lessons to learn how to draw and paint like a professional.

Florence always remarked that she had more passion than talent and never thought anything she created would ever be "museum quality" like the artists she admired. Whenever she found a particular artwork that she really liked when she was younger her father would quietly make note of it. If she was lucky, which was often the case, she would receive something she had revered for a birthday or Christmas gift.

Florence owned several large, valuable paintings before she left home. When she first married Edward their apartment was too small for most of her art collection so she kept them stored at her parent's home. I remembered how excited she was to finally be reunited with them when she moved into the dream home Edward built for her.

Every room contained a couple impressive paintings that either she or Edward had managed to acquire. There were so many that their home was starting to look like a museum. Edward had mentioned several times the need for a museum in Toledo.

In addition to the paintings, they of course had several extraordinary pieces of glass art. Some of these items were made by Libbey Glass and some were acquired over the years from overseas. Not many museums displayed glass as artwork, but after the huge interest in our display at the World's Fair a couple of years ago she knew there were others that shared this interest.

Edward invited me to his home that evening after work. We arrived to find Florence staring at a painting over the sofa in their parlor. We were both pleased to see that she was up and around. "Are you planning to move that?" Edward asked as we entered the room.

"Oh no, well at least not now," she replied and Edward looked at her in confusion. "I'm putting together a list of all of our art pieces. You know, we have quite a vast inventory of treasures. I started thinking today that maybe all our jokes about a museum should be taken seriously."

"What do you mean?" Edward asked still confused.

"I think we have such a fine collection that maybe we should seriously consider displaying it for the public to enjoy. My father has some empty buildings downtown, and maybe we could set up a temporary display and see what happens."

"That sounds like a great idea. I know a few of my associates at the Club who would be interested too," Edward replied. He always liked the idea of a museum in his hometown. If nobody else was going to start one, maybe they should do it.

"Red, you wouldn't believe how much we already have between us. We could fill a wing of the New York City Museum of

Art!" Florence said excitedly. The more she had been thinking about this today the more convinced she became that Toledo needed an art museum.

"I bet you're right, but no living art, ok?" I said seriously, thinking of Spark.

This reply got Florence laughing. "I was trying to keep that quiet, even here, but that was just unbelievable today," Florence said as she stepped closer to her husband and said, "You never cease to amaze me Mr. Libbey. There is certainly never a dull moment since you came into my life."

"I may be called a lot of things, but dull has never been one of them!" Edward quipped. He looked happy to be joking and teasing with his wife. "Red and I wanted to take you out for dinner at the Club tonight. You've had a full day of work, here and at the factory today. You deserve a little pampering and an exquisite meal," he said candidly.

"You know, that sounds like an excellent idea," Florence said as she hugged her husband. This was exactly what he had been waiting for, the old Florence he'd been missing for so long was back.

"Good, and if we see any art enthusiasts there we can talk to them about the art display."

"Deal," Florence replied.

Edward was so glad Florence was finally ready to go out in public. It had been too long since she'd been out for an evening of fun.

The Club was fairly full I noted as we entered. I recognized many familiar faces as we entered the lobby. There were over a hundred members now, so on any given night dozens would be in the dining room, or in the Centennial room playing billiards. The hostess greeted me and the handsome couple and led us to Edward's favorite table by the large bay window. A few people stood to greet us as we passed by.

When we were seated Florence said, "Edward thanks for suggesting this tonight. You've been very patient with me and I'm sorry that I've not been so outgoing lately."

"There is no reason to apologize, I'm just glad you were in the mood to go out tonight. I hope I had something to do with your improved mood and it wasn't all due to you know who this morning," Edward said hopefully. Actually he didn't need credit for her higher spirits he was just content to see they were elevated.

Florence smiled, "I must admit that did have an effect on me, but without you I wouldn't have ever had a clue about it. So I guess you get some credit too."

I could see that meant the world to Edward. I knew he felt like somehow he had let Florence down when their son died. It wasn't in his control, but he was her husband and felt like there must have been something else he could have done to save him, although there was not. It was nobody's fault, it was just his time.

God must have needed him more he told her over and over, when he found her crying alone in the nursery. It was the only thing that got him through it he confessed to me. He was devastated when his mother and father had died, but it was nothing compared to the heartbreak of losing his son. It just wasn't the natural order of things. A son was supposed to outlive his parents not the other way around. Even with all his training for the ministry he still didn't understand how and why these things should happen to anyone.

I had no answers.

Chapter 50

"Where's the new Spark of my life?" Florence yelled excitedly as she entered the lab.

Florence sure didn't want to disrupt us men at work but she couldn't stay away from Spark. I couldn't blame her. She thought about what she could do, almost missing the most obvious solution. What had she been working on all week? Artwork. And what was missing from their collection? A portrait of Spark! She certainly couldn't hire someone to do it. She would have to do it herself.

"The more I thought about it, the more I'm sure I can convince Edward of its importance. Of course, I won't be able to show it to anyone outside of our club but it would be an important part of my personal collection, what do you think, Red?"

"Are you asking me because you want to surprise Edward or are you afraid to ask for his approval?"

"You know, I accepted the fact that Edward kept Spark a secret from me, but you may be right that he might not understand me keeping such a secret from him, especially if it involved Spark."

Florence didn't need too much cajoling to agree that everything would go smoother with Edward if she had the plan all worked out and ran it by him for approval. She figured she would need a couple of weeks to get Spark sketched out properly. Drawing portraits from live models was not her strong suit, but if she didn't do it, who would?

Florence felt it was important to capture Spark on canvas even if only the five of us ever saw it. If anyone else ever happened upon it she would say she was trying her hand at fantasy art which was becoming more common in 1896. Most would think that genre to be out of character for her, which is why she could say she was trying to keep it hidden. She would feign embarrassment of anyone knowing that she fantasized about dragons.

With Edward's blessing in hand, Florence returned the following day eager to start. First she wanted to talk with me to find out the best time of day to study and draw Spark. Spark was kept fairly busy during the day I reminded her. Spark was now rather critical to the operations so I preferred the work be done in the evenings. Fortunately, this arrangement was alright by Florence.

Edward worked late most evenings anyway so Florence could come in the late afternoon for a few hours and go home when Edward was ready. This was also ideal since she would be coming in after shift change and there was a smaller number of employees around. This would reduce the number of people she would have to pass by.

I met Florence at the front gate that first afternoon and walked her inside. Nobody would think anything of her visiting at that time of day, especially with Edward around. I escorted her to Edward's office where we found him jostling some papers on his desk. Florence promised Edward that she wouldn't scream and scare Spark this time.

"I'm glad you thought of this Florence. I will enjoy having a portrait of him. I just wish we had thought of it sooner so we could have had one from his first days here." Edward remarked.

"You wouldn't believe it, but he fit in the palm of my hand back then," I said remembering fondly that feeling of holding Spark in my hand that first time.

The people in the plant we passed by were so engrossed in their work they didn't bother looking up as we passed through their areas. We quietly descended down to the sub-basement without notice.

We found Connor working on an experiment under the microscope when we entered the room. He stopped right away and came over to greet our newest member.

"Florence, it's great to see you again. I'm usually down here alone at this time so I'm glad to have company," Connor said smiling and waving her over to look at his work.

As Connor spoke, Spark woke up and scurried over towards Edward. Edward petted him and then pulled Connor aside to discuss something while Florence got acquainted with Spark.

"I'm going to be spending some time with you, Sparky!" Florence said happily walking towards Spark.

Florence pulled out her sketchbook and pencils. Then she walked around the room trying to select the best place to seat her model. She saw Spark settle down in one area and she decided to sit back and study him for a while. She wanted to get some measurements of him and thought she could do it tomorrow but then she remembered that engineers were in charge of this project.

"Connor do you happen to have any measurements of Spark?"

"Certainly. We take stats on him weekly. I have his height, weight, and everything on a graph chart," Connor said helpfully.

"Of course you do," exclaimed Florence clapping her hands in a joyful manner, "if I could look at it, I think that would really help me out and save some time."

"I'll leave you to your assignment dear." Edward said winking at Florence as he retreated towards the door.

Florence looked down and blushed. She waited until Edward was out of sight and then looked up impatiently as she got down to the business at hand.

Edward came and picked Florence up when he was done for the night. "I was so engrossed with my drawing I didn't realize how much time had passed," Florence said as she looked up at Edward.

"Would you look at that--" Edward said and was cut short.

"No fair peeking, I'm not ready for you to see this yet." Florence said sternly as she pushed Edward away and covered her drawing with a cloth.

The next few evenings went along pretty much the same as the first - until Friday. Robert was there in place of Connor when she arrived. Robert usually worked later at night but he was covering a few hours early for Connor today. Florence, like the rest of us, found she enjoyed Robert's youthful, high spirited energy in the room.

It wasn't long before I saw him admiring her drawings. He complimented her on capturing Spark's image but he thought the renderings were a little stiff and uninspiring. It wasn't Florence's fault. Her model was usually laying quietly and resting while she worked. She didn't have much opportunity yet to see him action, supplying energy to the furnace, running in the yard or flying.

Robert had not told or shown anyone else how he flew on Spark's back. However, for Florence he was willing to make an exception. It was a secret, inside a secret, that was too wonderful to keep to himself anymore. For the sake of art, he figured he could justify it. After all, wouldn't an action portrait of Spark be more compelling and authentic?

Naturally I knew about Robert's nighttime rides with Spark. I was the one who tamed Spark to ride long before Robert joined the team. But I wasn't ready to pronounce this to Robert. He thought I was a very conservative old gentleman and I didn't mind keeping up that façade. After all, I had trained Spark well and knew that he wouldn't take Robert very far from the safety of our factory.

I figured if Robert still thought he still had to keep this a secret from me he would remain cautious of being detected. This would keep him alert for danger without my having to tell him about Mr. Lee's warnings. I don't know that I really believed anyone was after Spark anymore, but it didn't hurt to be vigilant. While Robert took off with Spark, I would scout the perimeter of the factory yard for any signs of trouble. Then I would watch and follow them, undetected, back to the safety of the basement.

"Florence would you be able to work on your project later tomorrow night? I can get you home afterwards so Edward doesn't have to wait. I want you to see an experiment I'm working on with Spark. It might be something you want to capture in a drawing." Robert said, almost in a whisper, as I pretended not to listen.

"You know, Edward will be out of town tomorrow so that will work out fine," Florence said. She was looking forward to seeing Spark in action she remarked teasingly to Spark as she petted his head.

I was down the hall in another room looking for spare parts when Florence showed up the next night at the appointed time looking eager to witness the experiment. Robert stood chatting with her at the door, not realizing I was just steps away, and explained that what she would see was something extremely confidential that he had not shared anyone yet, including his father. He said he wanted to wait until it was perfected before bothering the others. Actually, I figured he was concerned that I would put a stop to it and he wasn't ready to give it up.

Robert looked at Florence and realized she wasn't properly dressed for the excursion he had in mind. "What happened to wearing long pants like I advised?" he said looking over her fancy dress and impractical high heeled shoes.

"Oh, I didn't think you were serious. I don't know what looking unfashionable has to do with it. I don't even think I own any long pants," Florence giggled as she brushed past him and entered the office.

I just rolled my eyes. It wasn't about fashion, it was about practicality and safety. I hoped that Robert would have the sense to walk her over to our closet and pull out one of the extra jumpsuits and a pair of work boots. Traipsing in the woods in high heels would only slow them down and they may have to make a quick getaway if they were spotted.

I grinned as I watched Robert pull the more suitable clothes from the closet and tried to hand them to Florence. I could tell she wasn't used to taking fashion advice from young men. Finally, after seeing that he was not going to give in on this, she took the clothes, and with a huff of exasperation went into the closet to change.

"Well, that looks like a good fit. Don't worry, Edward won't see you," Robert said and muttered under his breath, "at least I hope not." He placed the leash on Spark, turned to Florence and said, "Follow me."

"We're going in there?" Florence questioned as Robert opened the door to reveal a dark tunnel. She looked hesitantly back at Robert. She couldn't imagine what would be in there. She seemed to have second thoughts about this as she gently entered the tunnel and looked around.

Robert just smiled reassuringly and said, "Don't worry, you are perfectly safe. You are here with me and a dragon. What could go wrong?" and with that Florence laughed nervously.

Florence brushed aside her feelings of unease as they walked along the dark hall. The next thing I knew she was climbing through a window with a dragon breathing down her back. She looked relieved to be outside. She wouldn't let on to Robert at the time, but later revealed how she was starting to feel claustrophobic in that tunnel.

Now it seemed her thoughts were full of concern wondering why they were outside and who could see them. Robert as if reading her mind said, "This is a very secluded area. Nobody can see us from here." (Nobody but me, I chuckled to myself.)

"Do you bring Spark out here often?" Florence asked as it seemed Spark knew his way around. "Oh yes, every day. He needs his exercise too." Robert said and then provided more instruction, "We're going to walk a little ways on this path to the pond and then I can show you what I've been working on with Spark."

Florence must have been so concerned about the tunnel, and where they were going, that she didn't notice the bag Robert was carrying. When the three reached the pond Robert set down his bag. I hung back far enough not to be noticed, but close enough to keep an eye on them.

"What is the most special thing about Spark, Florence?" Robert asked her very seriously.

"That he is here, for one. I know Edward admires his fire-breathing capability, but to me, I'm fascinated with his wings and how fast he must be able to fly."

"A woman after my own heart!" Robert chuckled and then got a little red-faced at the way Florence looked at him.

She was quite a stunning lady I admitted to myself and not for the first time. I knew Robert would be so lucky to find someone like Florence to marry someday. Robert went to his bag and pulled out a saddle. Florence's eyes were wide with astonishment as she tried to process what was coming next.

As I expected, Robert walked over and strapped the saddle on Spark and turned to Florence. "I've been testing the ability to fly with Spark. It is such an amazing feeling. I can't tell my father about this. He is not that adventurous and he'd also be furious if he knew Spark left the property."

I bit my tongue. I wanted to jump out there and show my son just how adventurous I was and demonstrate my flying tricks with Spark, but I held back.

"I'm sure Edward wouldn't be too happy either. But I think a creature has the right to do what he was born to do and Spark was born to fly," Florence responded.

"I figured it was safer if I went with him, just to make sure he returned, but he's taken a few solo flights and always comes back. I only take him out on dark nights like this and late enough that it's unlikely he would be seen upon landing or take off. If you like I will show you how it works with a demonstration?" Robert asked a question, but there is really only one way I think anyone would answer that, making the question unnecessary.

In an instant, it seemed, Florence saw the two ascend and disappear in the clouds above. In a few minutes they were back on the ground next to her. "Robert that gave me goosebumps! What does it feel like being up there?"

"Spark, could you do that again with Florence?"

Spark bent his head down gesturing Florence to climb aboard. Florence clambered onto the saddle without any hesitation. If she had any qualms she might have lost her nerve thinking about the consequences of a crash, or death. Robert made sure the straps were well fastened around both of them and whispered in Spark's ear to go gently.

The next thing you know Florence was flying through the air. She would have screamed, not in terror, but in pure joy, but I think the rapid descent took her breath and voice away. Soon enough she would barely be able to recognize the factory, but what she could see, the tops of trees, the Maumee River, and tiny specks that were the tops of houses, was magnificent. I was a tinge jealous as I watched them go.

Soon they were flying through and above a cloud. To me flying was always a wonderfully, strange sensation. It was undeniably the best feeling in the world. I hope she is enjoying the flight I thought as I scanned the area for signs of trouble.

She seemed quite disappointed when she realized Spark was descending for a landing. "When can I do that again?" Florence asked screaming as giddy as a school girl.

As they proceeded back to the office, I could hear Robert trying to justify to her why this was not just a joy ride with Spark. He, just like his old man, saw it as a huge business advantage with many applications. I bristled with pride realizing how much he thought like me.

Robert thought Spark could be employed to fly above the plant someday to allow for easier inspection of the roof to check for damage. His flights could be useful to deliver important documents or to speed up pickups if they needed a part or something from a supplier. Need to get to a meeting in a hurry? Spark could get you there faster than any train. What Robert didn't know was that I had already tested all that. I already used Spark to run a couple deliveries. In fact, the most important errand was getting Edward transported to see his baby's first day on Earth! If only Florence knew that back then!

Florence could tell Robert had been thinking about this for some time. He actually had some very practical ideas that Edward would love, except for the fact it could expose the existence of Spark to the world. I knew that could pose a grave danger to him.

What Robert didn't know was that there were men out there that would kill to get their hands on Spark. Luckily those men didn't know where Spark was and I was determined to keep it that way. The dream of flight for business would have to wait.

What would the world be like if we could all fly around like Spark? It sure would speed up getting places I thought. You could get from one part of the world to another in a day. Now that would be progress!

"Clearly, that was the greatest thing ever," Florence said to Robert as they returned to the office. Robert said how brave she was and that he was glad he was finally able to share a flight with someone. The opportunity with Florence was not something he had ever thought about until he heard she was coming to draw Spark. Now that he had Florence on his side he hoped she would find a way to get through to Edward about his ideas.

"I know what you're thinking and someday I will find a way to broach the subject of flight with Edward," Florence said reassuringly to Robert.

Florence imagined that Edward was up for any adventure so the thought of flight wouldn't scare him. The problem that she didn't fully appreciate was the potential danger of someone seeing Spark. It would be hard to convince Edward to take such risks. For now, she would just have to revel in the memory of her first time flying in the air. I secretly hoped she was inspired with all the new images she had to work with and that it would resonate in her drawings tomorrow. She thanked Robert for the adventure and asked him to escort her home.

I was pleased to see, over the following days, Florence's paintings taking on a new life. Several showed the grace of Spark's wingspan outstretched and traveling above the tree line. The thrill and excitement she surely felt that night on his back was somehow captured in her still drawings. Just looking at them I felt like I was transported there with him.

When Edward stopped in one night to check on her progress he looked stunned. "Florence you don't give yourself enough credit. These drawings make me feel like I'm in the clouds with him. I can't believe you can draw all of this from your imagination. Simply amazing, darling!"

I saw Florence share a quiet look at Robert and his eyes pleaded with her to keep quiet which apparently she fully intended to do.

"Just being around Spark has ignited something in me. I never drew animals before, except horses, so I wasn't sure how this was going to go. I'm glad you like it, but it's not finished yet, so I need to get back to work."

Chapter 51

By the turn of the century, with his companies running smoothly, Edward told me of his desire to direct his attention to more community projects. He wanted to create a legacy. He wanted some way to share his passion for art with the townspeople that had embraced him so fully. He felt a great way to give back for generations was to implant a curiosity and love for art in everyone.

There were not many towns the size of Toledo with an art museum. In fact, not too many folks at the turn of the century had access to art or the means to learn about the great artists. When Edward talked with me about his idea, I responded enthusiastically, "I think that is a wonderful idea Edward. Truthfully, I always thought art was something only for the upper class, until Florence..."

"Sadly, I agree that is the way it has been, but I think we can change that. Art should be accessible to anyone."

Edward filled me in on the new idea that he had already pondered with Florence. She believed they could start with a small show to display art to the public and peek their interest. The Gardner building downtown was one area that I agreed made sense. It was in a good location near the business district which would help attract people.

"Of course, you know Florence, her main objective is to make it available for the children in the community. She's already planning to talk to some school teachers to find out how to get them involved. You never know where the next Rembrandt could be hiding she always says," Edward said chuckling.

"What about the employee clubhouse at the plant? She could set up a workshop and provide some lessons for the worker's kids and families. You know I was so impressed with her latest paintings, and it is a shame we can't display those to the public!"

"Don't even dare think that, Red!" Edward said jabbing me in the shoulder while shaking his finger at me.

Someday, I said to myself, someday.

As the full scope of Edward's idea sank in, I just knew it would work. Undertaking something in art education was just a natural fit for Florence. After all, her grandfather Jesup had started the University of Toledo, and was a big proponent of the value of an education. Florence and Edward already had a big collection of artwork. All they needed was a place where they could share it with others.

Florence told me that being exposed to art at a young age was so important to her development. She took years of piano and art lessons when she was a child. Her parents insisted she take them but she didn't mind. She enjoyed drawing and painting more than piano, but she was glad now that she had learned to play music too.

I was now fully enchanted with the idea of a museum for Toledo. "Let me know what I can do to help Edward," I started to say, and Edward quickly interrupted me.

"I know of a few others in town that are avid art lovers and collectors. I'm calling them together at the Club for a meeting tomorrow night, why don't you join us? I know you'll find it worthwhile."

The next night we met Edward's guests in the regal Board Room. The Board Room is an intimate, private room on the fourth floor. The room is fairly small compared to the others, but it is so rich with detail. The carved window valances, wooden trim around the room, and the elaborately engraved wood of the bar was a sight to behold. The room also held a couple of Edward's favorite paintings that he gladly donated for display. Edward used this Board Room for many important meetings over the years, but today's meeting felt especially notable.

The small group assembled around the table and Edward quickly began to fill us in on the purpose of the meeting. "As we have discussed many times over the years, Toledo is in need of an art museum. This would be so beneficial to the community and could be a real gem for generations. There are several glass collectors and a display of glass in the Glass City is a given, but I want it to be a place that embraces and exhibits all forms of art. I envision a museum with glass, paintings, sculptures, pottery, jewelry, textiles, and more."

I looked around at the audience and noted that Edward had managed to gather all the appropriate players. A few members of the Tile Club, who were local artists, were mingled between art collectors such as Robinson Locke of the *Toledo Blade.* Mr. Locke was an avid art collector and would surely have items to display.

David Stine, the architect who had designed Edward's home, and our World's Fair mini-factory, was also in the crowd. David was eager and willing to contribute financially to the museum and suggested that they reach out to other Club members like Carl Spitzer and Jay Secor.

"If we can outline a plan, I would certainly talk with Carl and Jay. I've viewed their extensive personal art collections and I'm sure they would be interested in investing in this project," David informed the group.

Edward added that he was very familiar with Carl's collection and was certain he could convince him to get involved.

The group spent the next two hours hashing out several details. When we were satisfied with the progress of the initial plans David stood up and announced, "I'm very excited about this project and know it will benefit the citizens of Toledo for generations if we get their support. I'd like to suggest we formally confirm our commitment to this mission and nominate Edward to be our President."

The announcement got a round of applause as Edward turned a light shade of red. Edward wasn't one to embarrass easily but he was taken aback as he realized how much he wanted this project to succeed. Edward humbly agreed to the appointment after a little prodding by the rest of the group who wouldn't allow any other outcome.

We all left energized and ready to do our part for this new venture. It seemed like no time at all before we were securing investors for funding, finding art to display and settling on a location for the art gallery. It wasn't going to exactly be a full-fledged museum, like the one in New York City. But over time, we knew it would be one of the top museums in the world with Edward in charge. For now, the gallery would be housed in a leased building downtown, but it was exciting just the same.

Edward was in charge, but he also had a small group of investors that were eagerly working to secure a more permanent home for the museum. The group of seven took the idea of a museum and made it into reality. A great feat for a small, but mighty, group of avid art collectors.

What the initial museum lacked was focus, but it still garnered wide-ranging appeal. "The exhibits should have something to suit everyone's tastes," Florence remarked as she worked beside Edward as we reviewed the small collection of donated items one evening.

It was a shame Florence couldn't display her dragon painting, but Edward was too paranoid about the talk it could generate. One slip of the tongue could unravel the secret we had been hiding for years. It wasn't worth the risk to him. He was normally a risk taker, but understandably he was ultra conservative on this issue. The velocity of the damage it could unleash would be impossible to stop. The only way we could mitigate the risk was to avoid disclosing any inkling of it.

While Edward wouldn't allow the paintings of Spark to be viewed in public, he did permit other dragon items into the museum. He owned a wonderful sword that had a dragon figure etched around it that he decided to donate to the museum. The item was made in Japan in the 1600's and Edward had picked it up on one of his many overseas trips.

"I wager you have several other dragon themed items that could be displayed to pay homage to Spark. I always admired the large painting of *Saint Michael and the Dragon* you have. Will you put that on display, at least for a little while?"

"Oh yes, that 1797 painting by Benjamin West is one of my favorite paintings too. Funny, I didn't know how real that image could have been when I purchased it," Edward said laughing.

"I hate to part with my Ewer Dragon glass that I purchased when we vacationed in Italy, but I think the children will adore it," Florence said happily as she pulled it off the shelf.

That exquisite glass was made around 1600 and would feature nicely with the glass displays. We'll have the most extensive displays of glass, I thought, as I reflected on all the museum quality art that came from our factory artists over the years. I was excited to think how our artists would feel to see their work on display in a museum!

Florence's father was always looking for ways to improve Toledo and was onboard about the potential of a museum from the beginning. Maurice was pleased to see how happy it made his daughter and he would do anything to support her with this important project. Florence's focus on the children of Toledo and her desire to provide them access to an education of art was inspiring.

Temporary displays were set up and promoted heavily by the Libbeys. Florence worked tirelessly to encourage school teachers to bring their students to see the exhibitions. She convinced her friends to loan their art for exhibits. She worked to get funding to bring in guest lecturers and contacted reporters to get articles published in the newspaper. Anything she could think of to promote the dream she did and it worked.

Maurice saw how popular the temporary gallery quickly became and he wanted to help make it more permanent. He was so anxious to help that he found a way to hasten a real museum into reality. Edward's father in law came to his aid again with the gift of a parcel of land.

Maurice thought the property he owned on Monroe Street would be the perfect home for a permanent museum. Edward was grateful to Maurice for the generous offer. He was reminded again how lucky he was that he had Maurice and Mary, and of course their daughter in his life.

Now that a permanent site was secured and with a blossoming art collection, the group was able to focus on constructing the building and growing a member base. If members would pay to join they could get it built that much sooner. How could they get more members to sign up already, I wondered?

When the project wasn't progressing fast enough for Edward's liking he issued a promise and a challenge to the citizens of Toledo. The newspaper said Edward would donate $400,000 if the people would match it. It seemed that before the newspapers were even widely distributed, the money was raised. It did my heart good to see the citizens quickly rally behind the project. I was so proud that my fellow Toledoans supported Edward's vision.

When the museum was up and running, Edward realized that it would need new displays from time to time. Edward was already worried that the novelty of the museum would wear off and visitors would dwindle. Most manufacturing towns like Toledo didn't have an art museum. What would it take to keep it going, I pondered?

"You've got that wandering look in your eye, Edward. Where are you thinking about going off to now?" I asked, knowing that he was already planning out a trip in his mind.

"Florence what are your thoughts about Egypt? I've always dreamed of going there," Edward said referring to my question.

"You can't go there without me," Florence stated sternly. A trip to see the pyramids was something she always dreamed about when she was younger. It always seemed like the most exotic place she told me more than once.

"I'd love to bring back a mummy or two for the museum. Can you imagine how much the children would adore seeing that on a school field trip to the museum?"

Florence was thrilled, "Oh, we could have a whole wing dedicated to Egyptian artefacts!"

Florence got right to work figuring out an itinerary before Edward changed his mind. There was so much to see and probably not enough time to do it all. "Any chance you are going to turn this into a total business trip? I know it's hard for you to resist looking for new customers, but I want some of your time too."

Not soon after that discussion the Libbey's were sailing across the world to Egypt. They wouldn't be alone. I had read recently how more and more wealthy businessmen from the United States were traveling to Egypt for adventure and treasures. Everyone was intrigued by the pyramids and archeology thanks to the romantic stories being written in the papers and the recent discoveries of ancient tombs by archeologists.

The trip to Egypt was probably the best expedition for the Libbey couple. They told everyone it was a business trip for the museum but I knew they took time for fun too. Riding on camels in the desert was one of the many highlights of the trip Edward raved about to me as he showed me a photograph as proof of his exploits.

"Well, don't you look dashing all dressed up in your grey suit and tie!" I said laughing loudly at the absurdity of it.

"Come this way, Red, I want you to see the hundreds of artefacts and two mummies I secured for the museum."

"Wow, your museum will be world famous! People will be coming from all over the country just to get a look at a mummy, I reckon!"

"I'm not concerned about the whole country coming, but if it gets the local kids interested in coming to the museum that will make me happy. I think we have enough Egyptian pieces that we will have to build a separate wing," Florence responded as she looked over all the jewelry, figurines, small statues, pottery and fragments of rocks adorned with hieroglyphic writing.

"I know something else that will get the kids to come-"I started to say but abruptly stopped myself.

Chapter 52

By 1923 Florence was ready for retirement. Her heart was longing for California, where she had enjoyed her most important day, which was giving birth to her son. Eventually she would find a way to convince Edward that Spark was in good hands with the Wynston boys.

Edward was torn, but in the end he couldn't deny Florence her dream. They settled in Ojai and I promised to visit now and then with Spark. I was true to my word until Edward's death in 1925.

I helped Florence with the arrangements to get Edward's body back to Toledo for burial. Before being buried at Woodlawn next to his infant son, Edward was placed in the Sculpture Court of his Art Museum for a few days. The town was devastated upon hearing of his death. Thousands came to the museum to pay their respects to my friend, the man who had turned Toledo into the world-renowned "*Glass City of the World*."

Florence was heartbroken at the loss of her husband. Shortly after Edward's funeral and burial we had a long talk and discussed Edward's final wishes. Florence told me that Edward was always worried about his journals falling into the wrong hands. She asked me to burn his papers as she didn't have the heart to do it herself. It was the least I could do.

"Edward gave me so many great years. He really embraced life and loved his adopted Toledo town, didn't he?" Florence said as she brushed away the tears running down her cheeks.

"We talked about what to do with our money when he died and he wanted me to have it all and then donate the remainder to the museum when I die. But Red, I've thought it over and I've decided to donate most of the money now so that people can benefit from it. I don't need much to live on."

"That's a beautiful idea," I said as I wiped a tear from my eye. *(That generous gift continues today, allowing the museum to offer admittance to everyone free of charge. Their money is still being used to procure works of art to add to the collection and continues to provide funding for maintenance.)*

After Edward died, I didn't know if I would have the heart to fly with Spark anymore. But I couldn't let my son down so we continued our work with Spark at the factory and kept him hidden from others and well protected.

Chapter 53

Red's story ended shortly after he buried Edward. His son Robert said Red's zest for life slowly faded after Edward passed away. Red had trained Robert well and knew he was ready to take the helm of supervising Spark. He had no doubt that Robert would build on his work and teach the next generation. That is exactly what Robert did.

My name is Drake Wynston and now you know my family's story. I can't tell you how pleased I was to join the family tradition at the glass factory. Yes, you may have realized that my dad had a wry sense of humor. My name Drake means *Dragon.* So he named me after his secret, but I wouldn't learn that until I was older. So ironically my full name translates to *Dragon Friend.*

Spark was very old when I met him but I couldn't tell by looking at him. He moved around and was just as playful as I heard he was as a youngster, from my ancestor's descriptions. My dad harped on me from day one about the honor, duty, sacrifice and secrecy that came with the job title of Dragon Master. I never took that lightly.

The dangerous nature of this secret getting out is what kept my family members from speaking out before now. After all this time has passed, and the originators of this event long gone, the dangers have greatly diminished as well.

Spark has aged quite well and he's still very active. Sadly though some of his yard was lost to progress. Parts of the Greenbelt Parkway now drive through his old stomping grounds. The nearby I-280 highway, while convenient to employees who may live further from the plant, is a little too close for my comfort. Taking Spark out for adventures, is a little more challenging, with all the streetlights and traffic, than it had been for Grandpa Red. Challenging, but not impossible.

I've found ways to get Spark up and flying. I look forward to that as much as he does. While I don't worry about the same dangerous man that was on Edward's mind, I must be careful to evade planes, helicopters, satellites and now drones. The obstacles I have to avoid just make our trips all the more satisfying to me.

I have maintained the family tradition as it was started over a hundred years ago. And I have treasured every moment I had with Spark. I knew I was given a rare opportunity and I have cherished it. After a quarter century of work though, I have come to change my view on one point.

I think all this secrecy is no longer necessary. I know many people used to kill big game for sport, and some still do, but conservation of wild animals is more embraced now. There are even laws protecting endangered animals. While it is true dragons are not on that list, that is only because Spark and any others remaining have been kept so well hidden that nobody knows that dragons exist.

I want Spark to come of out of the shadows and perhaps be reunited with his kind. That is one reason why I have brought you my story. I'm also looking for the next Dragon Master. I want to find someone who I can train to take my place as I have no children to pass on my torch to. Finally, I want to share Spark with the world and allow people to know him as I do, as a sweet, adorable, fun-loving dragon who happens to be an expert furnace engineer. Would you like to join me? Drop me a note at the factory and tell me why you'd be the best apprentice.

Wow, I now feel as though a huge weight has been lifted from my shoulders. I am feeling a wave of relief and satisfaction come over me. I'm finally free from a lifetime of secrecy! I know that revealing this secret to you was the right thing to do.

I believe in mankind. I believe there are thousands out there like you that will understand my plight. I now know you will do the right thing and protect the dragons and welcome them out of the darkness that they have been living in for generations. You can allow them to bask in the light of day with no worries of being hunted. I know you will come to understand and cherish him as much as I do.

The last thing I wish for is that you find a way to reunite Spark with his family. For I'm certain there are others out there, like me, still protecting the few dragons that walk this Earth. I would do it myself, but I'm afraid I'm running out of time. My health has been deteriorating quickly these last few months and I fear I don't have the strength to make another journey.

Can you grant my last wishes? I would be forever grateful knowing that Spark is well taken care of when I'm gone. He deserves the chance to see that he is not alone and not the last dragon.

Now, if you think back and recall any "tall tales" from a friend swearing they had seen something that looked like a dragon flying over the sky in Toledo, you should rethink your reaction of doubt. For now you know, they really did see it, they got a glimpse of Spark playing around above his hometown. If it was one of my lucky days, I was right up there with him, riding on his back. Those were the most magical times of my life.

Thank you for your patience and understanding as I told you my story, the story of my heritage and the story of the glassmaker that changed the world. And now when you pick up your glass I hope you will feel more proud to know that the extra sparkle in the glass is due to the magic of our wonderful Spark.

Old photo of Spark, maybe the only one ever taken.

ACKNOWLEDGMENTS

Many thanks go to my family, Alex, Kyla and Bram for giving me time and support to create this story. Special thanks to Kyla for drawing the cover of my book.

To my sister Erin, thanks for all your reviews, critiques and encouragement. Your enthusiasm and support pushed me along when I wanted to abandon this quest.

To my Dad, Patrick Roach, whose creativity I try to emulate just a little bit. Thanks for always being there and having everything I need (even if you can't always find it!).

Stacey, Jeff, Sean and Rachel, thanks for your support and excitement about my project, and for wanting to acquire it even before you knew what it was all about!

William A. Foley, who always listens and supports my zany ideas. Thanks for being a great role model and friend for all these years.

I'm indebted to Arthur H. Smith, who provided me with the opportunity to work for such a wonderful company. His vast knowledge and enthusiasm for the industry sparked my interest to learn more about the history of the glass city.

Special thanks goes to Susan A. Kovach for her continuous support and friendship. I am grateful that she is in my corner and always supportive of my creative concepts. I appreciate her guidance, for continuously pushing me to excel, and for being the first to embrace my idea of Spark!

To all my present (and past) associates of Libbey around the world, I thank you for everything you do to keep Edward's dream alive. I'm grateful to know and work with you every day. I hope my version of our company amused and delighted you! I raise my Libbey glass to *toast 200* to you all!

Wendy Daudelin was born and raised in the Toledo area. She was a teacher before being enticed into working at the glass company. She was inspired to write this book to clear up the mysteries surrounding the glass city and any doubts about dragons not being real. Wendy lives with her fabulous family, delightful dog and an ever expanding houseful of glassware. CLEAR AS GLASS is her debut novel.